Y0-BTE-263

# Islam in the European Union
## Transnationalism, Youth and the
## War on Terror

# Islam in the European Union
## Transnationalism, Youth and the War on Terror

Edited by

## Yunas Samad and Kasturi Sen

**OXFORD**
UNIVERSITY PRESS

# OXFORD

UNIVERSITY PRESS

Great Clarendon Street, Oxford OX2 6DP

Oxford University Press is a department of the University of Oxford.
It furthers the University's objective of excellence in research, scholarship,
and education by publishing worldwide in

Oxford  New York

Auckland  Cape Town  Dar es Salaam  Hong Kong  Karachi
Kuala Lumpur  Madrid  Melbourne  Mexico City  Nairobi
New Delhi  Shanghai  Taipei  Toronto

with offices in

Argentina  Austria  Brazil  Chile  Czech Republic  France  Greece
Guatemala  Hungary  Italy  Japan  Poland  Portugal  Singapore
South Korea  Switzerland  Turkey  Ukraine  Vietnam

Oxford is a registered trade mark of Oxford University Press
in the UK and in certain other countries

ISBN  978-0-19-547251-6

Typeset in Minion Pro
Printed in Pakistan by
Kagzi Printers, Karachi.
Published by
Ameena Saiyid, Oxford University Press
No. 38, Sector 15, Korangi Industrial Area, PO Box 8214
Karachi-74900, Pakistan.

# Contents

**Section 4: Discrimination, Legalization and the War on Terror**

# List of Abbreviations

| | |
|---|---|
| ATCSA | The Anti-terrorism, Crime and Security Act |
| EC | European Commission |
| EU | European Union |
| FRA | Freedom of Religion Act |
| GCHQ | The UK Government Communications Headquarters |
| IMF | International Monetary Fund |
| MI5 | The UK Security Service (internal) |
| MI6 | The UK Secret Intelligence Service (external) |
| NATO | North Atlantic Treaty Organization |
| OECD | Organization for Economic Co-operation and Development |
| OPEC | Organization of the Petroleum Exporting Countries |
| PKK | Kurdistan Workers' Party |
| RRA | Race Relations Act |
| RRAA | Race Relations Amendment Act |
| SDP | Social Democratic Party |

# Acknowledgements

This publication is the outcome of a conference, conducted under an Accompanying Measure, (HPSE-CT-2002-60064) 'Youth, Gender, Transnational Identities and Islamophobia' by the European Commission under its Fifth Framework Programme, in 2003. We wish to acknowledge the active support of the Scientific Officers: Andrew Sors, Fadila Boughanémi, Angela Liberatore, Giulia Amaducci, Aris Apollonatos and Ronan O'Brien, and administrative support from Vanessa Marinof. We wish also to acknowledge all those who contributed to the conference. Our special thanks go to Robert Cliquet, John Eade, Catherine de Wenden, Czarina Wilpert, Thijl Sunnier, Tazeen Murshid, Charles Husband, Marco Martiniello, Kumar Murshid, Imran Khan, Shareefa Choudhury, Suresh Grover and Samar Mashadi. We would like to express our thanks for the administrative, technical and editorial support provided by Lizzie and Peter Hamilton, Sally Foord-Kelcey and Tom Harrison. Finally, we are grateful to Ameena Saiyid, Managing Director, Oxford University Press, Pakistan and her staff for their contribution and efficiency, and to the anonymous reviewers for their comments.

# Note On Contributors

**Claire Alexander** is a lecturer in sociology at the London School of Economics. Her research interests are in the area of race, ethnicity, masculinity and youth identities. Her main publications include *The Art of Being Black*, OUP, 1996 and *The Asian Gang*, Berg, 2000. She is co-editor of *Beyond Difference, Ethnic and Racial Studies*, (July 2002) and *Making Race Matter: Bodies, Space and Identity* (Palgrave, forthcoming 2005).

**Jocelyne Cesari** is Principal Research Fellow at the National Centre for Scientific Research (CNRS). Her training, professional experience and academic expertise are in political science, the Middle East area and Islamic studies. She has written numerous books and articles on Muslim minorities in France and in Europe, and their transnational links with the Muslim world at large. On behalf of the European Commission, she is currently coordinating the 'Network On Comparative Research on Islam and Muslims in Europe' (Nocrime: see website: www.euro-islam. info). She is currently Research Associate at the Centre for Middle Eastern Studies at Harvard University.

**Tufyal Choudhury** is a lecturer in law at Durham University. He is author of the OSI report, 'The Situation of Muslims in the UK'. He was previously a research associate at the Centre for Public Law at the University of Cambridge, and is co-author with Professor Bob Hepple and Mary Coussey of Equality: 'A New Framework—Report of the Independent Review of the Enforcement of UK Anti-Discrimination Legislation'. He is also consultant to the discrimination law project for the UK human rights group, JUSTICE.

**Godfried Engbersen** is a full professor of sociology at the Erasmus University of Rotterdam, the Netherlands. He has worked at the Universities of Leiden, Utrecht and Amsterdam. In spring 1996 he was a visiting professor at the Centre of Western European Studies at the University of California, Berkeley. Engbersen is a member of the Amsterdam School for the Social Sciences and a member of the board of the Social Sciences Council of the Royal Netherlands Academy of Arts and Sciences (KNAW). He is the author of more than 15 books on social inequality, migration and the welfare state. Since 2002 he is (with Erik Snel) the Dutch correspondent for the continuous Reporting System on Migration (SOPEMI) of the OECD. He is also a member of the Dutch Advisory Committee on Aliens Affairs (ACVZ). His current research deals with issues of irregular migration and the interrelation between transnationalism and social integration.

**Masoud Kamali** is Professor of Social Policy at MidSweden University and Associate Professor of Sociology at Uppsala University, Sweden. He is currently leading a European Commission project called, 'European Dilemma: Institutional Patterns and Politics of "Racial" Discrimination', which is a comparative study in eight European countries. The home page of the project is: http://www.multietn.uu.se/the_european_dilemma/index.htm. He is author of seven books published in English, Swedish and Persian, including: *Distorted Integration: Clientization of Immigrants in Sweden*, Multiethnic Papers, 1997; *Revolutionary Iran: Civil Society and State in the Modernization Process*, Ashgate, 1998 and in Persian, *Jame-eye madani, dovlat va novsazi dar Iran-e ma'aser*, Markaze bazshenasi-ye Islam va Iran, 2002; *Kulturkompetens i socialt arbete*, Carlsson, 2002; *Enghelab-e Iran dar asr-e jahanishodan* (Iranian Revolution in a Global Perspective) (in Persian, *Nashr-e digar*, 2003) and *Multiple Modernities: The Case of Iran and Turkey* (Liverpool University Press, 2005).

**Imran Khan** is a solicitor and specializes in what have become known as 'impact cases'. He made his name with the Stephen Lawrence case, which resulted in a government inquiry into how the police and authorities had failed a black family. The Macpherson report in 1999 put the term 'institutionalized racism' into common usage. Since then he has represented the parents of Victoria Climbié, the little girl brutally killed by her aunt, and again, failed by the authorities, and the family of a young Asian, Zahid Mubarek, who was murdered by his cellmate, a known violent racist, at Feltham young offenders institution. At present he is working with Michael Mansfield QC, challenging the sentences meted out to Asian rioters in Bradford, many of whom were imprisoned for up to four years in spite of being first-time offenders.

**Les Levidow** has been involved in the Campaign Against Criminalising Communities (CAMPACC) since early 2001. Based in London, the campaign has made various links with the general movement against the 'war on terror' and against the US–UK attack on Iraq in particular. Over many years he has also helped to build solidarity with people targeted by state terror in Northern Ireland, Palestine, Chiapas and Colombia.

**Aminah Mohammad-Arif** is a researcher at the CNRS and is affiliated with the Centre d'Etudes de l'Inde et de l'Asie du Sud (Paris). She is the author of *Salam America, l'islam indien en diaspora*, CNRS Editions, 2000, translated into English in 2002 by Anthem Press.

**Konrad Pêdziwiatr**, a sociologist and anthropologist by training, is a PhD student at the University of Leuven, Belgium. He became interested in Muslim communities in Europe through his research on the Christian minorities in Middle Eastern countries such as Turkey, Syria, Lebanon and Egypt. He has written his Master's thesis on 'The Persistence of Islam: Religion and Identity Amongst the Pakistanis in Britain' (University of Exeter). He has been a Marie Curie Research Fellow at the University of Bradford, and worked as a researcher at the Centre for European Studies at the Jagiellonian University (Poland). He has published articles about Islam in Europe in various academic journals and major Polish and international newspapers.

**Yunas Samad** is a senior lecturer in the Department of Social Sciences and Humanities, Director of the Ethnicity Social Policy Research Unit at the University of Bradford, and Deputy Director of the South Asia Research Centre, Geneva. His research interests are 'race' ethnicity and multiculturalism; religion and nationalism; ethnicity and nationalism and identity politics. He is the author of *A Nation in Turmoil: Nationalism and Ethnicity in Pakistan 1937–1958*, Sage, 1995; co-author with John Eade of *Community Perceptions of Forced Marriage*, Foreign and Commonwealth Office, 2003; co-editor of *Culture Identity and Politics: Ethnic Minorities in Britain*, Avebury, 1996; guest editor for a 'Special Issue on Muslims in Europe', *Innovation: European Journal of Social Science*, 10 (4), 1998.

**Kasturi Sen** is a social scientist who has worked on public health and development issues for the past twenty years. She has a doctorate from the University of Exeter (1986) in Islamic studies, sociology and economics. Between 1993 and 2004 she coordinated several multi-centre studies for the European Commission in South Asia and the Middle East. The most recent project was an international meeting on Citizenship and Young People of Muslim Origin in selected countries of the European Union (2003–2004) in collaboration with the University of Bradford. She was a Visiting Professor at Jawaharlal Nehru University's (New Delhi, India) Centre for Social Medicine and Community Health between January and March 2004, and between 1996 and 2004 was based at the Institute of Public Health, University of Cambridge as Senior Research Associate. She is currently undertaking a migration policy review for the European Commission. Her interests are broad and include a special interest in political economy of health care and in the multiple aspects of labour migration. Among her recent publications are: K. Sen and A. Sibai, 'Transnational Capital and Confessional Politics—paradox of the health care system of the Lebanon' in the International Journal of Health Services Research, 2004 and Restructuring Health Services: changing contexts and comparative perspectives, (eds.) Zed Books, London, 2003.

**Ian Talbot** is Professor of South Asian Studies and Director of the Centre of South Asian Studies at Coventry University. His research interests focus on the modern history of the Indian subcontinent, with particular specialization in the following areas: history of the Punjab region during the colonial era; Punjab politics and the emergence of Pakistan; the impact of Partition on the Punjab and Bengal; Pakistan's political development since 1947. He is author of *Pakistan: A Modern History*, Hurst, 1999; *India and Pakistan*, Arnold, 2000; co-editor with G. Singh on *Punjabi Identity: Continuity and Change*, Manohar, 1996 and with G. Singh on *Partition and Region: Bengal, Punjab and the Partition of the Subcontinent*, Oxford University Press, 1999.

**Bryan S. Turner** is Professor at the National University of Singapore in the Asia Research Institute and previously was Professor of Sociology and Professorial Fellow at Fitzwilliam College, Cambridge. His areas of interest are medical sociology (body and society); political sociology (citizenship and human rights); sociology of religion (Islam); social theory (classical). He is the author of *Weber and Islam: a critical study*, Routledge, Kegan & Paul, 1974; reprinted with a new introduction in 1998; *Marx and the End of Orientalism*, Allen and Unwin, 1978;

*Citizenship and Capitalism: the debate over reformism*, Allen and Unwin, 1986; *Religion and Social Theory*, Sage, 1991, and a second edition with a new introduction; *Orientalism, Postmodernism and Globalism*, Routledge, 1994; editor of *Orientalism: Early Sources* Routledge, 12 volumes, 2000; editor of *Islam: Critical Concepts in Sociology*, Routledge, four volumes, 2003; co-editor with P. Hamilton of *Citizenship; Critical Concepts*, Routledge, two volumes, 1994: co-editor with F.E. Isin of *Handbook of Citizenship Studies*, Sage, 2002. He is the editor of *Citizenship Studies*; co-editor with Mike Featherstone of *Body & Society*; co-editor with John O'Neill of the *Journal of Classical Sociology*.

# Preface

A number of important and relevant developments have occurred since the completion of this book for the European Union. Many of the chapters could have been updated to accommodate them, but the recent bombings in London have made the publication of the book a matter of urgency. There are two connected strands within these developments, one being the bombings in London and Madrid and the other being the success of the 'No' vote in the referendum in the Netherlands and France on the European constitution. Both have increased the focus on European Muslims and revived the longstanding hostility towards the policies of multiculturalism that have been gathering momentum for a while. Within this context there is also a climate of rumour and counter-rumour, where the so-called terrorist actions have been judged before being fully investigated. The Labour government of the United Kingdom, for example, continues to vehemently deny any link between the bombings in London and the unsanctioned invasion of Iraq and its subsequent slide into civil war. This preface will summarize some of the current perceptions of Muslims in Europe, referring mainly to indigenous British Muslims but also to Muslims in France, Spain and the Netherlands.

A number of popular explanations have been provided for the events in London in July 2005. A view driven particularly hard by neo-conservatives is that violent activities are an intrinsic feature of Islamo-fascism, akin to a pernicious virus that needs to be dealt with by firm action. Some of the more enlightened members of the Liberal Democrat party as well as some Labour backbenchers see a more direct link between the London bombs and the government's foreign policy, particularly in Iraq. This view has been supported and reinforced by a recent leaked report from the Middle East section of the Foreign and Commonwealth Office.[1] However, there is an alternative view that is largely being ignored due to the climate of fear and hysteria perpetuated by the government and its security services and reflected daily in the popular press. This view emphasizes the social and political construction of endemic violence. Many chapters in this book suggest that the growing threats of violence and acts of terrorism are products of deprivation and alienation, and that socio-economic development is the key, not only in the UK but also in countries directly affected by the 'war on terror'—notably Afghanistan and Iraq. The reality is far more complex than the stereotyping of Islam as a 'violent' Other, and such an overtly simplistic and racially prejudiced analysis will fail to address the problem of growing violence.

There is another element that has altered the context, and needs to be highlighted. This has been provided by globalization. Inequality, poverty and social discontent are long-standing phenomena, and action has been restricted to particular contexts. However, in recent decades, one result of globalization has been to link foreign policies and radical ideology through transnational networks. The impact of foreign policy and current neo-liberal alliances, especially between the UK and the USA, is all too often visible in detail and with great speed on TV screens and on the Internet. This has clearly had the effect of inflaming some individuals, and lighting fires of violence in others. From a more academic and removed perspective, the argument that appears to be raging among social scientists is whether this is a top-down or bottom-up process.

What is happening to the Muslim diaspora in Europe and specifically in the United Kingdom? Unlike their North American counterparts—a much more successful group—Muslims in the UK are predominantly part of a racialized underclass and the descendents of labour migrants, who on a range of social indicators suffer from multiple deprivations. While neo-conservatives have drawn strong parallels between the group led by Mohammad Atta, responsible for 9/11, and Mohammad Siddique Khan, the alleged ringleader of the July 2005 London atrocities, they argue incorrectly that these are middle-class, well educated perpetrators motivated primarily by ideology. They claim that this is a 'top-down' process simply because it fits in well with the globalized policies of the 'war on terror'. The solution advocated is to deal with the perpetrators of hate in order to destroy their ideologies of hate and destruction, thus legitimizing the war on terror. More precisely, they call on Muslims to address this malignancy amongst them in order to solve the problem. However, this view is inherently false. As has been well established by now, those taking to arms are from radicalized youth throughout the world. They are not part of a defined entity but are more amorphously linked by the experience of dispossession and dislocation, spurred on by a burning desire for justice, which is expressed through violence.

A more careful reading of the biographies of the so-called London bombers, for example, provides a different picture to that which has been conveyed by the popular media and even by 'thinking' journalists. Nearly all the named individuals appear to have originated from the poorest parts of Leeds, the Beeston area, euphemistically called 'Chav' town, where most lived in social housing or with their parents. Only two, Siddique Khan and Shezad Tanweer, went to university (Tanweer dropped out) while the others barely completed secondary school education. Much has been made of the fact that Siddique Khan was a teacher. In fact, he was not a fully qualified teacher: he was a teaching assistant, a position usually filled by unqualified personnel to provide classroom support for the teacher. All the rest had casual employment working in market stalls, living off benefits or working for their families. Muktahr Said-Ibrahim and Yasin Hassan Omar appear to have had criminal records. The latter was designated a vulnerable adult after leaving foster care, while Hasib Hussain also came from a very vulnerable background. None of them were from a group of upwardly mobile and educated youth.[2]

These social origins are clearly important because, as with the Madrid train bombers, and if these men are the perpetrators of the London bombings, this is where anger tempered by hate philosophy becomes explosive. Two key variables are important in this process of radicalization. These are marginalization and deprivation. Unemployment or dead-end jobs and racism, in particular, make young men (and in some cases, women) angry and susceptible to transnational influences. Drifting away from their communities increases their isolation and makes them vulnerable to the philosophy of hate. The upshot is that those who have reasonable employment prospects and are integrated within particular ethnic communities are less likely to be influenced by transnational processes, which include the daily TV and Internet diet of violence and killings. This alienation is compounded by the security measures introduced to deal with the war on terror, which are stretching liberal democratic values to their limits: stop and search and trial where evidence is not revealed to the defence lawyers or the defendant add to a simmering and explosive situation.

The London bombings are a clear example of globalization, fuelled by real events that have allowed the various aspects to come together in such a frightening manner. It is not a question of jihadis parachuting into the locale and fermenting problems, but the locale reaching out to the global for succour, support and skills that can turn nebulous ideas of hatred forged in a crucible of deprivation and marginalization into a dreadful reality. An enquiry by MI5, MI6, the listening station, GCHQ and the police puts pay to the top-down view as they found no evidence of an al-Qaeda mastermind or senior organizer. Rather, these were two home grown, self-sufficient groups that were largely unrelated but consisted of 'clean skins', and the attempted bombings of 21/7 were copycat ones.[3]

Why is such anger deflected into revolutionary theology and not criminal behaviour? The biographies of some of the participants suggest how this has happened. Here, anger is stoked by events taking place in the Muslim world: Palestine, Chechnya, Kashmir and now Iraq. The unabated deluge of imagery from the mainstream media, particularly satellite television, beamed into living rooms, has been stirring passions among all those concerned with justice, but in particular among Muslims throughout the globe, since the target populations are unfortunately predominantly of Muslim origin. The military interventions of the USA and the UK are a constant reminder to the youth in Europe of the misery of some Muslims and the direct links between the terrible events and their own governments.

It is in this cauldron of anger that radical ideology connects with individuals. Salman Rushdie and others in the US have raised the call that Islam in general needs reformation.[4] This can only sound like sanctimonious humbug, ignoring the past fifty years of Washington's policy in the Middle East that has been supporting and promoting autocratic and conservative regimes, an illegal five decades of occupation of Arab lands by Israel, and regimes who have consciously promoted traditional Islamic interpretations in the struggle against Arab socialism and movements for democracy.

Fareed Zakaria has perhaps a more nuanced, but equally flawed argument, which is that the events unfolding are part of a revolutionary ideology, akin to a virus infecting Islam.[5] Well, if it is a virus then it a genetically modified virus created in the laboratory of Afghanistan by the US. It was in the intervention against the Soviet invasion, led by geo-political interests, that a so-called virulent ideology of violence was developed. It suited 'Foggy Bottom' as long as it served its purpose. First it turned Peshawar into the University of Jihad and the global focus for Islamicists throughout the world, where ideas were exchanged and contacts established, and which provided opportunities for a meeting of minds as well as access to military training, equipment and technologies. Next was the first Gulf War and the establishment of

American military bases in Saudi Arabia, which turned al-Qaeda against the West and in particular the USA for this act of sacrilege. The final piece in the jigsaw was Bosnia and this was for two reasons.

Firstly, it was a great shock to Muslims in the European Union to see indigenous co-religionists being subjected to genocide. The symbolism of the 7 July atrocities taking place on the tenth anniversary of the 10,000 massacred in Srebrenica cannot be lost. However, the mendacity of the US in supporting jihadis (hopelessly failing in the policy of differentiating between good and bad jihadis), and arms shipments sent to Bosnia from Iran to circumvent the United Nations arms embargo and to bolster the Bosnian forces in the face of the Serbian onslaught, backfired dramatically. It brought shocked Muslims from western Europe into contact with jihadis. Omar Saeed Sheikh, a graduate of the London School of Economics, who was sentenced to death for the murder of Daniel Pearl, went to Bosnia as a charity worker and was radicalized by the events in Europe to become involved in the Kashmir insurgency.

The alleged Pakistan connection, a legacy of the Afghan War, has been an important element in the London bombings. Some of the bombers visited Pakistan where al-Qaeda has an established network dating from the Afghan war that has been involved in numerous assassination attempts on President Musharaff. Although *madrassas* have been singled out they are not responsible *per se*, though some have been infiltrated by extremism. Meanwhile, the al-Qaeda leadership is constantly on the move between and across the porous and rugged mountainous border between Afghanistan and Pakistan. The border regions are littered with secret weapons dumps, while even the remotest regions have access to the Internet, satellite phones and satellite televisions, allowing them to continually monitor the media and remain in contact with their compatriots throughout the world. There are more Pakistani troops on the border than the 25,000 combined allied forces in Afghanistan: this reduced level is due to the US launching the second Iraq war. The fact is that the Americans took their eye off the ball, failed to capture or kill Osama bin Laden, and then diverted troops to Iraq, thus failing to anticipate the opposition that the occupation would face in the region.

Iraq is also a factor, and the second Iraq war has had a double impact. Firstly, it has become a *cause célèbre*, a burning injustice that infuriates Muslims as well as non-Muslims throughout the world, but tips a handful into extremist action. Many of these militants are likely to be those who have suffered at the hands of the occupying forces. Iraq has become the greatest propaganda victory for al-Qaeda, allowing them to trump the voices of moderation and conciliation. Secondly, and more importantly, the deposing of a secular though cruel despot who had kept a tight lid on religious extremism has led to the creation of a power vacuum, which has been occupied by jihadis with the greatest of ease since the liberal opposition are either killed or have turned into yet another diaspora. Iraq has thus become a magnet for 'wannabe' jihadis from around the world, including the UK, but mainly from the Arab world, where they can acquire on-the-job training and mastery of the arts of war. Iraq has replaced Afghanistan as the academy for the military training of jihadis. A hypothetical US withdrawal from Iraq would not resolve this problem, as the ensuing chaos would allow for the continued training of militants. With the likelihood that the USA and its allies will be involved in the country for the next decade, Iraq will provide the clarion call for al-Qaeda recruits. The West and its allies are tensing themselves for the anticipated return of veterans from the Iraq imbroglio, coming back to infect a new cohort of Muslims with radical ideology and military know-how.

It is important to see al-Qaeda as a global phenomenon linking numerous and disparate local groups primarily through ideology. Globalisation makes it greater than the sum of its parts, by synchronising local activities and acting as a catalysing agent to make inert elements volatile. July 2005 appears to have been the month when various local agents attempted to coordinate their activities. The assault on Ayodhya (India), the multiple bombings in London, Turkey and Egypt and the sharp increase in Iraqi insurgency all have the signature of al-Qaeda sympathisers. Its ability to act as a catalyst and its role as an exemplar is resulting in the emergence of units such as the Pakistanis and others involved in the London bombings that are undetected by the security 'radar'.

Globalization of 'blowback' requires a rethinking of foreign policy, as it is the result of short-term aims that is producing long-term problems. Iraq has become the magnet for 'wannabe jihadis', including those from the United Kingdom, and these 'chickens' have yet to return to roost—which is clearly cause for concern. However, jihadis will only succeed if they connect with discontented, marginalized and discriminated youth in the Muslim diaspora. Widening conflict would be the greatest political victory for the jihadis, resulting in even greater numbers heeding their call to violence. To address this problem, social needs must be addressed wherever sources of potential foot soldiers exist, along with a reform of US foreign policy in the Middle East that makes them so angry, and only then can the leadership that produces this theological perversion be isolated and rooted out.

This brings the global back to the locale and challenges somewhat the growing tendency to blame violent events on the evils of 'multiculturalism', thereby ignoring the important role played by political and social factors. The referendum for ratifying the European constitution failed in France and the Netherlands for many reasons. Among these were important factors relating to the provision of equal rights of citizenship for Muslim residents. In France, while there may have been an array of complex reasons (economic, social, political) for the 'No' vote, one aspect that played an important role was concern about Turkey joining the European Union, and the role this might play in the troubled relations with Muslims. This relationship has become increasingly tense with the introduction of legislation that bans the wearing of religious symbols and artefacts in schools. In the case of the 'No' vote in the Netherlands, one of the concerns again was with its resident Muslim population who were not considered to be sufficiently Dutch. The right-wing politician, Pim Fortuyn, for example, mobilized considerable electoral support for his anti-Muslim campaign, and this hostility was reinforced by the murder of Theo van Gogh by a Muslim. There were a number of reasons for the 'No' vote, but the concern with Muslim immigration and debates around multiculturalism and its inadequacies played an important role. What is increasingly evident is a growing hostility to Muslims and to notions of multiculturalism in the UK in particular, but also in France and in the Netherlands, even prior to the July 2005 bombings in London, but with these attacks this hostility has become much more explicit and significant.

David Davis, an aspiring leader of the UK Conservative party, made a major statement on multiculturalism, linking it to the suicide bombings in London and arguing that the bombings were a product of segregated communities that were not sufficiently British. Muslims suffered from dual loyalty, a consequence of multiculturalism, and they needed to be more integrated and to adopt British norms.[6] There are a number of criticisms that can be made against multiculturalism: it fails to address economic disadvantage and marginalisation while celebrating cultural difference. Representatives of communities are primarily elderly religious men, and women and young people are excluded from the process. However, David Davis's criticism of multiculturalism is unsustainable. The segregation of communities is not merely a product of cultural preference but is behaviour that is grounded in deprivation and marginalization. These communities are segregated not because of a policy of multiculturalism but because of poverty. Furthermore, culturally segregated groups that are middle class are hardly ever referred to in the criticism of multiculturalism. The working class marginalized groups suffering multiple deprivations are always the focus of this critique. Muslims need to be more 'British', whatever this is, and their treatment of women is unacceptable. The treatment of women is not because of their religious beliefs but reflects the rural origins of the majority of Muslims in this country. Social class is an important variable in this discussion, and the Muslim middle class treatment of women is much closer to the so-called British norm. The claim that Muslims are not adequately British is usually expressed in terms of their inability to speak English. While this may be true of the elderly population, which is a minority, the majority of young Muslims growing up in Britain are English speakers who are deeply embedded in their local environment, speaking with local accents and proud of their local heritage.

The suggestion of discarding multiculturalism so that Muslims could be assimilated to become more British and hence loyal, and would not therefore engage in terrorist acts, is fatally flawed. It would not have this intended result, and in fact, would create a situation that increases the propensity for violence and reduces the loyalty of the Muslim community. This is because the demise of multiculturalist policies would increase poor socio-economic integration, reduce involvement in the labour market and weaken ethnic bonds by trying to assimilate these communities. These are the two factors that are associated with increased transnational influence. It is the unemployed or those not involved in meaningful economic activity and those who have drifted away from their communities who may be influenced by the promoters of hate. An assimilation strategy based on debunking multiculturalism would simply accelerate this process and increase the potential for militants to emerge. The other consequence of such a policy U-turn would be that Muslim communities would feel threatened, turn inwards and become less cooperative with the authorities. It should be remembered that the police in the July bombings received crucial information from family members and friends from the Muslim community in their investigation. Without the support and assistance of the Muslim communities the police investigation would have been very difficult, and multiculturalism plays an important role in keeping communities engaged with the authorities.

The baby should not be thrown out with the bath water, and legitimate criticism of multiculturalism can and should be made to refine the policy. Socio-economic marginalization is an obvious area that needs to be engaged in an innovative manner and one which does not trigger the white backlash ever ready on the sidelines. The far right has found a receptive audience in the white working class when it argues that multiculturalism is positive discrimination for ethnic minorities at the expense of the white population. While this may be patently incorrect, it resonates well with the hardships that marginalized groups across the board experience: economic policies that address the socio-economic problems of the Muslim minority must be linked to programmes that also benefit the white working class. The whole emphasis on multiculturalism of faith communities must be revisited and secular dimensions of it need to be legitimized and incorporated, with special emphasis on women and young people. Muslims cannot be treated simply as a 'faith' community. They must be viewed as a social entity with considerable diversity of opinions and views just as in mainstream British society.

**Yunas Samad and Kasturi Sen**

## NOTES

1.  Martin Bright, 'Leak shows Blair told of Iraq war terror link', *The Observer*, 28 August 2005.
2.  Ian Herbert, 'Family struggles to understand why students become 7 July Bus Bomber', *The Independent*, 2 August 2005. Terry Kirby, Cahal Milmo and Terri Judd, 'Just two normal boys who played football in the park', *The Independent*, 27 July 2005. Brian Brady and John Philips, "Confessions" lifts lid on London bombing plot', 2 August 2005, news.scotsman.com. Vijay Dutt, 'London bombs wanted to avenge Iraq', 1 August 2005, www.hindustantimes.com. Abul Taher and John Elliot, 'Bombing suspects tried to have moderate Imam sacked', 31 June 2005, www.timesonline.co.uk.
3.  Jason Bennetto and Ian Herbert, 'London bombings: the truth emerges', *The Independent*, 13 August 2005.
4.  Salman Rushdie, 'The Right Time for An Islamic Reformation', 7 August 2005, www.washingtonpost.com.
5.  Fareed Zakaria, 'How to stop the contagion', *Newsweek*, 1 August 2005.
6.  David Davis, 'Why cultural tolerance cuts both ways', *The Daily Telegraph*, 3 August 2005.

# Introduction

The role and position of Muslims communities in Western Europe has received increasing social and political contemplation in recent times, along with the general interest in Muslim societies and Islam. Attention started with the Iranian revolution, gaining momentum with the Rushdie controversy, the headscarf affair and the reverberations spawned by the Gulf Wars, reaching its apogee with 11 September. The study of Muslim societies and communities has changed from an esoteric interest of the select and close-knit few, mainly academics, to become a major concern of policy makers, the media and the public at large. Lamentably, the predominant interest was from a security paradigm and Muslims were perceived as a threat from within and without; a bridgehead for Islamic terror emanating from the turmoil in Muslim countries. The neo-orientalist perspective, exemplified by Samuel Huntington and *The Clash of Civilizations* (1998) thesis, was influential in policy circles both in Europe and the United States. This perspective is challenged in this volume by locating Muslim communities in their social and policy context, particularly the youth, and exposing the biases that exist in studies on them.

While in the popular consciousness of Europeans, Muslims have just popped up, their presence pre-dates contemporary interest. They have been established in most European countries for nearly fifty years, and in France and Britain their presence goes back to the nineteenth century as a by-product of the empire. However, social scientists and policy makers had, until the 1980s, investigated Muslim migration and settlement within migration paradigms. Muslims were represented either as nationals of third world countries or as racial and ethnic minorities. Prior to the 1960s, Islam was alien—there were few mosques and settlers and it was during the 1950s and 1960s that Muslim labour migration and settlement, either as guest workers or economic migrants, took place. With the recession of the mid-1970s, immigration policy to Western Europe changed and primary migration came to a halt. However, the size of Muslim communities continued to grow as a consequence of family reunification. Today, the highest Muslim presence as a percentage of the total population is found in France (it also has the largest population in absolute numbers followed by Germany and then the UK) while the lowest rate is found in Great Britain (see Pêdziwiatr's chapter).[1]

The transformation of migrant labour into settled communities with a growing population born in Europe saw the beginning of explicit political participation. As citizens educated with a European mindset, political activity by Muslims for Muslims was not surprising. It was generally believed that the secularization thesis (in its various forms) would, over time, result in these minorities losing their religious distinctiveness and becoming assimilated into the secular norm of European civil society. However, like other religious groups, evangelical Christians and Hindu nationalists, religious identification has increased in the era of globalization. In Western Europe, a number of organizations (Muslim Council of Britain, Conseil Francais du Cult Musulman, Zentralrat für die Muslime in Deutschland, Muslim Council of the Netherlands, L'Exécutif des Musulmans de Belgique and Förenade Islamiska Församlinger i Sverige) emerged representing Muslim interest on the national level. The ground realities also indicated an increasing conspicuousness of Islam represented by the proliferation of *halal* food outlets, mosques, graveyards, Islamic bookshops and charities, and demands within education for practices and norms acceptable within Islam. In some sense, the reunion of families and the transformation of migrant labour, consisting entirely of men, into mixed gender communities with multiple generations naturally brought new demands on the social context that they were now living in. It was the needs of families and the emergence of a younger generation that made Muslims more prominent in their diasporic location. These internal developments resonated with external ones, where political Islam becomes much more active in the Muslim world; in Turkey, Iran, Philippines, Afghanistan, Pakistan, Indonesia and Trinidad, Islamic movements challenged the regimes. With the break-up of the USSR and Yugoslavia, Muslim entities emerged from the reconstitution of the socialist bloc. In the USSR, Uzbekistan and other central Asian states emerged as independent nations, but where nationalities were denied nationhood, there were separatist movements as in Chechnya. Similarly, with the break-up of Yugoslavia, Muslim political entities of Bosnia and Herzegovina, Macedonia and Kosovo emerged. However, the intrusion of international events into domestic politics exemplified by 9/11 extenuated cultural differences between Muslims and the society they settled in, resulting in a backlash against them.

## The Other within

There are two parallel debates, the security paradigm and the discussion on European identity that problematizes Muslims. The former argument is well rehearsed and will be covered briefly. In the post-cold war era, academics, such as Samuel Huntington (1998), Bernard Lewis (1990) and Gilles Kepel (2002) argued that a new paradigm was needed to understand the changing realities. With the collapse of the Berlin Wall, the old certainties of the left–right dichotomy that was dividing the world and societies was replaced by new antagonisms with Islam versus the West. For Kepel, the Rushdie controversy in the United Kingdom and the 1989 headscarf affair in France were indicative of the activation of political Islam among the diaspora, as Khomeini attempted to extend his influence from Muslim countries to Europe. Huntington, pursuing a similar approach on a much grander scale, argued that the demise of the cold war meant that the new antagonism would be based on culture, and he conceptionalized this 'brave new world' into culturally differentiated areas. For him and Lewis, Islam, and not simply 'fundamentalism', was irreconcilable with Western values, and were destined to collide. The events of 11 September reinforced the increasing insecurity that Western states felt about Muslims, and invigorated the perspective that this minority had to be viewed from a security paradigm. The unjustifiable fear that Islamic 'fundamentalism' was establishing itself among Muslim minorities in Europe was reinforced by the knowledge that a jihadi cell involved in 9/11 was based in Europe. There was a knee-jerk reaction that was even reflected by prominent social scientists: Ralph Darehndof argued for the defence of Western values against terrorism; Anthony Giddens wrote that governments needed to clamp down on immigration flows so that they did not give sustenance to extreme right-wing parties (see Kamali's chapter). In the moment of crisis, Muslims became the new folk devils, vilified by the great and the good. There was an assumption that Islamic radicalism was establishing itself in the European context through a top-down process whereby jihadis were being parachuted into the fertile terrain of inner city ghettos. This whole perspective of viewing minorities from a security paradigm will be questioned thoroughly, and alternative perspectives for understanding the social processes, particularly among young Muslims, will be looked at.

The second policy theme that intercepts with the security issue is the question of the emerging European identity. This issue has been implicit in the evolution of the European community to the European Union, and has now become explicit with expansion, which brought in a number of Eastern European countries. The whole issue of expansion has raised explicitly the question of how and what shape this identity will take that will provide a common sense of belonging to a disparate collection of nationalities. It raises the question about where the construction of boundaries of 'us' and 'them' should be located. With Muslim minorities being the largest minority group within the European Union, estimates range between 10 and 15 million (Glavanis, 1999), the blurring of these boundaries of 'us' and 'them' and the construction of the 'other' become extremely pertinent and relevant. Clearly a security perspective in relation to Muslims would construct them as the 'other' within, and would lead to substantial numbers of people being excluded from this new European identity.

The European Convention (2003), which considered the European constitution, is a very good example of the issues that are at stake, and how this process of construction of a European identity is taking place. Ireland, Spain, Portugal and Poland argued that Christianity is a core characteristic in the make-up of the European identity, and backed the call by Pope John Paul to the European Convention that the constitution should have a role for God. The Catholic Church is preparing a major rolling campaign of seminars and presentations to press home its point (THES, 2003). President Chirac resisted this approach but conceded the 'Christian origins of European civilization' (*EU Business 2003*). Ultimately, Valery Giscard d'Estaing omitted any explicit reference to Christianity in the document that was presented to the European Council meeting in Thessaloniki in June 2003. This reflected the influence of the northern states that wanted a more secular approach that resonated with their civil societies, over the southern states that were more sympathetic to the approach of the Vatican. The draft treaty referred to the traditions of democracy in Greek antiquity, and elaborated on the values of the Enlightenment. Equality, freedom and respect for reason were the guiding principles that were drawn from the cultural, religious and humanist inheritance from Europe's past. There is obviously a tension between the kinds of values that are celebrated as European and their historical baggage. Clearly, the presence of Muslims has implications in terms of the construction of European identity; the construction of Muslims as the 'other' within has implications in terms of social policy in general. These biases are disentangled by challenging assumptions that are central to the arguments of both the neo-orientalists and European identity.

## EUROPE AND MODERNITY

European identity has been inextricably linked with the emergence of modernity, and this conflation is not something that is merely apparent in the debates around identity within the European Union, but also among social scientists. Gerard Delanty (1995) asks which Europe we are talking about. His analysis clearly points out that there have been multiple Europes throughout history, and these different Europes have had centres that have changed over time. The ancient Greeks provide the intellectual source for much of European thought. However, for the Greeks, their notion of identity was that there were Greeks and barbarians, and these barbarians could be found in those areas that we today call Asiatic or European. It is also difficult to differentiate Greek intellectual flowering from the knowledge of the ancient world that was transmitted from Babylon and ancient Egypt. The dichotomy of Orient and Occident is also highly problematic in antiquity; for the Greeks, the Occident was based in Asia Minor, and the Orient consisted of territories that were beyond that. The Romans did not view themselves as a European power. They had an empire that was based firmly in the eastern half in the Mediterranean basin, and was more oriental than Western. Hence, ancient Rome and Greece are problematic bases for constructing a European identity. The idea of Europe emerges much later in the Dark Ages, when the Mediterranean fell under the control of Islam, and the Occident began to embrace the north-west of the continent. The idea emerged when Europe was under siege and suffered military defeats by Islam in the south. The acceptance of Christianity by the northern tribes from the Franks to the Vikings allowed for the ascendancy of Charlemagne who styled himself as the father of Europe. It was with the abandonment of the Mediterranean for the Baltic that the identity of Europe emerged.

Christianity was inextricably associated with this European idea. However, there is a question to be raised: which Christianity are we talking about, Roman or Byzantine? Rome had Europeanized an Asiatic cult, Christianity, in the eighth century, and during the evolution of the Christian church it bifurcated into one that was based in Rome and the other that was based in Constantinople. The Greek Orthodox Church became orientalized while the church that was based in Rome was adopted as the identity of Western Europe. This tension between the two churches was explicitly demonstrated during the Crusades. For medieval Europe, the Crusades galvanized an identity around Christianity, even though the Crusades only captured Jerusalem for a short while before the forces of Islam retook it. It is pertinent to note that in the course of this conflict the European Crusaders sacked Constantinople, the centre of the Byzantine church, and hastened its demise. The Normans, the ascendant power in Europe, annexed the remaining Byzantine cities that were located in Italy (Delanty, 1995).

The final point about the multiplicity of Europe is related to Islam. As Bryan Turner (1994) points out, when Islam initially emerged it was viewed as a Christian sect, and for a substantial period of time it occupied parts of southern Europe, Spain, Sicily and the Balkans. It is difficult to make a case that Islam was not part of what we see today as Europe. In the nineteenth century, Turkey was seen as a European power, hence the adage, 'the sick man of Europe' that was common in Victorian parlance. There are multiple Europes that have existed over different historical periods, and contemporary notions of Europe are a product of shifts in balances of power that took place in the early modern period, between the West and the Rest.

The alternative is to link European value to modernity, and this is the approach that the Convention (2003) took. The Enlightenment was a multi-faceted phenomenon with positive and negative legacies that need to be examined critically. Positive aspects are the emergence of democracy, secularism, scientific reasoning, equality for citizens, and freedoms and rights. These are the notions celebrated as those European values that can be considered traceable back to the Enlightenment. There is a dark side of Enlightenment that is associated with scientific racism, colonialism and the Holocaust. Giddens (1990) has persuasively argued that modernity produced a state structure that was more efficient at fighting wars than empires and kingdoms. This efficiency in war translated into colonial empires, and was a defining factor in the construction of the West. The term, 'the West' simplifies complexities that disguise the fact that not all of Europe is the West, and not all of the West is Europe. The West is modern, includes Western Europe, North America and Japan and is juxtaposed with the Rest, which is traditional. The idea of the West is a concept central to the Enlightenment, and is a characteristic that helps to define 'us'. The Rest assists in the definition of the West through the construction of the 'other'. Neither term is homogeneous, and both constructions change over space and time, but these are important concepts that are formed in Enlightenment, and influence the Enlightenment process as well (Hall, 1992).

Orientalism promotes this division between the West and the Rest: it reinforces the idea that Europe, the West and the USA are in opposition to the Orient, the East and the 'other'. Orientalism has multiple meanings, and can be used geographically to look primarily at Asia. Edward Said's (1978) use of Orientalism was specifically related to the Middle East and Islam. Orientalism was the defining 'other' that assisted in constructing modernity. Classical social scientists' Eurocentric theoretical observations were in opposition to orientalism. Weber's Protestant work ethic juxtaposed the diligent and economically rational Occident with the lazy, licentious and superstitious Orient. Marx argued that Oriental society was inherently despotic, and hence not conducive to the development of capitalism.

Masoud Kamali (2003), in his chapter, argues that the dichotomy between the West and the Orient is false. There are multiple routes to modernity, and there is a need to challenge Eurocentric assumptions of modernity that see it as a single, universal and homogeneous process. Hall (1992) reiterates this point, arguing that there is no master narrative for modernity. Kamali examines the relationship of Islam and modernity in the case of Turkey and Iran. It is the impact of military defeat on the Ottoman and Persian Empires that initiates a process searching for alternative paths to modernity. Taking Giddens' argument that a modern state was excellent at waging war, it forced elements within these pre-modern formations to respond by modernizing the state and producing new model armies. In this search for alternative paths to modernity, to resist primarily British and Russian imperialism, elites from Turkey and Iran were impressed by German and Italian fascism. The process of modernization was looking for alternative routes that were emerging from less powerful European nations. Democracy was also an important aspect of this development and important social groupings in both of these countries were promoting democratic reforms. While modernization of the state, explicitly the formation of modern armies, was more successful, the democratization of society was not so successful due to intervention from the West. Demand for democracy in Iran in the 1950s led to US intervention and the downfall of the Mossadeq government, and in the case of Turkey, the Kemalists, supported by NATO, kept the religious parties from coming to power. Western intervention in the case of Iran ultimately led to the fall of the Shah and the rise of Khomeini, and in the case of Turkey, it supported numerous military coups removing legitimately elected governments, the most recent example being the fall of Demirel.

This interconnection and intimacy between alternative paths of modernity and Islam are recreated in recent times with the emergence of jihadi Islam. Ian Talbot persuasively argues that Europe and the USA played a major role in the construction and emergence of jihadi Islam as a new political force. This goes back to the Soviet invasion of Afghanistan and the use of guerrillas to fight a covert action against the occupation. The USA persuaded Pakistan to become a front-line state, and used its considerable influence to get Saudi support for the operation. Saudi Arabia matched dollar for dollar US contributions to the war. The USA and its Western allies supplied arms, and turned a blind eye to the production and smuggling of drugs to the West that funded covert action, and acts of misogyny and savagery carried out by their allies. Peshawar became the grand meeting place for Islamicists from all over the world. They came from all over the globe, encouraged to do so by the USA and its allies, to train, form networks, provide resources, set up charities and generally exchange ideas on the prosecution of jihad in different parts of the world. What emerges is a transnational social movement that transforms the true meaning of jihad into being primarily understood as physical conflict. Abdallah Azzam's revolutionary reinstatement of jihad, which explicitly incorporated martyrdom, was responsible for this development (Cook, 2005). Once this transformation had taken place, it was possible for those who conducted their local jihad in different parts of the world to rally to the calls of Osama bin Laden and his global jihad against the USA. The first Gulf War was the crucial turning point, where groups who were acting as proxies for the USA and the West began to turn against their former masters. Even though bin Laden declared jihad against the 'Jews and Crusaders' in 1992, the USA was still using jihadis as their proxies in the conflict in Bosnia and Kosovo (ICG, 2001).

The construction of the West and the Rest is based on a notion of European identity that draws on Islam as the 'other'. This occurred in various ways in the past with the construction of European identity around Christianity; it is deeply embedded in the Enlightenment process and is reflected in the way that Eurocentric theories are constructed by classical social scientists. It is also reflected in the way that Europe and the West intervene in Muslim countries by derailing democratic processes, and in the construction of jihadi groups. The reality is that the West is inextricably, and on multiple levels, inseparable from the Rest, and these dichotomies have little substance in either history or policy.

Delanty (2000: 65) has argued that the alternative is to develop post-national citizenship and identity that overcomes the dichotomy of 'us' and 'them', inclusion and exclusion, et cetera. He refers to a 'reflexive transformation of existing national conceptions of group membership', built primarily on the recognition of shared sovereignty where significant inroads into national sovereignty have taken place on the supranational and sub-national level. National citizenship is based on birth and descent while post-national citizenship is based on residence. European citizenship, as adopted by the Maastricht Treaty, is an example of post-national citizenship. Delanty develops Jurgen Habermas' (1998) argument of 'constitutional patriotism' where identification is with normative principles of the constitution. This form of citizenship and identity is not anchored in the state, territory, cultural heritage or shared conceptions of community. European expansion is developing a post-national society based on a European-wide political, public sphere embedded in shared political culture: a shared political culture founded on civil society, not national culture, represented by interest groups, non-governmental organizations and citizen-based movements and initiatives. Constitutional post-nationalism for Delanty has to be rooted in civic communities, which are discursively constituted. European civil society does not exist but a transnational civic community, a virtual community, is being realized.

## GLOBALIZATION, TRANSNATIONALISM AND FUNDAMENTALISM

Muslim communities in Western Europe are undergoing considerable social change and a far more useful explanatory approach is to locate it within the wider process of social transformation taking place, rather than attributing it to developments within the Islamic world. With the postmodern term there has been an increasing engagement with micro sociology accompanying the demise of the meta-narratives. Lyotard's incredulity of the meta-narrative of progress, development, science, class, et cetera led him to embrace the postmodern condition of uncertainty and rhetorical play (Hall et al., 1992). The focus of micro-narratives, in part, was to investigate cultural identifications as free-flowing dramaturgical processes resulting in hybrid formations unhindered by structure. The smorgasbord approach to cultural identifications was criticized by Lash and Urry (1994) in their writings. Their critical concern was the absence of structure in postmodern theory, and they argued for the continued salience of institutions in understanding contemporary social change. The changing nature of work or the lack of work due to post-Fordist development in flexible production and mobile labour has had a considerable impact. The process of social change in work was reinforced by globalization and the translocation of production processes to the Pacific Rim.

Deindustrialization as a consequence of globalization and the changing nature of work are major factors in the decline of the meta-narrative and the emergence of a European underclass—an underclass that is primarily populated by ethnic minorities, who in Europe are mainly Muslim. These populations suffer lower rates of employment (52.7 per cent employment rate compared to 64.4 per cent employment for European citizens), more so for women. Ethnic minorities are over-represented in risky sectors of employment, the grey economy, and are exposed to health risks. Well-educated and skilled migrants are often unable to find work appropriate to their level of skill, and accept employment with lower skill requirements and less pay (CEC, 2003). Here, the focus is upon micro-narratives that are circumscribed by marginality and exclusion with specific reference to Muslim minorities, the product of a specific type of migration, which are over-represented in the deindustrialised zones. At the European level, the underclass, whether in Britain, France, the Netherlands or Germany, is populated largely by Maghrebians, Turks and South Asians who are predominantly of Muslim origin.

Postmodernity has been complemented by globalization, which has led to the collapse of time and space resulting in the disembedment of cultural products from their spatial origins. De-territorialization of cultural products results in transnational flows of people, finance, ideology, images and technology that sidestep boundaries of nation-states (Appaduri, 1990). There are a number of aspects of transnationalism that are pertinent to understanding the social change taking place among Muslims settled in Europe. Transnationalism, the movement and flow of cultural artefacts, specifically relates to a number of areas pertinent to ethnic minorities in Europe. Vertovec (1999) indicates that transnationalism, as the spanning of the borders, has transformed ethnic diasporas from the classical understanding of people dispersed, into people who are situated 'here and there', simultaneously connected by strong networks spanning the globe. The old diasporas of yesterday have become the transnational communities of today, and Muslims have strong networks both as ethnic and religious communities.

The process of transnationalism also produces cultural hybridization of identity free from kinship and territory (Cohen, 1997). Hall has argued that in the diaspora, cultural identities are reformulated, resulting in new ethnicities, which are linked to new ethnic and new religious movements (Hall, 1996; Gillroy, 1987). There is also the world economy, where strong identities and global networks of mutual trust operate. While there has been considerable focus on global corporations, small economic players also need to be accounted for, and are probably more relevant when considering the Muslim underclass. The flow of remittances, and financial institutions, ranging from banks and money changers to informal banking networks have come under increasing scrutiny post-9/11 for their linkage to jihadi groups. Transnational political activity, the intersection of the global and the local, encompassing both cosmopolitan and essentialized identifications, introduce the politics of the homeland as well as movements with wider agendas. The case of Muslim mobilization against Salman Rushdie, the Gulf War, the spillover of Islamic upsurge in Algeria and the support among some European Muslims for the al-Qaeda network are examples of transnational politics in the European context. The disjuncture between territory, subjectivity and collective social action has also seen the rise of virtual communities, virtual politics and networks. The Internet has become the home of ethnic and religious mobilization representing a range of opinion among Muslims (Vertovec, 1999). It is clear that transnationality is an integral and recognizable feature of Muslim minorities in Europe (Samad, 1998). Among Muslims, there are a plethora of transnational networks and associations, both in consumption and production of media, politics, religious activity, cultural artefacts, economic activity, fashion and food. Transnational identifies are cultivated and supported by a variety of 'ethnic institutions' in Europe, often solidifying in resistance to racism and religious bigotry, renewed and reinvented through contacts with the country of origin and other members of the diaspora (Raj, 2000; Glavanis, 1999).

Barber (2003) theorizes the process of globalization as being a collision between the forces of aggressive economic and cultural globalization, McWorld, versus the forces of tribalism and reactionary fundamentalism, jihad. For him, the issue is not about Islam. It is about militant fundamentalism and the dialectical interdependence of these two oppositional sets of forces. The process of McDonaldization and Coca-Colaization, the cultural and economic homogenization of the global economy results in cosmopolitan identifications that revel in hybridity and postmodern irony and play. Meeting resistance from essentialist forms of identification, ethnic, nationalist or religious, which contest this homogenising process by emphasizing authentic diversity. Barber's choice of metaphor is problematic; there are numerous debates about how fundamentalism can be defined. Turner (1994) argues that it is not useful to conflate all religious traditions as fundamentalist, and uses the term specifically to consider where religion enters into politics. Globalization of religion actually increases fundamentalism but the collapsing of conservative with modernist variations in Islam is unproductive. Political Islam is Janus-faced, castigating traditional Islam as deviant from the true path and simultaneously challenging the West with alternative strategies of modernity. It does this by entering the realm of politics, which is a clear departure from the practices and behaviour of traditional Islam. The real threat to all religious faith comes from postmodern consumer lifestyles with their cut-and-paste approach that undermines faith-based belief systems (Turner, 1994). There are serious questions concerning meta-theory and its empirical verification on the ground. A number of writers in this collection challenge these arguments by examining the process from the bottom up, and this will be covered later in the introduction.

Robertson has questioned the top-down approach to globalization driven by transnational corporations homogenizing culture, and instead argues that there is a reverse process that simultaneously has a heterogenizing effect. The inter-reaction of the global only develops significance when it intersects with micro-processes in the locale (Robertson, 1992). The global/local inter-reaction results in the hybrid cosmopolitan identifications and new ethnicities as argued by Stuart Hall (1992) and Paul Gillroy (1987). Kaldor (2003) and Samad (1998) argue that simultaneously essentialized identifications are being produced in the locale which are hybrid and new. Muslims are reconstructing identity as an interaction between transnational and local processes; a development more advanced among the youth of the Muslim population.

## YOUTH, GENDER AND MULTICULTURALISM

As pointed out, identifications are constructed in the locale and are mediated by social policy. Multiculturalism has become the policy of choice to deal with diversity, and in the process has become globalized and, in turn, mediated in the locale by place and space (Jackson and Penrose, 1993), resulting in various relationships between structure and power (Hall, 1992). Clearly there is considerable variation in multiculturalism, strong multiculturalism refer to societies that have policies and procedures to govern difference while weak multicultural societies are simply culturally interogeneous with no social policy relating to governance (Hall, 2000). Overall multiculturalism predominates in Europe and three different approaches emerged in the incorporation of Muslim minorities. While a number of European countries—Sweden, UK, Belgium and Holland—have, with varying degrees, adopted group rights (recognizing different aspects, some religious, other ethnic) as the basis of managing minorities, other countries, in particular France, have resisted this approach and emphasized individual rights to be paramount. However, even in France there has been some movement in recent times towards the recognition of group rights in an implicit manner. The final category is represented by Germany where minorities are treated as guest workers, and policies and practices are based on the assumption that they are non-citizens and without political rights but have social rights only. It is important to qualify the differences in national experience in terms of legislation and policy, which have a significant influence on the conceptualization and operation of multiculturalism. Thus, there are considerable variations in multiculturalism in Europe, and ironically, the results are strikingly similar, with minorities across the board being marginalized and excluded, and forming a major part of the European underclass. Muslims are concentrated in temporary and insecure work, with rates of unemployment ranging from two and a half times to five times the unemployment rate of the indigenous population and low rates of health cover (see Pêdziwiatr's chapter).

Multicultural policy acts directly or indirectly as a mediator for transnational influences and gives it a degree of authenticity and legitimacy. The common themes that emerge, in spite of the local variations, are the essentialization of identifications, the gendered and generational representations of community and the emphasis on authenticity, resulting in older, male religious leaders emerging as community representatives. Multiculturalism from this perspective silences the voice of the young, women and gays. Anti-essentialist approaches to multiculturalism argue that community is a contested terrain and can be deconstructed along the lines of gender, class, generation, sexuality and political allegiance. Collective identification is a multi-vocal dialogue between different aspects shifting over time, space and place (Hall, 1996; Ranger, 1996).

Youth is also a fraught and ambivalent category where young people actively negotiate cultural process, not simply react to them, forming hybrid and new identifications from standard cultural artefacts (Amit-Talai & Wulff, 1995). Youth are at the forefront in the negotiation of tradition and postmodernity in a globalized world, levering open spaces to negotiate generational differences and generating new forms of social constructions. These spaces are being denied by countervailing influences of elder generations and society attempting to re-culturalate or assimilate them (Samad, 1997). The emergence of essentialist hybrid identifications has been linked to processes of social exclusion, racism and xenophobia (Hall, 1996; Gillroy, 1987; Samad, 1997). The search for purity and authenticity among young Muslims is resulting in a fractured and disarticulated politics of identity that results in the emergence of hybrid Islamic identification: a fractured identification divorced from Islamic tradition and practices, an inventive process whereby Islam is re-imagined and reconstructed in the diaspora as a vehicle for assertion of the self and being as well as acts of violence and crime (Samad, 1998; McLoughlin, nd). It is significant that the Muslim population is youthful in comparison to the white population, and while comparative figures are problematic and scarce, it is indicative that in the United Kingdom 50 per cent of Muslims are under 25 while in Belgium 35 per cent are under 18 (see Pêdziwiatr's chapter).

Transnational processes intervene in these developments taking place in the locale. Ideologically, Islam appears to be well placed to take advantage of globalization and transnationalism. It conceives the Muslim community as a world community, not recognizing nation states as legitimate in religious terms. The theoretical arguments suggest that the Islamic concept of *Ummah* would make Muslims more susceptible to transnational Islamic movements, which would have a profound societal impact, generally and specifically. As Paul Lubeck (2003) argued, contemporary Islamic activism is neither local nor bounded by nationality, but is multifaceted and potentially global. The *Ummah* is a transnational ideology, which is grounded and reinforced by pilgrimage and Sufi and religious networks. These characteristics are reformulated by the information revolution, providing for new networks to emerge.

The long-term consequences of such arguments, if supported by evidence, would exacerbate racism and xenophobia, impacting on general relations between different communities. Godfried Engbersen, in his study, challenges this simplistic understanding of transnationalism and 'fundamentalism' in the European locale. His evidence suggests that high degrees of social integration of Muslims result in strong ethnic identities and weak transnational influences; conversely, unemployment leads to greater affiliation to transnational influences emanating from the country of origin. He demonstrates clearly the inter-reaction of transnational influences with underlying factors, particularly marginalization and social exclusion, which encourage or depress transnationalism.

The second consideration is the discourse of the search for essentialist and authentic identification among the youth. Impressionistic formulations suggest that 'fundamentalism' is appearing on the ground. However, evidence collected by Cesari and Samad have a strong contra-factual effect for this argument. The ethnicization of religion, where Islam becomes an identity marker, a source of pride and simultaneously a sign of integration, is a different phenomenon from increasing religiosity and the rise of Islamic 'fundamentalism'. Young Muslims are losing rapidly their ability to speak Arabic, Farsi, Punjabi, Turkish or Urdu, and are more familiar in the language of their adopted country, and this is an indication of the degree that they have become Europeanized. The shift in identity is also reinforced by the way that Islam is represented in the media and by neo-orientalist discourse. The two are complementing each other in producing this shift, and combine the engagement of young Muslims with popular culture. Rap songs, tattoos and graffiti, essential aspects of popular culture, are reinterpreted through Islamic metaphors and idioms. Young Muslims, like other young people in their rebellious phase, adopt Islamic rhetoric to remain within the outer boundaries of community, which is circumscribed by discrimination, racism and xenophobia, and yet present a provocative and challenging imagery to mainstream society.

Gender is an important variable in this process, with young women adopting Islamic modes to challenge gender-oppressive community practices and gain control over their bodies and lives. Islam is considered to be a liberating ideology from the conservative cultural practices of their elders, and allows women to make life choices in relationship to education, employment and marriage. The wearing of the veil has become a highly complex and political activity; complex in that there are numerous considerations that are involved in the veiling of women, ranging from misogynist practices to liberation theology (Naguib, 2002). Some young women see the wearing of the veil as a political response to mainstream society, demonstrating their authenticity and identity. There is little evidence to suggest that young men or women's identity shift is actually being influenced by transnational processes. It is primarily a generational issue where young people are trying to redefine their identification vis à vis their elder generation within a context of marginalization and exclusion. Overwhelmingly, identity politics reflects social change through migration rather than that of resistance to the corrosive influence of postmodernity and globalization.

Social class is an extremely important variable, having significant impact on life trajectories and responses of young Muslims. In the European context, young Muslims are the descendants of labour migrants and have low educational attainments and relatively low degrees of professionalization. In parallel with their white counterparts, they have become part of the working class culture that is slipping into the grey/black economy and criminal activity. Violence, riots and ghettoization and other social problems associated with Muslims are indicative of the marginalization that impacts upon them and are over-represented in the prison population, (in France and Germany there is a 5:1 ratio of Muslims to local populations, and in the Netherlands and Belgium there is 6 and 8:1 ratio respectively). See Pêdziwiatr's chapter. Aminah Mohammad-Arif's case study of South Asian Muslim youth in the USA clearly brings out this variable. With US immigration controls acting as a filter, allowing only professionals to enter, South Asian Muslim youth are highly educated and have high aspirations that make them have the same aspirations, desires and attainments as their middle class counterparts; the representation of them is not as rioters, gangs or as segregated communities.

## Islamophobia

The emergence of Muslim identity is misrepresented by the media who whip up moral panic and xenophobia about the globalization of Islamic fundamentalism: a moral panic that intersects and reinforces existing racist outlooks and xenophobic discourses, forming new combinations of discrimination. Huntington's thesis, *The Clash of Civilizations* (1998), is a typical but flawed example of the reworking of orientalist ideologies that reinforce the tropes of folk devils and demonization of Muslims. In the era of globalization, new orientalist ideologies are refashioned, continuing to demonize Islam rather than exploring conditions that generate marginalization and social exclusion. Consequently, Islamic groups in many European countries argue that a new phenomenon has emerged, Islamophobia, in the post-cold war world: a negative stereotype of Muslims that justifies their oppression and violence at multiple levels.

Racism and orientalism have a long historical legacy intimately tied to the formation of modernity but reconstituted over different historical periods in various ways. Islamophobia's historical legacy is found in orientalism; there are multiple strands that juxtapose Christian Europe versus Islam, and the process of otherization is also found in the construction of modernity. Huntington's argument simply resurrects these orientalist discourses in the context of a post-cold war world. The categories; racism, xenophobia and anti-Semitism, are common terms but Islamophobia is a more recent coinage, which only emerged in print in 1991 in the USA. It is the reformulation and reimagining of orientalist discourse in a new context. Not the most elegant of terms, it was defined by The Runnymede Trust's report as a 'useful shorthand way of referring to dread or hatred of Islam—and therefore to fear or dislike of all or most Muslims' (Runnymede, 1997: 1). The phenomenon has become much more explicit in the last twenty years. Islamophobia belongs to a family of racisms that include anti-black, anti-Asian, anti-Turk, anti-Arab, anti-Irish, anti-Jewish and anti-Roma forms of racism.

There are, however, two strands that are common in the family of racisms. One strand, a visible difference, focuses on pigmentation, body and hair type, and differentiates around notions of racial differences. The other strand highlights cultural differences, religion, language, dress, and kinship patterns, and emphasizes these differences as a way of framing differentiation and hierarchy (Gilroy, 1987; Wieworka, 1995; Barker, 1981). The postmodern increasing sensitivity to cultural identity makes the emphasis on cultural difference a reference point for discrimination consistent with contemporary trends in social change.

Post-9/11, Islamophobia has become intensified with the fear of terrorism conflating with general unease with Muslim populations settled in Europe. Evidence collated by the European Monitoring Centre on Racism and Xenophobia post-9/11 shows that there has been an increase in low levels of physical violence in most EU countries, and verbal abuse, harassment and aggression has become more widespread. Muslim women, particularly those who wear *hijab*, asylum seekers and others who appear to look like Muslims or Arabs have been subjected to threats and violence, and mosques and Islamic cultural centres have been targeted. Neo-Nazi and far right groups have increased their activity in a general context where xenophobic sentiments have increased. While most politicians have attempted to engage in inter-faith and inter-community dialogue, some have attempted to gain political capital, particularly where concerns with terrorism conflate with immigration. It was also noted that sensationalism of stereotypical representation of Muslims increased in the media (Allen & Nielsen, 2002).

Claire Alexander demonstrates that Muslims have become the new folk devil, and representations seamlessly portray them as terrorists, rioters and criminal gangs, resulting in moral panic. The moral panic triggers neo-orientalist discourses in social policy where conceptions of culture that privilege religion become the dominant mode of understanding by media and policy makers. A triple demonization of Muslims has taken place, particularly in the UK, where a conflation of religious militancy and cultural misogyny merges with ghetto masculinity and criminalization. Islamophobia's impact in social policy is resulting in an inability to see violence as a social phenomenon emerging from social exclusion and economic marginalization. The impact of moral panic and the construction of Muslims as new folk devils leads to them being demonised as terrorists, rioters and criminal gangsters.

## DISCRIMINATION LEGISLATION

Comparative approaches to central issues of governance and citizenship indicate specific social policy issues that need to engage with Muslims, and youth in particular. Tufyal Choudhury's study shows that there are difficulties in investigating comparative social policy on the European level for a number of reasons. The issue of statistical evidence is clearly a difficulty that still has to be engaged with. Statistical comparability is an issue because data collected in terms of immigrant and citizen does not necessarily compare like with like. In the case of Germany, citizenship is exceedingly difficult to acquire even when younger generations of migrants are born there, while in the UK and France, citizenship is acquired much more easily. Ethnicity is recorded in the UK, but only in the 2001 census was religion included. In the case of Italy, there are no statistics on ethnicity, and this has been used as a defence by the authorities against accusations of discrimination. Germany has legislation that prevents the collection of data on ethnicity. In France, religious data is illegal, and in Spain it is mainly due to lack of political will. Without statistical data, it is difficult to gauge the degree of discrimination and its significance.

Discrimination legislation also varies. There is no comprehensive legislation on discrimination in Germany or Spain. In Italy, constitutional anti-discrimination provision is complemented by legislation dealing with direct and indirect discrimination, but low public awareness has resulted in little use of this protection. France has a comprehensive discrimination law that is framed within the republican principle of equality for individuals. Muslim claims challenge this notion of equality, and France does not recognize minorities or group rights, but this position is slowly changing with the establishment of a Muslim council by the authorities. The legislation includes direct discrimination, but this is not clearly defined as it clashes with republican ideals. In the case of the United Kingdom, there is no comprehensive anti-discrimination act except in Northern Ireland. The Race Relations Act does not cover religion or incitement to religious hatred, though some minorities, Sikhs and Jews, are covered through indirect legislation. The MacPherson Report defined institutional racism, but it has the same weakness as the Race Relations Act in that it does not cover religion. Similarly, in Belgium, religion is not included in the legislation, and this lacuna has been exploited. The General Act on Equal Treatment in the Netherlands, however, covers religious discrimination and has been actively used, resulting in case-law (Open Society Institute, 2002; Glavanis, 1999).

Tufyal Choudhury's chapter argues that there is a clear need for EU legislation on discrimination which includes religious discrimination. There is at present an EC directive covering employment, but its scope needs to be widened and made more extensive. This recommendation follows the US example that has introduced a Freedom of Religion Act (FRA). The motives for implementing the FRA were dubious at best: it was designed to capture the moral high ground, allowing the USA to pontificate on religious freedom to third world countries, and in particular, to Muslim states. The act comprehensively covers Muslims, and there have been a number of cases, mainly in employment, around the issue of wearing beards and *hijab* that have successfully used the legislation in a court of law (Moore, 2002). At present the act has been temporarily suspended because of the war on terror.

Terrorism legislation, according to Les Levidow, has had a pernicious impact on Muslims, resulting in the criminalization of Islamic 'fundamentalists', refugees and asylum seekers, and creating moral panic. The Terrorism Act of 2000 in the UK had a broad definition that stigmatized community networks and community activists. The Terrorism Act of 2001 in the UK created further difficulties for Muslims; the Act unilaterally produced a UK definition of terrorism for which there is no international consensus. The international community is divided by the debate that one man's freedom fighter is another man's terrorist, but the UK definition was open-ended and made to apply globally. Its intention, according to some writers, was to frighten people and curtail their right of freedom of speech. The Terrorism Act of 2001 extended police powers, allowing arrests, mainly of Muslims, for indefinite periods. So far 562 arrests have been made under the Act but only 97 have been charged with 14 convictions (there are some large cases pending) (The *Guardian*, 5/8/2004), it was also used to make collective arrests, where even the families of individual suspects were taken in for questioning by the police. Ordinary illegal activity now became portrayed as terrorist plots, such as the ricin poison case. Imran Khan raises the key question, 'On what grounds and what circumstances should the state be able to criminalize the activity of its citizens?'—a question raised by legal experts. The unease with the legislation has been reflected in the upper echelons of the judicial hierarchy, and Lord Woolf reminded the establishment that they should avoid making the mistakes of the Second World War and the rounding up of aliens. Such scenarios are permissible with the Act that affects asylum seekers, refugees and foreigners.

Levidow's chapter suggests that Britain has attempted to influence the European Union and make them adopt similar draconian legislation on terrorism. Under UK influence, the EU's war on terror has led to the banning of a number of Muslim groups and the increased regulation of refugees and asylum seekers. The EU council redefined terrorism in a similar style to the United Kingdom. This has resulted in group approaches to policing and punishment becoming permissible across Europe, resulting in entire communities being treated with suspicion and hostility, their economic resources threatened through the freezing of property, cash and business accounts, all in the name of terrorism. Formal and informal banking networks in the Muslim communities have been subject to intense scrutiny or have been shut down and Muslim charities have been adversely affected. It is resulting in a failure to differentiate between legitimate political activity and terrorism—an increasingly worrying development as many refugees and asylum seekers are political activists who have been persecuted in their countries of origin. The moral panic has led to the stereotyping of Muslim parties and organizations as a source of insecurity and concern. Consequently, there has been a blurring of the distinction between political activity, community networks, immigration issues and organized violence. Muslim communities are treated as dangerous, and their networks are under suspicion for having links to terrorism. Human rights activists are arguing that anti-terror legislation is an attack on democracy *per se*, and needs to be changed. Human rights should not be sacrificed on the altar of security.

The question that comes to mind is, what will be the Muslim communities, response to the 'war on terror' in the long run? This is primarily a battle of hearts and minds, and without their support al-Qaeda and its allies will not find fertile ground to work in. However, media moral panics construct Muslims as folk devils, which leads to misguided, inappropriate and aggressive legislative responses. The banning of the veil in French schools or the excessive use of anti-terrorism laws in Britain carries the risk of alienating Muslims, in particular the youth, who are explicitly conscious of their rights as citizens. Individual European nations as well as the European Union need to provide the space for Muslim communities that allows for their incorporation as citizens based on equality. There needs to be recognition that there is an identity shift taking place, that appearance and essence are different things as Muslim youth become European and what the French see as threatening—Muslim women wearing *hijab*—can be turned around as in the UK, which allows Muslim police officers to wear the *hijab*. Instead of challenging the law it can become a symbol of law enforcement. This does not necessarily mean that all conservative

Muslim demands should be met, but meeting some of the issues allows for the disaggregation of Muslims into a range of opinions and positions. Ultimately for the youth, only substantive efforts on the central issues of access to the labour market and legislation against, and monitoring of, discrimination, in particular Islamophobia, will reassure them that they have a place, and their contribution is welcomed, in the new Europe.

Yunas Samad

## REFERENCES

Allen, Christopher and Nielsen, Jorgen S., Summary Report on Islamophobia in the EU after 11 September 2001, European Monitoring Centre on Racism and Xenophobia, Vienna, 2002.

Amit-Talai, Vered and Wulff, Helena (eds.), *Youth Cultures: A Cross-Cultural Perspective*, Routledge, London, 1995.

Appaduri, Arjun, 'Disjuncture and Difference in the Global Cultural Economy', in Mike Featherstone (ed.) *Global Culture: Nationalism, Globalization and Modernity*, Sage, London, 1990.

Barber, B.R., *Jihad vs. McWorld*, Corgi Books, London, 2003.

Barker, Martin, *The New Racism*, Junction Books, London, 1981.

Cohen, Robin, *Global Diaspora: an Introduction*, UCL Press, London, 1997.

Cook, David, *Understanding Jihad*, University of California Press, Berkeley, 2005.

Commission of the European Communities, *Communication from the Commission to the Council, The European Parliament, The European Economic and Social Committee and the Committee of the Regions on Immigration, Integration and Employment*, Com (2003) 336 final, Brussels, 2003.

Delanty, Gerard, *Inventing Europe: Idea, Identity, Reality*, Macmillan, Basingstoke, 1995.

Delanty, Gerard, *Citizenship in a global age: society, culture, politics*, Open University Press, Buckingham, 2000.

EU Business, www.eubusiness.com. 11 September 2003.

The European Convention, Draft Treaty Establishing a Constitution for Europe, submitted by the President of the Convention to the European Council meeting in Thessaloniki on 20 June 2003, CONV 820/03.797/1/02 REV 1, 2003.

Giddens, Anthony, *The Consequence of Modernity*, Polity Press, Cambridge, 1990.

Gilroy, Paul, *There Ain't No Black in the Union Jack*, Hutchinson, London, 1987.

Glavanis, Pandeli M., *'Muslim Voices' in the European Union: The Stranger Within. Community, Identity and Employment*, Final Report, Brussels: European Commission. Targeted Socio-Economic Research (TSER) SOE1-CT96-3024, 1999.

Glavanis, Pandeli M., 'Political Islam within Europe: A Contribution to an Analytical Framework', *Innovation*, Vol. 11, No. 4, 1998.

Habermas, Jurgen, *The Inclusion of Other: Studies in Political Theory*, MIT Press, Cambridge, MA, 1998.

Hall, Stuart, 'New Ethnicities' in Donald, J. and Rattansi, A., *'Race' Culture and Difference*, Sage, London, 1992.

Hall, Stuart, Held, David and McGrew, Tony, *Modernity and its futures*, Polity Press/Open University, Cambridge, 1992:333.

Hall, Stuart, 'Politics of Identity' in Ranger, T., Samad, Y. and Stuart, O., *Culture, Identity and Politics: Ethnic Minorities in Britain*, Avebury, Aldershot, 1996.

Huntington, Samuel P., *The Clash of Civilizations and the Remaking of World Order*, Touchstone Books, London, 1998.

ICG, *bin Laden and the Balkans: the Politics of Anti-Terrorism*. International Crisis Group Balkans Report No.119, 2001.

Jackson, Peter & Penrose, Jan (eds.), *Constructions of Race, Place and Nation*, UCL Press, London, 1993.

Kaldor, M., *Global Civil Society: An Answer to War*, Polity Press, Cambridge, 2003.

Kepel, Gilles, *Jihad: The Trail of Political Islam*, I.B. Tauris Publishers, London, 2002.

Lash, S. and Urry, J., *Economies of Signs and Space*, London, Sage, 1994.

Lewis, Bernard, 'The Roots of Muslim Rage', *The Atlantic*, September, 1990.

Lubeck, P., Lipschutz, R. and Weeks, E., 'The Globality of Islam: Sharia as a Nigerian 'Self-Determination' Movement', Conference on Globalization and Self-Determination, Queen Elizabeth House, University of Oxford, 4 2003.

McLoughlin, Sean, "An Underclass in Purdah?' Discrepant Representations of Identity and the Experiences of Young-British-Asian-Muslim Women', *Bulletin, John Rylands Library*, (nd).

Moore, Kathleen, 'The Politics of Transfiguration: Constitutive Aspects of the International Religious Freedom Act of 1998', in Yazbeck Haddad, Yvonne and Smith, Jane I. (eds.), *Muslim Minorities in the West: Visible and Invisible*, Altamira Press, Walnut Creek, 2002.

Naguib, Saphinaz-Amal, 'The Northern Way: Muslim Communities in Norway' in Yazbeck Haddad, Yvonne and Smith, Jane I. (eds.), *Muslim Minorities in the West: Visible and Invisible*, Altamira Press, Walnut Creek, 2002.

Open Society Institute EU Accession Monitoring Program, *Monitoring the EU Accession Process: Minority Protection Volume II Case Studies in selected Member States*, Open Society Institute, Budapest, 2002.

Raj, Dhooleka S., 'Who the hell do you think you are? Promoting religious identity among young Hindus in Britain', *Ethnic and Racial studies*, Special Issue Vol. 23, No. 3, 2000.

Ranger, Terence, 'Introduction' in Ranger, T., Samad, Y. and Stuart, O. (eds.) *Culture, Identity and Politics: Ethnic Minorities in Britain*, Avebury, Aldershot, 1996.

Report of the Runnymede Trust Commission on British Muslims and Islamophobia, *Islamophobia: a challenge for us all*, The Runnymede Trust, London, 1997.

Robertson, Roland, *Globalization: Social Theory and Global Culture*, Sage, London, 1992.

Said, Edward, *Orientalism*, Pantheon Books, New York, 1978.

Samad, Yunas, 'Ethnicity, Racism and Islam: Identity and Gender and Generational Debates' in *Multiculturalism, Muslims and the Media: Pakistanis in Bradford*, unpublished manuscript produced as part of the research conducted for the ESRC (Award number L126251039), 1997.

Samad, Yunas, 'Media and Muslim Identity: Intersection of Generation and Gender', *Innovation*, Vol. 11, No. 4, 1998.

*Times Higher Educational Supplement*, 1/8/2003.

Turner, Bryan S. Orientalism, *Postmodernism and Globalism*, Routledge, London, 1994.

Vertovec, Steven, 'Conceiving and researching transnationalism', *Ethnic and Racial Studies*, Vol. 22, 1999.

Wieviorka, Michel, *The Arena of Racism*, Sage Publications, London, 1995.

## NOTE

1. There are a number of problems associated with statistics across Europe. In France collecting data on religion is illegal, in Germany the data is for non-citizens and in the United Kingdom only in the 2001 census was the religion category included. In the Netherlands, Belgium and Sweden the Muslim populations are estimates drawn from the number of foreigners resident (see Konrad Pędziwiatr's chapter).

# SECTION 1

# Islam in Europe:
# Theoretical and Empirical Overview

The first chapter of this book focuses on demography and representative organizations among Muslim minorities of Europe through careful assessment of demographic and statistical information. It highlights varied histories in the origin and process of migration and its important impact upon the structure and composition of the constituent populations. This in turn has affected the nature of social and political organization in each of the countries under consideration. This chapter also looks specifically at policies relating to Muslim minorities and their organizations in France, Belgium, the United Kingdom, Germany, the Netherlands and Sweden, and provides a rich source of background information on these communities. This serves as the contextual basis for the ensuing discussion of diverse Islamic culture and polity in the remainder of the book. The first chapter, in particular, highlights the demographic youthfulness of Muslim communities, and the difficulties these communities experience in nearly all of the countries in question in achieving social and political recognition. A similar theme is taken up by Turner in the second chapter, where the image of Muslim culture and polity is described as being historically steeped in 'otherness' in the Western European tradition. This, Turner argues, is intrinsic to the 'Orientalist' academic tradition, which has so powerfully shaped the dominant paradigm in the study and understanding of Islam as an unchanging, static and regressive force. In turn, this outlook has acted as a self-fulfilling prophecy, reinforcing separation, suspicion and to some extent, mutual hostility. Turner sets this perspective in the economic and social dislocation created by neo-liberal policies, particularly in the social and economic sectors of many European countries. The chapter explores the devastating consequences of the combination of this paradigm and the lack of recognition, creating at the national and global level an underclass that serves as the firm basis for religious revivalism.

# 1

# Muslims in Europe: Demography and Organizations

*Konrad Pêdziwiatr*

## EMERGENCE OF MUSLIM COMMUNITIES IN EUROPE

The fact that Islam is the second largest religion in Europe is the result of relatively recent immigration processes. Despite significant differences in the national typology of such processes, one may also point out some common features. One such common factor is an increasing trend towards restriction; following a period of an open door policy, due mainly to the need for cheap labour, immigration laws in most countries of the EU have become increasingly restrictive. They have been narrowed down to the acceptance of new migrants only for family reunification, refugees fleeing persecution, professionals who have already acquired jobs, and finally, students wishing to study. Thus, while up to the mid-1970s, migrants of Muslim origin arrived in large numbers as a complement to the labour force, from the mid-1980s onwards they have arrived mostly as political refugees.

In France, for example, although migrants from the Muslim world had already begun to settle in the nineteenth century, they did not arrive in significant numbers until the end of the Second World War. In the 1950s, Muslims who arrived in France were mainly of Algerian origin and were followed by immigrants from Morocco, Tunisia, sub-Saharan West Africa (mainly Senegal and Mali) and Turkey. In response to the economic recession of the mid-1970s, French immigration controls were to rapidly tighten and restrictions were introduced. Between 1977 and 1981, for example, France subsidised migrants to return to their countries of origin. The aim of this policy was to achieve the return of one million people. However, this policy met with little success, and the eventual formal registration of 130,000 clandestine settlers in 1981–2 could be interpreted as a clear admission of its failure (Nielsen, 1992).

As in most European countries, the first phase of the migration of Muslims consisted predominantly of males seeking work. Algerian migrants had already begun to bring their families over in the 1950s, but the process of family reunification in the case of the other Muslim groups began much later. Despite differential migration patterns during the earlier phases, various Muslim population groups had reached roughly the same gender distribution by 1982 (ibid.). Although there were numerous immigration barriers, France remained an attractive destination for many migrants not only from the Maghreb but also the Middle East. A recent Eurostat study has revealed that some 29 per cent of Moroccans and 10 per cent of Turks emigrating from their countries chose to go to France (Eurostat 2001).

**Emigration from Turkey and Morocco**

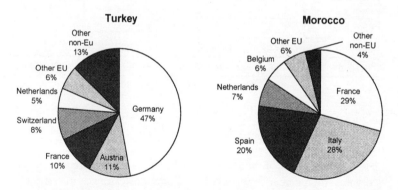

Figure 1
*Source*: Eurostat (2001) Statistics in Focus: Why Do People Migrate?

The settlement of the second largest Muslim population in Europe on the territory of Germany began from 1961. It is not a coincidence that the date of the erection of the Berlin Wall, which blocked the entry of East Germans, is also the date when a bilateral recruitment agreement was signed between Turkey and Germany, to ensure a steady supply of cheap labour. A guest worker scheme was also established with other Muslim countries and recruitment agreements were signed with Morocco in 1963 and with Tunisia in 1965.

The pattern of immigration into Germany was altered during the economic recession in the mid-1970s and during the following decade, when a growing number of refugees from various parts of the world including Turkey, Iran and Arab countries began to arrive in the country. This form of immigration was further strengthened in the 1990s, with the arrival of the political refugees from the former Yugoslavia, Palestine and Afghanistan. Today the migration flow into Germany remains one of the highest in Europe (see Figure 2). Without this immigration, however, Germany would have experienced a population loss.

**Total immigration in selected European countries**

|         | 1996    | 1997    | 1998    | 1999    |
|---------|---------|---------|---------|---------|
| Belgium | 61,522  | 58,849  |         | 68,466  |
| Denmark | 54,445  | 50,105  | 51,372  | 50,236  |
| France  |         |         | 100,014 | 57,846  |
| Germany | 959,691 | 840,633 | 802,456 | 874,023 |
| Holland | 108,749 | 109,860 | 122,407 | 119,151 |
| Sweden  | 39,895  | 44,818  | 49,391  | 49,839  |
| UK      | 258,000 | 285,000 | 332,390 | 354,077 |

Figure 2
*Source*: Eurostat Yearbook 2003: 93.

Until the beginning of the 1960s, entry into the UK by citizens of British colonies and member countries of the Commonwealth was unrestricted. The first Commonwealth Immigration Act of 1962 introduced restrictions on immigration into the UK. Although it was intended to discourage Pakistanis and people from Commonwealth countries from migrating to the country, it turned out to have the opposite effect. The 'unintended effect' of the 1971 Immigration Act was that a significant number of Pakistanis and immigrants from other countries entered the UK, in an effort to 'beat the ban' (Shaw, 1994). On the other hand, the closing of the gates of labour immigration also generated an inflow of migrants in larger numbers, because of the already existing networks of migration—the 'chains' of migration in which seamen and soldiers acted as the first links. The voucher system, briefly introduced under the 1962

Act (until the end of 1967) further strengthened the existing pattern of migration: that is, migration through the family and kinship networks. From the 1970s onwards, the immigration flow has been restricted mainly to family reunification and asylum migration, which has not taken place without difficulties for immigrants due to the application of strict criteria for entry.

As with the situation of the United Kingdom and France, Muslim migration to the Netherlands is characterized by post-colonial links. However, the flows into the Netherlands have not been as substantial in number as with France and the UK. Among the immigrants arriving to the country after the Second World War there were only pockets of Muslims from Indonesia and the Moluccans (former colonies). More numerous groups started to arrive from Dutch Guyana (Suriname) at the end of the 1960s and especially so in the years before it proclaimed its independence from the Netherlands (1975).

The arrival of the immigrants who today make up the largest Muslim groups in the country started in the 1960s. The recruitment agreements were signed with Turkey in 1964 and with Morocco in 1969. In recent decades one has seen the arrival of a growing number of asylum seekers from specific parts of the Muslim world. In the 1980s, they arrived mainly from Iran and Iraq, while in the 1990s the arrivals were mainly from Somalia and Afghanistan, reflecting political tensions and crisis in each of those regions (Maréchal, 2002: 156).

The emergence of a Muslim migrant population in Belgium has similar roots to that of the Netherlands and Germany. The main waves of such migration began in the early 1960s, when agreements were signed with Morocco and Turkey. This was followed at the end of the 1960s with agreements to import workers from Algeria and Tunisia. In contrast to the Netherlands, Belgium had few relations with the Arab Islamic world during colonial days. By 1974, its government had begun to impose strict conditions for the entry of foreign labour. Belgium, however, continued to remain one of the most liberal countries in Europe as far as policies on family reunification are concerned.

The main inflow of workers from Muslim countries into Sweden began in the mid-1960s; Muslims of Turkish and Yugoslavian origin were the first Muslim groups that settled in the country. These were followed by smaller groups of Moroccans, Pakistanis and Egyptians. As elsewhere, the nature of Muslim immigration changed in the 1970s, towards family reunion, but in Sweden another channel of immigration emerged, namely that of the entry of refugees.

Sweden had been until the late 1980s the country with the most liberal refugee policy in Europe. As a result, many Turks, Iranians, Palestinians and Lebanese refugees arrived in Sweden. It is important to note though that many migrants coming from the so-called Muslim countries were not Muslims.[1] This is one of the reasons why it is a particularly difficult exercise to estimate the actual numbers of Muslims in Sweden.

## FAMILY REUNIFICATION AND INSTITUTIONALIZATION OF ISLAM

The primary motive for the migration of people from Muslim countries to Europe was economic, as with most other migration processes. Many came with the firm intention of returning in order to enjoy the fruits of their labour in retirement. In fact, many of them did return to their native land, but a significant number did not and the longer they stayed, the more powerful the mythology of a future return they built up. This perception acted as the rationale for the endurance of hardship at work and in their living conditions, in order to save as much money as possible, which could later be sent to their country of origin. Yet another function of the 'myth of return' was to legitimize continued adherence to the norms and values of their home country, and to condemn assimilation with the culture of their host society (Greaves, 1996: 58).

Though, on the whole, the classic myth was fulfilling its functions very efficiently, there were some exceptions; for example, 'single male' migrants in early post-war Britain were partially affected—as many researchers have suggested—by the 'corrupting influences' of the host society (Shaw, 1994: 41). Apart from the individual daily prayers and 'rites of passage', religious practices hardly existed during this period. There were no 'purpose-built' mosques, nor were any organized religious activities part of the set-up for Muslim immigrants at that time. Muslim migrants to France, Germany and other European countries were not there in order to pray to Allah and proselytize (to perform *dawah* among the host society), as some *ulama* (Muslim scholars) would have liked, but rather to earn money. As 'inter-continental commuters', they did not care much about religion at this early stage of migration. The practice of religion was 'over there', back home, but not in France, Britain or Germany. Talking about the

Pakistanis in Britain, Jones, for example, notices that 'the migrant lived and worked in Britain on behalf of his family, who, it may be surmised, prayed on his behalf' (Jones, 1993: 24). The locus of religion was with the family, as it was in the case of migrants from other ethnic groups.

It should not be surprising, then, that the role of Islam as a way of life, governing not only religious practice and morality but also social relations, marriage, divorce, kinship, economic and political relations, grew enormously following the arrival of wives and children. Thus, their arrival, which took place mainly in the 1970s, marked a turning point in the establishment of Islam in the countries of the EU.

First of all, reunion with family had a strong conservative influence on lifestyles within the Algerian, Pakistani, Turkish and other large Muslim communities in Europe. Shifting from a sojourner status—sustained by the myth of return—to permanent settlement meant, *inter alia*, the end of 'bachelor lifestyles' for many immigrants of the era of single-male worker migration. In the UK, behaviour that would previously pass without comment—as the lonely immigrants sought comfort among local women—began to be regarded as deviant, and hence was frowned upon (Ballard, 1994: 15). Thus, along with the emergence of 'community' through family reunification, some of the conventional norms rooted in social relations, through the practice of Islam, began to be established. The lack of social engagement and absence of welfare facilities in the early days of family reunification meant that many gladly turned to faith as solace. This would have been reinforced by low levels of education as well as the rural origin of many immigrants of all faiths, where religious organizations had played an important welfare function in the absence of any other public provision.

Secondly, family reunion also widened the scope for interaction among migrants of Muslim origin within the host society. As Nielsen has observed, men on their own had interacted only minimally with the wider environment, but with the arrival of women and children these interactions became somehow inevitable (Nielsen, 2000). Health centres and schools, for example, were the main institutions in host societies with which the immigrants began to interact. Since the communities were young with a high proportion of women having children, these interactions, once established, were quite frequent.

With the increasing interaction with the host society and its institutions, Islam as a way of life and as an expression of particular meanings and values began to play an increasingly important role in the lives of migrants in several recipient countries. The context thus began to change to being an active one. This was a significant factor in the establishment of a new form of 'identity'. The identity and function of the Muslim migrant ceased to be merely an individual matter for the individual migrant; through obtaining access to social services such as education the migrant had entered the wider social sphere where the issue of the Islamic faith became an increasingly important and more 'public' matter. However, this process was to become established only through the creation of a significant number of Muslim organizations.

Muslims in the countries of the European Union have organized themselves in many ways. They have established institutions ranging from mosques, prayer halls, schools, halal butchers, religious radio stations, own language newspapers to representation through political parties. In some cases they have managed to appoint Muslim chaplains in hospitals, prisons, armed forces, and have successfully lobbied for changes in state policies regarding various issues affecting migrant communities of Muslim origin.[2] As a result of such efforts, some have managed to create what sociologists have described as the 'plausibility structure' (Berger, 1969: 42), reflected by a network of social relations within which some core religious beliefs and values are articulated.

The establishment of various Muslim organizations, which are a vital element of a system of 'coping', has enabled the first generation of immigrants to pass on some of the values of the Islamic faith to their children born in non-Muslim countries, which is an issue of considerable concern for the first generation of migrants. In recent years, however, a different kind of Muslim organization has come to the fore. The marginalization and exclusion experienced by migrants of Muslim origin in most countries, as evidenced by this book, had fuelled the desire among migrants of Muslim origin for their own representative organizations. As a result, the issue of representing Muslims in a dialogue with state institutions has been placed very high on the agenda of most Muslim organizations established in Europe. To some extent, this is also a result of the request put to Muslim migrant communities by individual European states, which have requested a 'single voice' of representation to deal with the needs and demands of Muslim communities. As Dilwar Hussain has observed, this request was in itself an illustration of wishful thinking due not only to the diversity of origin, but also because Muslim migrants had generally not been very skilful at forming representative, coordinating bodies that effectively reflect diversity by race, class and locality (Hussain, 2003: 245).

## PROFILES OF MUSLIM POPULATIONS AND THEIR REPRESENTATIVE ORGANIZATIONS

### General remarks

The common problem of most research on Muslim minorities in Europe has been to identify those who would consider themselves Muslims, and their socio-economic characteristics. Despite evidence of common features in the growth and development of the Muslim populations in EU countries, there is no single methodological approach to their quantification. The differences in the way governments have pursued policies of integration have also had direct implications for the way in which the identity of individuals is represented in official statistics.

European states differ not only in the way in which they represent individual and group identities in statistics, but also in the frequency and manner with which they collect data on their populations. The differences in time, locality and definition apply to the whole population and not to Muslim migrants alone. Early initiatives by the European Parliament to standardize the practice of the decennial census, including the type and form of information collected, have not been successful. Some countries have moved towards register-based statistics while others have not (Glavanis, 1999).

Despite the efforts of Eurostat there is also little standardization across countries in the dissemination of population statistics, either in format or in their detail. This is one of the reasons why it is most difficult to find data on the characteristics of Muslim migration to Europe on the Eurostat website. With the exception of the UK, which in the 2001 census included the question on religious identification, the official population statistics available for the other countries are simply unable to provide an accurate reconstruction of the emergence and growth of the Muslim population. It is, however, clear that without changes in the form of data collection, future estimates of the size of Muslim populations based on the indirect measurements will become less and less accurate. The estimates which rely on some form of demographic projections will also be increasingly problematic, since changes in the European Muslim population cannot be modelled simply as a function of net migration and natural increase (both extremely difficult to foresee); models would also have to include assumptions about movement between non-Muslim and Muslim populations in the form of inter-marriages and conversions (or a decline in practice of faith), and about religious practice among the offspring of such unions. Given the number of uncertainties involved, it seems certain that estimates derived in this way would have to fall within a very wide margin of error.

Finally, it is important to stress that the profiles of Muslim communities presented below show only some of their features, depending on the availability of data. This can almost certainly be improved upon by a more exhaustive search of sources in the individual countries concerned. The task here, however, has been to provide an overview of what may be gleaned about Muslim populations across Europe, utilizing data that is relatively freely accessible in the public domain.

## Muslim populations in selected European Countries

| Country | Estimate | Source |
|---|---|---|
| France | 4,000,000-5,000,000 | Buijs, F. and Rath, J. (2002) |
| | 4,155,000 | Amiraux V. (2002) |
| | 4,000,000-5,000,000 | Maréchal, B., coord. (2002) |
| Germany | 3,000,000 | Buijs, F. and Rath, J. (2002) |
| | 3,040,000 | Maréchal, B. coord. (2002) |
| | 3,200,000-3,500,000 | NOCRIME www.euro-islam.info |
| United Kingdom | 1,591,000 | Office for National Statistics (2003) |
| | 2,000,000 | Choudhury T. (2002) |
| | 1,400,000-1,800,000 | NOCRIME (2002) www.euro-islam.info |
| Netherlands | 696,000 | Buijs, F. and Rath, J. (2002) |
| | 695,000 | Maréchal, B., coord. (2002) |
| | 920,000 | Statistics Netherlands (2003) |
| Belgium | 370,000 | Buijs, F. and Rath, J. (2002) |
| | 400,000 | Bousetta, H. (October 2003) |
| | 350,000 | Religious Freedom Report (2002) |
| Sweden | 250,000-300,000 | Buijs, F. and Rath, J. (2002) |
| | 350,000 | Religious Freedom Report (2003) |
| | 350,000 | Sander, A. and Larsson, G. (2003) |

Figure 3

## France

The Muslim population of France accounts for approximately four to five million adherents constituting some 7 to 8 per cent of the total population. One of the more recent estimates, based on the cultural definition of what it means to be Muslim, provides the figure of 4,155,000 (Amiraux, 2002: 74). However, there is no reliable data on the number of Muslims in the country. The collection of statistics on religious affiliation is not permitted, and the census does not ask questions regarding religion. The fact that a large part of the Muslim community was born in France and holds French nationality further hinders any estimation. Most of the children of Maghrebian immigrants or *beurs* (from the slang reconstruction of the word 'Arabe') and other Muslims who have French citizenship, for example, are simply indistinguishable from the non-Muslim majority in existing data based on citizenship or country of birth.

Muslims in France, like the followers of Islam throughout the world, are diverse in terms of culture, language and tradition. They come from different countries and belong to different ethnic groups. The most numerous group—almost three million—come from the Maghreb. Among these, some 1,550,000 are of Algerian origin; 1,000,000 of Moroccan origin; and 350,000 of Tunisian origin. There are also approximately 450,000 *harkis* or Algerian repatriates and their descendents. Other more substantive groups include people who emigrated from Turkey (315,000), the Middle East (100,000), sub-Saharan Africa (250,000) and approximately 100,000 Asians. France also has one of the highest numbers of converts to Islam. Again there is no reliable source for this although the figure of 40,000 is most often quoted (Maréchal, 2002: 69). One has also to take into account approximately 350,000 asylum applicants and illegal workers who are of Muslim origin (HCI Report 2001: 37-38).

Muslims are settled throughout the country, but there are concentrated communities in the regions of Marseilles, Lyons, Lille and above all, Paris. Within this general situation it is interesting to note that Moroccans are much more widely spread outside these centres than either Algerians or Tunisians. People of African descent are concentrated in and around the capital, with smaller communities in all areas of industry, especially around Lille. Although the majority of Muslims in France continue to live in big cities, one may also find an increasing number of them, especially those of Turkish origin, in rural areas. Apart from the greater Paris region, Turkish people are to be found mainly in the eastern regions centred on Alsace and Lorraine.

The latest national census in 1999 revealed more than three million 'foreigners', which constitutes some 5.6 per cent of the total population of the country of 58 million. This proportion increases to more than 15 per cent in some underprivileged districts where the majority of 'foreigners' are of Muslim origin. These numbers illustrate the extent of social problems experienced by Muslims in the country. The repercussions of these problems might be found in the areas of employment, health, education, security and others (INSEE, www.insee.fr).

Muslims, and especially the youth, are more strongly represented among the unemployed. One can observe a rise in immigrant entrepreneurship in France as well as in other European countries (Glavanis, 1999). Faced with a lack of employment options, self-employment has become a way of avoiding exclusion in the labour market. Immigrant communities and minority groups are skilfully utilizing social capital and ethnic niches in the economy in setting up their own businesses.

Seventy-eight per cent of French people have medical insurance, compared to just 57 per cent of migrants, which reflects the informal and insecure nature of their employment. French people tend to consult a doctor six times a year, the Maghrebians consult their doctor three times and the Francophone Muslim Africans only twice. One of the consequences of this situation might be the much higher infant mortality rate amongst the Maghrebian children (12 per 1000) compared to the national average (9 per 1000) (Glavanis, 1999: 99).

The EFFNATIS project (2001) has discovered a strong relationship between the level of education of children of immigrants and their gender. Generally, Muslim women are far more likely to have attained higher levels of education than men. The census data show that the number of unqualified workers among foreigners is twice as high than among the native French.

Muslim associations in the country have formed several federations to identify and represent common interests vis-à-vis the State. The national organizations that have sought recognition as the official representatives of the Muslim community including, among others, the National Federation of the Muslims of France (FNMF), the Paris Mosque, the Union of the Islamic Organizations of France (UOIF) and the Tabligh. These are the main players in the recently established Conseil Français du Cult Musulman.

## CFCM—Conseil Français du Cult Musulman

This representative board for Muslim worship in France was created in April 2003 after more than a decade of intense discussions between various Muslim organizations and successive Ministers of the Interior, ambassadors and scholars. It constitutes an elected national body in charge of issuing principal statements on central religious topics and embodying the partnership with public authorities nationally and locally. The CFCM is made of a general assembly and twenty-five regional agencies called the Conseils Regionaux du Cult Musulman (CRCM) in charge of the daily management of the Muslim communities' affairs, in particular relations with the French public administration. Among its aims and objectives are: to defend the dignity and interests of Islam (Muslim worship) in France; to organize an exchange of services and information between the places of Muslim worship; to encourage dialogue between religions; and to ensure a space for Muslim worship within public space.

## UOIF—Union des Organisations Islamiques de France

The organization established in 1983 in La Courneuve (Seine-Saint-Denis) is the strongest Muslim federation in the country. It is formed from a mixed ethnic group of Algerians, Moroccans and Tunisians, and has some 200 affiliated organizations. Ideologically close to the Muslim Brotherhood and the Tunisian spiritual leader, Rachid Ghannouchi, it strives for space for Islam in the public domain and refuses to limit the role of religion to the private sphere. Among its activities are: looking after mosques; organizing theological seminars and seminars on interfaith dialogue; and Islamic summer camps for the youth. It is the French branch of the Union of the Islamic Organizations in Europe. It manages the European Institute of Social Sciences of Saint Léger de Fougeret (Nièvre) for *imams* and religious educators (opened in 1992). The institute aims 'to give Islam stable structures responding to the needs of Muslims while taking into account the specificity of their surroundings.' The institute has 160 students from France and other European countries. Financial support for these groups is provided by the Arab Gulf States.

### FNMF—Fédération Nationale des Musulmans de France

The FNMF was established on the basis of the Moroccan networks in 1985 in Paris to counterbalance the Algerian influences in Islam in France. It was inspired by the Muslim World League's Paris office. It aims to meet the religious, cultural, educational, social and humanitarian needs of Muslims. At the moment it has about 70 affiliated organizations and among these are, for example, significant mosques on the outskirts of Paris such as those of Evry Mantes la Jolie and Asnières.

### IMMP—L'Institute Musulman de la Mosquée de Paris

The Paris Mosque (established in 1926) includes more than 500 local associations among its members. Until 1993, it was financed by Saudi Arabia. Today it is funded by the financial contributions of its members (a majority of whom are of Moroccan origin), and is closely affiliated to the Algerian Government. It has always been closely associated with various government initiatives. Its leader, Dalil Boubakeur, played an important role in the establishment of the Conseil Français du Cult Musulman.

### Tabligh

The Tabligh—a movement of Pakistani origin—is also a major actor within the Muslim community. The association of 'Faith and Practice', which belongs to this movement, is especially active in providing assistance and services to the residents of the so-called disadvantaged districts of Paris. The organization is based in the Ar-Rahma Mosque in Saint-Denis.

### CMTF – Le Comité Musulman des Turcs Français

It is the French equivalent of the German DITIB, which closely cooperates with the Turkish DIYANET (The Turkish Directorate of Religious Affairs of the Prime Minister's Office). It represents about 150 mosques in the country.

# Germany

There are approximately 2.8 to 3.2 million Muslims living in Germany (approximately 3.4 per cent to 3.9 per cent the population of 82 million). As in France, the national statistical office does not gather information about the religious affiliation of the country's inhabitants. Although on the website of the Federal Statistical Office[3] one may find information about the number of Protestants, Catholics and the followers of Judaism in the country, no data on other religious groups is provided. In contrast to France, the majority of Muslims in Germany do not possess a German passport. According to the Religious Studies Media and Information Service (REMID),[4] at the beginning of 2000 only 310,000 Muslims (including ethnic Germans who converted to Islam) had German citizenship, constituting some 10 per cent of the total.

Among a diverse Muslim population, the largest group consists of Turks, numbering 1.9 million, out of whom some 35 per cent were born in Germany. In addition to those of Turkish origin, there are larger numbers of Bosnian (over 150,000), Maghreb (over 120,000) and Afghan (almost 70,000) Muslims (Statistisches Bundesamt Deutschland, 2003). The majority of German Muslims are Sunnis. There are, however, significant groups of Alawites (340,000) and Shias (140,000) (REMID).

Muslims in Germany usually live in larger cities that are primarily in the western part of the country. Berlin, with more than 180,000 Turkish inhabitants, is the biggest single Turkish community outside of Turkey. Apart from the Turks, there are also many Iranians, Afghans and Palestinians who have settled in the capital. Other cities where one may find a large number of members of the above mentioned groups are Cologne, Düsseldorf, Duisburg, Munich and Hamburg. Ex-Yugoslavians live mainly in Munich and, together with the Turks and North Africans, in Frankfurt am Main and Offenbach (Maréchal, 2002: 77).

Research suggests that there is a widespread perception that poor living and working conditions are accepted as 'the norm' for immigrants. Unemployment represents one of the most serious conditions affecting Muslims in Germany. As Vogel and Cyrus have observed, the gap in unemployment between foreigners and Germans had widened from 0.7 per cent in 1979 to 8.5 per cent in 1998. Moreover, whereas only 38 per cent of unemployed Germans had no vocational qualifications in 1997, the figure among foreigners was 78 per cent. The unemployment rate among 16 to 21 year olds is estimated to be as high as 50 per cent

(Vogel and Cyrus, 2001: 31) thus reflecting the insecurity and vulnerability among this population.

**Unemployment rate of EU and non-EU nationals in 2001**
(per cent of their active population aged 16 to 64)

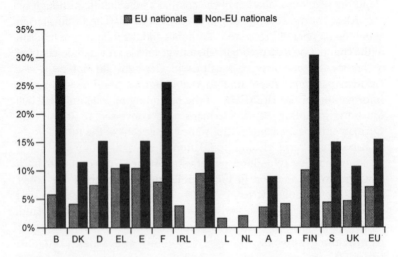

Figure 4
*Source*: LFS, Eurostat.

As mentioned previously, one of the reasons why foreigners have difficulties in gaining access to the labour market is that they do not have sufficient educational or vocational qualifications. However, as the children of families that often had poor access to education, they lack knowledge, opportunities and access for their own children, thereby placing them in a cycle of deprivation and condemning them to low-waged occupations. In addition, language problems act as a reason for children being sent by teachers to special schools, which additionally restrict their future prospects.

Social exclusion, as many studies have shown, is not simply a matter of material disadvantage or political marginalization. It also involves significant cultural processes. The report on 'Migrant Insertion in the Informal Economy' (Reyneri, 1999), for example, shows how criminalization of immigrants operates in the European countries. One of the results of this 'criminalization' of foreigners is their over-representation in prison. In Germany, the rate of imprisonment for natives in 1997 was 66 per 100,000 people, compared with 342 for foreigners, among whom the youth of Turkish origin had a large stake. It means that imprisonment rate for foreigners was five times higher than for natives. The same ratio of foreign to native imprisonment can be found in France, whereas in the Netherlands and Belgium it is six and eight times higher respectively. The authors of the report point out that many of the natives in these estimations are naturalized immigrants, so the immigrant/ethnic minority over-representation is actually even higher (Pallida et al., 1999: 26). Social exclusion reinforces the overall function of migration labour as a whole to serve as a low-skilled labour force, and is reflective of a wider level of exclusion and dispossession rather than being a condition intrinsic to migrant communities. The process of the criminalization of such communities is one effect of poverty and degradation, and operates at multiple levels.

In Germany neither the state nor Muslim groups have succeeded in appointing officials who could act as a representative link between the two parties. The traditional relationship between state agencies and the German churches has been used erroneously as the basis for interpreting the needs of Muslim migrant communities that remain diverse in origin and practice, unlike their German Christian counterparts. The opportunities for contact between Muslims and state institutions are thus diminished, and there is, as a result, a serious under-representation of Muslims in national and local level decision-making processes including in key agencies of the government, the civil service, in public appointments, in the media, among the police, the judiciary, the health service, education service, et cetera.

It is evident that a range of representative organizations exists in Germany despite the limitations placed upon civic recognition.

## ISLAMRAT BD—Islamrat für die Bundesrepublik Deutschland

The German Islamic Council was formed in 1986 with the cooperation of the World Muslim Congress, the Nurculuk Movement and the Friends of Islam. Its members are from various ethnic backgrounds, including German converts, although key roles are played by members of *Milli Görüs*, which has around 200 mosques.

## ZENTRALRAT MD—Zentralrat für die Muslime in Deutschland

The Central Council of Muslims in Germany was formed in 1994. It currently has around 20 organizations and networks affiliated to it, representing some 700 mosques and communities. It is composed of a broad ethnic mix. Among its aims are the improvement of the legal and material situation of Muslims in the country and the stimulation of debate among the representatives of the member organizations.

## DITIB—Türkisch-Islamische Union der Anstalt für Religion

Created by DIYANET (The Turkish Directorate of Religious Affairs of the Prime Minister's Office) in 1982, it represents the Turkish version of a 'laic' state-controlled Islam. Despite its official connection with the Turkish State, the DITIB is one of the few Muslim organizations in Germany which public opinion considers to be a legitimate partner for the German authorities. The DITIB brings in religious teachers from Turkey in an attempt to keep the religious connection with the Turkish state alive. The facilities offered by this organization are diverse and range from language courses to the provision of Muslim burial.

## AMGT—Avrupa Milli Görüs Teskilatlari/Islamische Gemeinschaft Milli Görüs

This is one of the most influential Turkish–Muslim federations in Germany, and was established in 1972. It has a wide range of activities ranging from Quranic classes to social and cultural activities and political/educational conferences. Having close links with the Turkish Refah Party, the AMGT advances a political vision of Islam. However, the organization remains ideologically diverse with the younger generation of German Muslims trying to utilize this entity to stake a claim in German society. Although the organization has never attempted to create a political party or challenge the political establishment, it is under close scrutiny of the *Verfassungsschutz* or intelligence services, which target groups potentially hostile to the constitutional order of the country. The AMGT has been publishing a journal known as the *Milli Gazzete* since 1995.

### VIKZ—Verband der Islamischen Kulturzentren

This organization is closely linked with the Suleymanci movement in Turkey, and was established in 1973. From its purely spiritual origin, the VIKZ has become increasingly political. It tries to achieve its political goals via mobilization through education. The organization has built a wide network of educational institutions in the country, and offers services ranging from weekend courses to the formation of *imams* (in Cologne). Although its activities have been less publicized than, for instance, those of the AMGT, it is also under the scrutiny of the security services.

## United Kingdom

As a result of the lobbying campaign run by a number of religious organizations (among others the Muslim Council of Britain) a question about religious identity was included in the last census in 2001. The topic was new to the census in England, Wales and Scotland although the subject had been included in previous censuses in Northern Ireland. The question, which in England and Wales was voluntary, was answered by 92 per cent of the population and revealed that Islam was the most common faith in Britain after Christianity (72 per cent) with nearly 3 per cent of the population, i.e., almost 1.6 million people describing themselves as Muslims (Office of National Statistics).[5]

Islam in the UK has a visible South Asian character. The largest number of Muslims originate from Pakistan (658,000—of whom 54.5 per cent were born in the UK), Bangladesh (260,000—of whom 46.6 per cent were born in the UK) and India (136,000). Together, Muslims of South Asian origin constitute almost three-quarters of the adherents of Islam in the UK. There are also sizeable groups from Cyprus, Malaysia and the Arab countries. In the Census data many of them are to be found within the category 'white', which accounts for 11.6 per cent of British Muslims. 6.7 per cent of Muslims in the UK are black and many of them come from African countries such as Somalia. The number of converts to Islam in the UK is estimated at about 10,000 people.

Muslims are not evenly distributed throughout the country. The active kinship and friendship networks and the process of chain migration have contributed to the concentration of Muslims in particular regions and cities. They are mostly to be found in the Greater London conurbation, where, according to the latest census, some

607,000 inhabitants are of Muslim origin as well as in some other areas of the South-East, the Midlands, West Yorkshire and South Lancashire. There is also a concentration of Muslims in the central Clydeside region of Scotland.

There are significant differences between various Muslim communities in terms of settlement patterns. For example, while Pakistanis are more dispersed nationally, Bangladeshis are concentrated in large numbers in fewer areas, particularly in the East End of London in such districts as Tower Hamlets (71,000—36 per cent of the population of the district are Muslims) and Newham (59,000—24 per cent). These districts have the highest proportion of Muslims in the country. Other large Muslim clusters are to be found in Birmingham (140,000—14 per cent of the total city population are Muslims) and Bradford (75,000—16 per cent).

The Muslim population in Britain is very young. Muslims aged zero to 15 years total 33.8 per cent (the national average is 20.2 per cent), and 18.2 per cent are aged from 16 to 24 (the national average is 10.9 per cent). There are also fewer older people; however, at the other end of the age scale, over 50 per cent of Muslims are under 25 years of age, compared with the national average of only 31 per cent. The fact that there are more Muslim children of school age than in other groups has implications for issues that are relevant to the education of relatively large numbers of Muslim children in areas with high Muslim populations. It is not uncommon in cities such as Birmingham, Leicester, Manchester or Bradford to find schools where 90 per cent of pupils are of South Asian origin.

Pakistani and Bangladeshi households in Britain tend to be larger with 4.7 and 4.2 persons per household respectively, compared with the rest of the population (2.3 persons). Muslims in the country often live in joint and extended families. There are also fewer single-parent families among Muslims than in other groups. According to recent data, 15 per cent of Pakistani families are single-parent families while the percentage for the white population amounted to 23 per cent, and 54 per cent amongst the black Caribbean population (White, 2002).

Research has shown that when the economic situation deteriorates, the unemployment rate of minorities rises faster than the rest of society (Modood, 1997). In the UK, even in cities with a relatively small minority population, they account for a disproportionately large number of the unemployed. As the Labour Force Survey (Spring, 2000) illustrates, Bangladeshis and Pakistanis are two and a half times more likely than the white population to be unemployed and nearly three times more likely to be in low-paid jobs. The proportion of young men from ethnic minorities without jobs is considerably higher than for young men in the white population with the same levels of education and the same qualifications.

As in the other countries, Muslims are over-represented in the prison population. Almost 10 per cent of British prisoners are Muslim. At the same time they are under-represented in the police, the judiciary, the civil service, the media and in public appointments.[6] This data can be misleading as it does not differentiate between citizens and foreigners, and many of those are non-citizens incarcerated for trafficking narcotics.

There is no official Muslim representative organization in the country. However, since the New Labour government came to power in 1997, it has been tacitly supporting the Muslim Council of Britain (MCB) created in the same year, which has strived to establish itself as the voice of Muslims in the country.

## UMO—Union of Muslim Organizations of UK and Eire

The Union of Muslim Organizations of UK & Eire (UMO) was the first national umbrella organization to be established in Britain in 1970 by representatives of some 38 organizations. The number of its affiliates grew over subsequent years but it was unable to attract the support of the larger organizations that had already become established. It attempted to lobby the national governments of the UK and Eire at a time when most decisions relating to Muslims were taking place at a local level. Its first objective was to 'realize' Muslim unity. The other aims of the UMO were to co-ordinate the activities of all Muslim organizations in the UK and Eire and to act as the representative body of British Muslims in negotiations with the British government as well as other governments and international bodies. For example, this organization offers help to individual Muslims to have the right to practise the tenets of Islam while at work. The UMO National Muslim Education Council also offers help to teachers, through the provision of guidelines and a syllabus for Islamic Education. The organization is a member of various inter-faith groups (Religious Education Council).[7]

## MCB—Muslim Council of Britain

The Muslim Council of Britain (MCB) is an umbrella organization, which was inaugurated on 23 November 1997 following three years of wide-ranging consultations at Brent Town Hall in Wembley by representatives of more than 250 Muslim organisations from all parts of Britain including Northern Ireland. In recent years the organization has been strengthened, and is now considered to be one of the most representative organizations of Muslims in the country. There are currently about 350 institutions affiliated to it, including mosques, education and charitable institutions, women's and youth organizations and professional bodies, both national and regional. The composition of the membership is ethnically mixed. The organization is opposed to labels such as 'ethnic minority', clearly favouring religious identification. As reflected by its website, the MCB's approach in dealing with civic affairs is one of participation, rather than agitation; when dealing with the government, it advocates constructive engagement. The MCB strives to deal with problems, and influence policies and outcomes through effective participation in the political process.

Among its aims are: to promote cooperation, consensus and unity in Muslim affairs in the UK; to encourage and strengthen all existing efforts being made for the benefit of the Muslim community; to work for a more enlightened appreciation of Islam and Muslims in wider society; to establish a position for the Muslim community within British society that is fair and based on due rights; to work for the eradication of disadvantages and forms of discrimination faced by Muslims; to foster better community relations; and to work for the good of society as a whole.

## MMP—Muslim Parliament

The Muslim Parliament was established in 1992 by the then Director of the Muslim Institute, Kalim Siddiqui, who had gained notoriety as a vocal supporter of the Iranian 'fatwa' or legal opinion against Rushdie. The organization published the 'Muslim Manifesto' in which it called for the establishment of islands of peace, harmony and moral excellence within British society, which it considered to be afflicted with numerous social problems. After the death of its founder in 1996, the organization appears to have lost its dynamism and to decline because of disputes over leadership. As a result of these disputes the Parliament's relationship with the Iranian state also broke down.

## MAB—Muslim Association of Britain

The Muslim Association of Britain was set up in 1997 by a group of Arab Muslims who felt largely left out in a country where representation is dominated by people of South Asian origin. The MAB website claims that it was 'established as an institution in an attempt to fill the gap in terms of Islamic *dawah* work in Britain, where it feels that the call for a representative Islam that encompasses all aspects of life is lacking. MAB tries to implement this through 'wisdom and good preaching'. The organization, which has about one thousand members, co-organized demonstrations with the 'Stop the War' coalition, which in September 2002 and February 2003 brought hundreds of thousands of people to the streets of London. Among its aims and objectives are: to spread the teachings and culture of Islam; to instil Islamic principles in the hearts of the Muslim community; to encourage good morals within British society; to assist the Muslim community in maintaining its integrity; and to foster within it ideals of Islamic conduct such as the worship of Allah, education and social relations, especially ties of kinship; to make Muslims aware of their duties towards the society in which they are living; and to promote an active role for the Muslim community in helping to solve the problems of British society, such as crime, drugs, unemployment, family disintegration, et cetera.

## The Netherlands

According to available statistics, there were nearly 920,000 Muslims in the Netherlands in January 2003. This number is 20,000 more than the previous year and some 294,000 more than in 1995. In 2003, Muslims account for 5.7 per cent of the total population of the Netherlands, compared with 4.1 per cent in 1995. The number of Muslims has increased strongly with the growth of the non-Western foreign population (see the graph below). More than 95 per cent of Muslims are of non-Western descent. This does not mean, however, that a large majority of non-Western foreigners are Muslims. In fact, only about 54 per cent of non-Western foreigners in the Netherlands are Muslims. Thirty-eight per cent of non-Western Muslims living in the Netherlands belong to the second generation.[8] As the Dutch statistical office predicts, the population of Muslims in the country is expected to reach one million in 2005.

### Growth of the Muslim population in the Netherlands

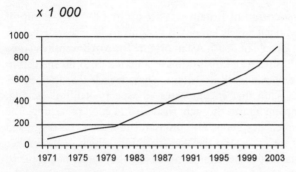

Figure 6
*Source*: CBS.

Most Muslims originally came from Turkey (nearly 320,000) and Morocco (285,000). Together they account for two-thirds of the total Muslim population of the Netherlands. Other smaller groups of Muslims come from Suriname, Iraq, Somalia, Iran, Afghanistan and Egypt. The Majority of the Turks and Moroccans have Dutch nationality.

As with other European countries, Muslims in the Netherlands are concentrated in urban centres. One may find them especially in four of the largest Dutch cities: Amsterdam, Rotterdam, The Hague and Utrecht. Whereas Muslims of Turkish and Moroccan origin can be found in all of the above-mentioned cities, the Surinamese are mostly concentrated in The Hague.

Members of the ethnic minorities, on average, are appointed to lower positions, and their jobs are often less secure than those of native Dutch employees with comparable education. They are also more often appointed on a temporary employment contract. Turkish and Moroccan employees in particular perform simple tasks that require little or no education. More recent data (Van Engelen, 2003) indicates a slight improvement in the position of ethnic minorities on the labour market (see Figure 7). However, in 1999, Moroccans and Turks were seven and nine times more likely to be unemployed than the native Dutch population despite a substantial proportion of the former group being from the second generation.

## Registered Unemployment in the Netherlands

|            | 1986/8 | 1992 | 1994 | 1996 | 1997 | 1998 | 1999 |
|------------|--------|------|------|------|------|------|------|
| Turks      | 44     | 333  | 36   | 34   | 30   | 27   | 18   |
| Moroccans  | 42     | 31   | 29   | 23   | 22   | 18   | 15   |
| Surinamese | 27     | 20   | 28   | 31   | 22   | 15   | 12   |
| Antilleans | 23     | 20   | 28   | 31   | 22   | 15   | 12   |
| Dutch      | 13     | 4    | 6    | 5    | 4    | 3    | 2    |

Figure 7
*Source*: Van Engelen, 2003 (National Employment Strategy)

One of the root causes of the poor performance of ethnic minority pupils is over-representation of non-native pupils in the so-called 'black schools' or schools where over 70 per cent of the student population belong to an ethnic minority community.

There is a general consensus that a high concentration of ethnic minority students in certain schools is counterproductive to the integration of young people. Moreover, the quality of teaching in such schools also tends to be lower than in schools with a better mix of pupils.

As with the situation in the United Kindom, there are no Muslim organizations officially recognized by the state, which could represent all Muslims in the country. The attempts to establish a representative body incorporating Muslims from different national backgrounds have been hampered as in many other EU countries by diversity of origin of migrants along national and ethnic lines; among the current groups, the following ones are supposed to be representative of Muslim migrants to the Netherlands.

## NCM—National Council of Mosques

The National Council of Mosques is one of two organizations in the country (beside the MCN—Muslim Council of the Netherlands) that claims to represent a large section of the Muslim community. The key player in this group is the Diyanet-controlled Islamic Foundation Netherlands.

## IFN—Islamic Foundation Netherlands

The Islamic Foundation of the Netherlands was founded in 1982 and covered 78 member associations in the early 1980s. It continued to grow slowly over the decades, and today is responsible for 140 mosques. It collaborates closely with the Diyanet, which provides the organization with *imams* whom it employs in its own member mosques.

## UMMON—Union of Moroccan Muslim Organizations in the Netherlands

The Union of Moroccan Muslim Organizations was founded in 1978 and covers some 100 mosques. Despite the assumed monarchical connections, mosques associated with UMMON, like other Moroccan mosques not associated with the umbrella body, have to find and employ their own *imams*, as they are not supplied by Morocco on the Turkish pattern.

## MG—Milli Görüs

This movement of the 'national view', combining orthodox Islam with Turkish nationalism, was established in 1982 as the Netherlands Islamic Federation. It runs various kinds of projects and presides over some 30 mosques as well as 60 youth and women's organizations.

## Belgium

The number of Muslims in Belgium is estimated at around 400,000 and constitutes some 4 per cent of the total population. As in other countries of the EU, the Muslim population in Belgium is very young. Almost 35 per cent of Turks and Moroccans, who constitute the largest Muslim groups in Belgium, are below 18 years old, compared to 18 per cent of native Belgians. One of the consequences of this situation is that one-quarter of the population of Brussels is under 20 years old and is of 'Muslim origin' (Bousetta, 2003: 8).

In the country's multicultural Muslim community, the largest groups are made up of Moroccans (230,000) and Turks (130,000). Members of the smaller groups come from Algeria (8,500), Tunisia (4,000) Bosnia-Herzegovina, Pakistan, Lebanon, Iran, Syria and Egypt. According to Maréchal, 113,842 people from 'Muslim countries' had acquired

Belgium citizenship between 1985 and 1997. In addition, every year at least 8,000 Moroccans and 6,000 Turks receive Belgium citizenship. There are also some 6,500 political refugees from the Arab–Islamic world in Belgium. The number of converts in early 2002 was between 3,000 and 15,000 (Maréchal, 2002: 21).

The spatial distribution of Muslims across Belgium reflects the nature and process of immigration. The greatest concentration is in Brussels with a significant remainder residing in the industrial areas of the French-speaking south. The Brussels conurbation is home to more than 50 per cent of the Moroccans in Belgium. They can also be found in Antwerp, Liège, Hainaut, in the region of Charleroi, and in Limburg. Half of the Turks have settled in Flanders, especially Antwerp, Ghent and Limburg. They live also in certain districts of Brussels (e.g. Schaerbeek, Saint-Josse) and in the Walloon area of Belgium in the region of Hainaut and Liège (Bousetta, 2003: 8).

The 'Muslim Voices' project, found significant differences between the two major Muslim groups in the country. While the Turks still remain a very close-knit community, maintaining many of their rural traditions (e.g., choosing spouses from their parents' villages), the Moroccans appear to be better integrated not only in the economic but also in the social, cultural and political sphere. They have, for example, a higher rate of mixed marriages with Belgians. The Turks, on the other hand, seem to master the country's language less well than the Moroccans and consequently they also fare worse in school (Glavanis, 1999: 94).

All groups of non-EU nationals are over-represented among the unemployed. As is illustrated in Figure 4, there were five times more unemployed non-EU nationals in Belgium in 2001.

In a country where Islam has been a legally recognized faith since 1974, there was until recently no representative organization for people of Muslim origin. Muslim groups were unable to organize themselves and agree upon a representative structure. Besides, strict criteria were required as preconditions for the formation of organizations. This was to ensure that Islamic 'fundamentalists' did not take over, and thus created a more complex accreditation process.

### EMB—l'Exécutif des Musulmans de Belgique (Muslim Executive Council)

The EMB was established in May 1999 and is responsible for the administrative management of Muslim worship in Belgium. It plays the role of a mediator between the state and Muslim communities in the country. Its responsibilities range from providing religious education in schools and educational training for *imams* to the appointment of Muslim chaplains in hospitals and prisons. The EMB is made up of some 17 members, seven Moroccans, four Turks, three converts and three members of other nationalities. The EMB has been receiving state subsidies since 2001. In 2002, the state supported the organization with 420,000 Euros, while the Catholic Church was given 350 million Euros.

### ICCB—Islamic Cultural Centre of Belgium

Until the establishment of the EMB, the ICCB had been the de facto representative of Muslims in Belgium. The ambassador of Saudi Arabia chaired its board of trustees. The land for the Centre was handed over to King Faisal in 1967, as a gift in exchange for donations he had made to set up the ICCB. The Centre was built with financial support of the Muslim World League.

### AEL—Arab European League

The AEL, since its inception three years ago, aimed to defend the civic rights of Arabs in Europe, and has attracted a following among the thousands of jobless, frustrated young immigrants who feel excluded by mainstream European society. Its leader, Abou Jahjah, often portrayed by the media as Belgium's Malcolm X, is a charismatic debater with an MA in international politics and fluency in four languages. The organization, together with a number of leftist parties, set up a party called 'Resist', and ran in the elections of 2003. Taking into account the popularity of its leader, its election achievements were relatively poor. However, Abou Jahjah had already announced the creation of a new political party, named the Muslim Democratic Party, which he expects to achieve better results in the next national and local elections in 2006. The AEL now has expanding branches, both in France and in the Netherlands and is attempting to become a pan-European representative force.

## MJM—Mouvement des Jeunes Musulmans

Like the AEL, the MJM also created a political party. Its Parti de la Citoyenneté et de la Prospérité achieved surprisingly good results in local elections in Brussels in May 2003.


## Sweden

There are approximately 350,000 Muslims in the country out of whom around 150,000 belong to, and participate in the activities of, Swedish Muslim congregations, 'recognized' by the Commission for State Grants to Religious Communities. Around one-third of the country's Muslims were born in Sweden. They belong to an extremely diverse community in which, unlike other European countries, there is no dominant group. Most of the Swedish Muslims are Sunnis. The number of Shias at the end of the 1990s was estimated at slightly over 60,000. The number of converts, mainly women married to Muslim men, is, according to Sander and Larson, not higher than 5,000 (Sander and Larson, 2003: 15).

Muslims in Sweden may be divided into seven different sub-groups: Turks, Arabs, Iranians, Africans, Pakistanis, Muslims from the Balkans and Muslims from the rest of the world. The Turkish Muslims were the first Muslim group of any size to come to Sweden, and until the beginning of the 1980s, they were by far the largest single Muslim community in the country. However, today they constitute less than 10 per cent of the total Muslim population. Amongst Arab Muslims originating from almost twenty different countries, Iraqis (52,000) constitute the largest group of which one-third is made up of Kurds. People from Lebanon, Morocco, Syria, Tunisia and Palestine make up roughly one-third of the Muslims in the country.

The Iranian group is the second single largest group of ethnic Muslims in Sweden after the Iraqis, with almost 52,000 individuals. The remaining four groups are smaller in size (Sander and Larson, 2003: 13-15).

Swedish Muslims live mainly in the major cities such as Stockholm, in the south and north-west of the city, in Gothenburg (mostly in the north, east and south of the city) and Malmö (in the city centre and south and east of the city). However, there are also some active Muslim communities outside big cities in urban centres with the population of 30,000 to 90,000. There are virtually no Muslims in the rural areas.

In Sweden, visible signs of religious affiliation (e.g. turban, shawl), especially in combination with dark skin colour, seem to be clear obstacles for obtaining work. Research shows that even in well-respected professions such as medicine, engineering and teaching, Muslims are facing discrimination and disadvantage, thus affecting their integration in employment and with society at large. The Muslims in Sweden, depending on their origin, have between four and ten times higher unemployment rates than native Swedes (Sander et al., 2001: 22). Many Muslims are employed in unskilled jobs in the service sector (restaurants and hotels) and in public institutions.

A high percentage of Muslims in the country live in socially disadvantaged areas. Their living conditions are lower than non-Muslim citizen. Their children attend schools struggling with social, financial and other problems. At least partly due to this situation, Muslim children tend to perform relatively poorly in school, with greater problems of conduct and higher dropout rates. Muslims see the education system as failing their children.

Neither the state nor Muslim groups have managed to appoint officials who can act as a link between them. One of the biggest obstacles to building a representative structure is the heterogeneity of the Muslim population. The reluctance of the state to deal with questions raised by Muslims concerning cultural issues such as food, education and dress has been yet another obstacle preventing dialogue. However, there are three organizations 'recognized' by the Commission for State Grants to Religious Communities, established in 1980 and earlier, from 1972, operating as the Council of Swedish Free Churches. They are not clearly divided along the ethnic or religious lines. However, IKUS is strictly Sunni. All three of them cover 75 per cent of the Muslim communities in Sweden. The three state-subsidised organizations are described below: FIFS, SMUF and IKUS.

## FIFS—Förenade Islamiska Församlingar i Sverige (United Islamic Communities in Sweden)

The organization was created in 1973 to fill a need among the Muslim communities for an umbrella organization. In 1977 it organized eight local groups or 'congregations'. Especially at the beginning of its activities, the FIFS engaged with a variety of Muslim communities, including Shias, Sunnis and communities of different ethnic backgrounds. By 2001, the FIFS claimed to have organized some 41 local congregations.

## SMUF—Sveriges Muslimska Ungdomsförbund (Union of Muslim Communities of Sweden)

This group was established in 1982 as a second national federation after a split within FIFS. At the time they claimed to have jointly organized 23 local congregations and had some 22,000 registered members. The majority of these were Sunnis of an Arabic-speaking background, but also included some Shiite communities. Today, the SMUF claims to organize 48 congregations.

## IKUS—Islamiska Klturcenterunionen (Union of Islamic Centres of Culture)

This group was created in 1984 following a split within the FIFS when the organization became eligible for state grants in 1987. IKUS has a leaning towards the Suleymanci movement of Turkey but it also looks after the welfare of some Somali communities and currently coordinates some 28 congregations.

## SMR—Sveriges Muslimska Råd (Muslim Council of Sweden)

The council was formed by FIFS and SMUF in 1990 to concentrate and centralize power and to demonstrate a more united front. The most active person in SMR is Mahmoud Aldebe who also led SMUF for some time. To some extent the SMR can be seen as his project. Among the aims of SMR are: to create mosques and Islamic schools; to create information material about Islam directed towards the non-Muslims in Sweden; and to take an active part in the public debate in society.

## CONCLUDING REMARKS

It is clear that Muslims in the countries covered by this book originate from very diverse social, political and cultural backgrounds, which makes it problematic to create any form of in-country representations. Demographically, however, migrants of Muslim origin are a youthful population, which is potentially invaluable to the European labour market where fertility is generally below replacement level, raising concerns over the support of a rapidly ageing population in terms of health and social care and pensions. Hence, migration from countries where Islam is the major faith has been important to the labour market of the major European countries (the United Kingdom, Germany, France and the Netherlands in particular).

The young generation of Muslims born in European countries usually possess not only formal citizenship rights but also a range of forms of tacit knowledge, competences and taken-for-granted assumptions, which allows them to engage constructively in citizenship activities: as research shows, citizenship (alongside religion) is often central to their self-understanding and assertions of who they are (Cesari, 2003; Lathion, 2003). With its help they have been seeking the recognition of their heritage and values in the public and private spheres. Thus, they have been following earlier groups (e.g. ethnic minorities or women's groups) that have been mobilizing around a particular identity for several decades.

The focus on religious rights as the primary right in relation to the allocation of civil liberties is an issue that requires further exploration in all the countries in question. What is evident is that as political pressure on Muslim communities increases, people are forced back into faith-led activities, as the only form of civil rights they can defend, rather than campaigning for better access to social and welfare services, education, employment and housing. This dependence on faith-led activity appears, however, to be a global phenomenon in the face of the retreat of welfare states, rather than one that is restricted to migrants of Muslim origin alone.

## REFERENCES

Amiraux, V., 'Studying Islam in Europe: Are there ties binding academics and politics', Conference paper, Erfurt, 2001.

Amiraux, V., EU Accession Monitoring Program (EUMAP), Report on France: "Monitoring Minority Protection in EU Member States", 2002.

Ballard, R., Desh Pardesh—The South Asian Presence in Britain, Hurst & Company, London, 1994.

Berger, P., The Social Reality of Religion, Faber & Faber, London, 1969.

Bousetta, H. and Maréchal, B., L'Islam et les musulmans en Belgique: Enjeux locaux et cadres de réflexion globaux, Fundation Roi Baudouin, 2003.

Buijs, F. and Rath, J., 'Muslims in Europe: The State of Research', essay prepared for the Russell Sage Foundation, New York, 2002.

Cesari, J., 'Muslim Minorities in the West: The Silent Revolution' in Esposito, John and Burgat, François, (eds.), *Modernizing Islam: Religion in the Public Sphere in the Middle East and in Europe*, Rutgers University Press, 2003: 251-269.

Eurostat (2001) Statistics in Focus: Why do People Migrate?

Eurostat (2002) Statistics in Focus.

Eurostat Yearbook 2003.

Glavanis, P. M., *'Muslim Voices' in the European Union: The Stranger Within. Community, Identity and Employment*, Final Report, Targeted Socio-Economic Research (TSER) SOE1-CT96-3024, European Commission, Brussels, 1999.

Greaves, R., *Sectarian Influences within Islam in Britain*, University of Leeds, 1996.

HCI Report (Haut Conseil à l'Intégration HCI), *L'Islam dans la République*, Documentation Française, Paris, 2001.

Hussain, D., 'Representation and Relationship with the State' in Esposito, John and Burgat, François, eds., *Modernizing Islam: Religion in the Public Sphere in the Middle East and in Europe*, Rutgers University Press, 2003: 251-269.

Jones, T., *Britain's Ethnic Minority*, PSI, London, 1993.

Lathion, S., *Musulmans d'Europe*, L'Harmattan, Paris, 2003.

Maréchal, B., (coord.), *A Guidebook on Islam and Muslims in the Wide Contemporary Europe*, Bruylant-Academia, Louvain-la-Neuve, 2002.

Modood, T., and Berthoud, R., (eds.), *Ethnic Minorities in Britain—Diversity and Disadvantage*. Policy Studies Institute, London, 1997.

National Statistics, Labour Force Survey, Spring, 2000.

Nielsen, J., *Muslims in Western Europe*, Edinburgh University Press, Edinburgh, 1992.

Nielsen, J., 'Fluid Identities: Muslims and Western Europe's Nation States'. Paper written for the project 'identity and citizenship' conducted by the International Center for Ethnicity, Migration and Citizenship, New School University, New York, 2000.

Palidda, S., Frangoulis, M. and Papantoniou, A., *Deviant Behaviour and Criminalisation of Immigrants*, European Commission, Brussels, 1999.

Religious Studies Media and Information Service (REMID): www.remid.de.

Reyneri, E., *Migrant Insertion in the Informal Economy, Deviant Behaviour and the Impact on Receiving Societies*. Targeted Socio-economic Research (TSER) SOE-2-CT95-3005. European Commission, Brussels, 1999.

Sander, Å. 'The Road From Musalla To Mosque: Reflections on the process of integration and institutionalisation of Islam in Sweden' in Shadid, W.A.R. & van Koningsveld, P.S., (eds.), *The Integration of Islam and Hinduism in Western Europe*, Pharos, Leiden, 1991.

Sander Å., Larsson G. and Kos-Dienes, D., *'State Policies Towards Muslim Minorities in the European Union'*, final report, 2001.

Sander Å. and Larson G.) *'Muslims in Sweden'*, 2003, available on: http://www.emz-berlin.de/projekte/pdf/Muslims_in_Schweden.pdf.

Shaw, A. 'The Pakistani Community' in Ballard *'Desh Pardesh—The South Asian Presence in Britain'*, Hurst & Company London, 1994.

Van Engelen, *National Employment Strategy*, 2003.

Vogel, D. and Cyrus, N., 'Immigration as a side effect of other policies: principles and consequences of the German non-immigration policy' in Triandafyllidou, A., (ed.), *Does Implementation Matter? Informal Administration Practices and Shifting Immigrant*

*Strategies in Four Member States*, Targeted Socio-Economic Research (TSER) HPSE-
CT-1999-00001, European Commission, Brussels, 2001: 9-38.
White, A., (ed.) *Ethnicity*, 2002, available on: http://www.statistics.gov.uk.

**Websites of National Statistical Offices**

L'Institut national de la statistique et des études économiques (INSEE): www.insee.frww.
insee.fr
Statistisches Bundesamt Deutschland (SBD): www.destatis.de
Office for National Statistics (ONS): www.statistics.gov.uk
General Register Office, Scotland: www.gro-scotland.gov.uk
Statistics Netherlands (CBS): www.cbs.nl
Statistica Centralbyrån (SCS): www.scb.se

**Websites of Muslim Organisations**
**France:**
UOIF:  www.uoif-online.com
IMMP: www.mosquee-de-paris.org
CMTF: www.diyanet.go.tr

**Germany:**
ISLAMRAT BD: www.islamrat.de
ZENTRALRAT MD: www.islam.de/?tree=zmd
AMGT: www.igmg.de
VIKZ: www.vikz.de

**Great Britain:**
MCB: www.mcb.org.uk
UMO: www.theredirectory.org.uk/orgs/umouk.html
MAB: www.mabonline.net

**Netherlands:**
UMMON: www.emim.be/assoc.php
MG: www.milligorus.nl

**Belgium:**
EMB: www.embnet.be
AEL: www.arabeuropean.org
MJM: www.mvjm.be
PCP: www.particp.be

# NOTES

1. In fact, a large number of Turks arriving in Sweden in the 1980s and 1990s were
   Syrian Orthodox Christians; equally many Lebanese were Maronites, and some
   Iranians and Palestinians were of Christian faith.

2. For example, in the UK the Muslim lobby united with other religious groups has managed to convince the government to include the question on religious identification in the census of 2001.
3. www.destatis.de accessed 10.11.2003.
4. www.remid.de accessed 10.11.2003.
5. If not stated otherwise the information in this section comes from the Office for National Statistics http://www.statistics.gov.uk or General Register Office, Scotland: http://www.gro-scotland.gov.uk.
6. http://data.webstar.co.uk accessed 11.11.2003.
7. Union of Muslim Organizations of UK & Ireland (UMO), *1970-1995: A Record of Achievement, 25 Years Silver Jubilee Magazine*, 1995: 6.
8. Muslims in the Netherlands are calculated on the basis of an estimate based on the number of foreigners in the Netherlands per country of origin, and the percentage of Muslims in the populations in these countries of origin. For people from Suriname, Morocco and Turkey, however, the percentage of Muslims was taken from the survey on the social position and use of provisions by foreigners in the Netherlands. The survey included a question on the religion of respondents. Statistics Netherlands, Voorburg/Heerlen, 2003, available on: www.cbn.nl.

# 2

# Orientalism and Otherness

*Bryan Turner*

## HISTORICAL FACTORS: RELIGION AND ORIENTALISM

Contemporary Western understanding of Islam is seeped in a deep historical tradition influenced by early Christian thought. Islam from a very early period was seen as a distinct threat to Christendom. The earliest evidence of this hostility and vilification is shown below, demonstrating the depth of animosity. The first Christian polemic by John of Damascus (d. 749) took the stand that the Prophet of Islam was not genuine and had plagiarized the Old and New Testaments in the time of Heraclius to form his own sect.[1] In the ninth century, Theophanes Confessor (d. 817) was the first Byzantine historian to write on Islam, and produced a derogatory biographical commentary on the Prophet of Islam that attempted to explain the success of Islam in terms of his cunning and the gullibility of his followers.[2] These prejudicial stereotypes of Islam were reproduced throughout the Middle Ages by Christian writers, and became taken-for-granted assumptions of Western criticism (Grunebaum, 1953: 43-4). The ideological threat of Islam was particularly acute in the seventeenth century during the conflicts between Protestants and Catholics, when translations of the Quran were seen to add yet more fuel to the conflagration of religious persuasions (Matar, 1998: 73-83).

There has subsequently been an extensive debate in Western scholarship about the negative conceptual framework within which Islam has often been understood and analyzed by Western humanities and social sciences. While the contemporary discussion about Western views of the Orient was unquestionably stimulated by Edward Said's *Orientalism* (1978), the controversy about the character of other cultures should be seen as one dimension of the more general problem of 'other religions', and thus to the ancient encounter between Christian protagonists and heretical antagonists. The basic dilemma is that Islam, Christianity and Judaism are variations of a generic monotheistic religion, but political processes that have constructed separate religious systems differentiate them. This division was sustained historically by the notion of Islam as a heretical sect and of Judaism as a betrayal of Christianity.[3]

Within the orientalist paradigm, the Orient appears in Western imagination as the forbidden 'other', which is both repulsive and seductive. Like the Muslim veil, the Orient is simultaneously hidden and inviting (Yegenoglu, 1998). It thus exists within a literary and visual tradition that is fantastic (Sweetman, 1988). The basic argument is that the Orient was constructed in Western perspectives as a permanent and enduring object of knowledge in opposition to the Occident as its negative counterpoint. This Western image of Islam and the East has proved to be remarkably enduring and consistent. Orientalism generates a concept of Oriental societies as stationary, and through the sedimentation of the divergent cultural phenomena of Oriental societies, orientalism converts the diversity of Oriental traditions into a unitary, integrated and coherent object of Western science. While the Occident is seen to develop through historical stages in terms of a series of modernizing, violent revolutions, the unhistorical and stationary Orient exists outside of history.

In this view, however, any simple dichotomy of West and East involves an attempt to impose a false homogeneity or unity on cultures which are necessarily heterogeneous and hybrid. They are in reality recalcitrant to simple classification because there is no authentic, original culture. There is only historical difference. We may call this issue, in an obvious reference to the notion of 'the imaginary', the problem of 'the originary', namely the legitimizing quest for authentic origins in a context of obdurate differences (Turner, 2001). These originary dichotomies encourage us politically to take sides, and thus to hand out praise, and blame for historical development.

The current debate about globalization inevitably raises questions about the interrelationships between the world religions in a shrinking globe. If there is the possibility of creating a form of global governance, then there are important questions about the co-existence of different world religions and different assumptions about citizenship within the 'global village'. In the mediaeval period, Islam developed as a world religion, but given the limitations of technology, transport and literacy, it could not exercise world hegemony (Grunebaum, 1953). Islamdom was constituted as an ideal that could never be fully realised in practice. With the globalization of communication systems and with the collapse of communism, Islam can, in principle, function as a genuinely global religion, and the pilgrimage to Mecca has served as an important factor of cultural integration in modern Islam. These global processes have increased conflict between Western political systems and Islam, creating in turn conditions for the growth of militant Islamic movements (Tibi, 1998).

Perhaps the principal consequence of global modernization is the constitution of 'religion' as a separate, differentiated and specialized sector of modern society—a cultural sector that is often thought to refer to, and assumed to manage, the private world of subjectivity and meaning. Religion in the modern world has been transformed into an institution that manages the problems that trouble individuals, namely, what they think, is of ultimate concern. Globalization and modernization have promoted the sovereignty of the individual (Abercrombie, Hill and Turner, 1986) and in turn individualism has converted religion into an activity within the private sphere.

Secularization and modernization made 'religion' in this sense a special 'problem of modernity', and thereby placed the question of 'religion' more explicitly in public discourse (Robertson, 1970). The effect of globalization is to export this Western pattern of religiosity as a general cultural theme of the world order. The Westphalian political settlement produced a world system of nation states, and this political system was based on the notion that the Wars of Religion (1550–1630) were an inevitable outcome of the persistence of religion in public life. Intolerance and violence were to be contained by confining religion to the private sphere (Thomas, 2000). This process of exporting an individualistic version of Latin Christianity, and global reactions to it, has been described as 'globalatinization', namely the alliance between Christianity, technology and capitalism (Derrida, 1998: 13). Fundamentalism attempts to ensure the dominance of religion in the public spheres of law, economy and government, and is thus a response to Weber's tragic vision of the separation of the value spheres. In the religious conflicts of the twentieth century, the Western model of denominational pluralism was increasingly adopted as the model of religious (and hence political) tolerance.

## Islamism and fundamentalism (perpetuation of Otherness)

Fundamentalism can be seen as a religious process that attempts to resist the melting-pot model of secularism, political tolerance and religious pluralism. In particular, fundamentalism resists the separation of religion and politics, whereby religion is confined to the private sphere. If we regard modernization from a sociological point of view as the differentiation of the various spheres of society (economy, politics, law and religion) into separate domains, then fundamentalism must be defined as the 'de-differentiation' of such separate fields of activity (Parsons, 1999). In this sense, fundamentalism is anti-modernization (Lechner, 2000). The growth of fundamentalist movements in Islam, Christianity and Judaism is often interpreted as a response to the disruptions of traditional life and values that result from globalization. Fundamentalism is seen to be a movement that preserves tradition against the cultural melting pot that follows global migration, tourism and mass consumerism. While Islamic fundamentalism has come to the attention of the Western media, fundamentalism has also been increasingly characteristic of other religions of Asia, especially Hinduism. Fundamentalism has become the target of Western criticism because it is seen to be incompatible with a liberal democracy that attempts to create an open and diverse public sphere (Tourraine, 2000). The further implication of this argument is that, since Islamic fundamentalism is anti-modern, it must be also anti-Western. These assumptions about Islam and religious fundamentalism have dominated recent political discussion, especially about the alleged 'clash of civilizations' (Huntington, 1997).

For Samuel Huntington, the clash is inevitable and deeply embedded in two different cultures, one that separates religion and politics, and the other that keeps them together. In more sociological terms, Huntington describes four causes of the contemporary growth of Islamic radicalism. The first is that there has been a significant and widespread Islamic resurgence in response to social and cultural modernization. These Islamic movements have provided a new consciousness at one level, but they have also offered welfare support to their followers, where governments have failed their local populations. A good illustration would be the 'Justice and Charity Movement' in Morocco, which offers educational and welfare support for marginal and deprived groups. Secondly, Islamic movements have mobilized and thrived on grievances, not only against the USA and its political allies, but also against national governments that have failed. There is a general sense of alienation from government, given the failure of both nationalist and communist movements to deliver sustained social development with egalitarian consequences. Muslim grievances against the West have been exacerbated by the territorial expansion of Israel and by overt Western support for Zionism. Such support for Israel must necessarily appear hypocritical, given the West's support of human rights legislation and aspirations in other areas, such as South Africa and East Timor (Ignatieff, 2001).

Thirdly, Islamic militancy has been further sustained by conflicts within Islam (for example, between Iraq and Iran) and by ethnic divisions within Islamic societies (for example, Afghanistan). However, the final causal argument is perhaps the most important component of Huntington's position, namely that the demographic growth of Islam has produced large numbers of mobile, unemployed and disaffected young men in the 16 to 30 age group who are ideal recruits to Islamic fundamentalism. In this context, the Islamic resurgence has given hope and inspiration to a variety of social movements, especially against the economic and military spread of Western societies. The fall of communism opened up a space for Islamic militancy, and the end of the cold war has intensified the historical division between the civilizations of the West and the Islamic world.

This characterization of fundamentalist Islam as anti-modern is problematic, not least because it makes it impossible to distinguish religious fundamentalism from political Islamism on the one hand, and from traditionalist Islam on the other. Fundamentalism rejects traditional Islam, because traditional Islam is seen as a compromised form of religious belief and practice that is subordinate to the Western secular influence. Because fundamentalism rejects both Sufism and traditional Islam, it would in many respects make more sense to regard modern fundamentalism as the modern heir of previous reform movements that sought to modernize Islam from within, in opposition to the West, namely the Wahhabi movement of Arabia and the Salafi movement that reasserted *Shariah*-minded Islamic orthodoxy against traditionalism and Sufi mysticism. We might reasonably define Islamic fundamentalism as a reformist movement in religion that has attempted to modernize and radicalize Islam in the name of its fundamental roots. There are clear parallels between Western Puritanism that developed a radical politics against the corruption of this world through a return to its religious roots.

The real struggle against the West is not about modernity and anti-modernity as such but a struggle against postmodern consumerism that threatens to undermine any religious authenticity by offering many experimental lifestyles that undercut religion as, in Durkheim's terms, the 'serious life'. Modernist consumerism offers to satisfy the basic needs of a mass market through Taylorist and Fordist methods of production, distribution and consumption. The classic joke of the modernist period of consumerism was that everybody could choose their own model of the Ford car, provided it was black. More technology has transformed production and consumption into smaller niche markets, developed methods of creating tastes rather than satisfying needs, and created commodities that shape the self through a consumerist fantasy. Postmodernity is the consequence of the fragmentation and differentiation of consumption, which has produced the commodified self and the consumer lifestyle (Featherstone, 1991). One characteristic feature of the postmodern economy is the manufacturing of celebrity as a mechanism for selling lifestyles as the mechanism for selling commodities (Rojek, 2001). The self becomes malleable because it is also the subject of fashion. Perhaps one remarkable feature of postmodern capitalism is that literally everything can be transformed into a commodity, a fact that was illustrated by the popularity of Osama bin Laden T-shirts in northern British cities that emerged after the American military activity against the Taliban. Through the emergence of niche markets, leaders of Islamism can achieve celebrity status and offer a lifestyle choice. The real challenge to Islam is not modernity but the postmodern fashioning of alternative selves and lifestyles that directly challenge the *Shariah*-minded puritanism of religious fundamentalism.

This challenge to religion through the seduction of Muslim youth by the fantasy world of cultural production, individualism and consumerist narcissism was perceptively analyzed in *Postmodernism and Islam* (Ahmed, 1992), and more recently explored in *Jihad vs McWorld* (Barber, 2001). Barber's theme is the clash between the universal consumer world (McWorld) and the tribal world of identity politics and particularities (jihad). The 'essential jihad' is the fundamentalist movement of Islam, and the essence of McWorld is McDonalds. These two realities produce two radically different forms of politics. 'Jihad pursues a bloody politics of identity, McWorld a bloodless economics of politics' (Barber, 2001). Although in his 'Afterword', Barber retreats somewhat from an exclusive identification of jihad with Islamic fundamentalism, the Islamic world does provide Barber with his most striking illustration of a committed politics. Whereas fundamentalist certainty results necessarily in antagonistic politics, McWorld is not a place for hot political emotions, but for pragmatic adjustment to contingencies.

The terrorist attack on New York can be taken as an unnerving illustration of the truth of Barber's dichotomy of politics in *Jihad vs McWorld*, because symbolically the World Trade Centre towers perfectly embodied the cool systems of exchange that advanced capitalism had promoted against the hot politics of diasporic people and their cultures. It would be wrong, however, to assume that Barber's typology is merely a reproduction of Huntington's 'clash of civilizations' in which again Islam is chosen as a compelling illustration of an inevitable conflict between the West and the rest, or Fukuyama's version of the end-of-ideology thesis. Barber's analysis is, in fact, more complex and more interesting than Huntington's dichotomous model of endless conflict or Fukuyama's model of inevitable evolution towards liberal capitalism. For Barber, jihad and McWorld stand in a dialectical relationship of mutual reinforcement. McWorld needs jihad as its negative other, while jihad requires capitalism or more specifically the USA as its contrast case. The cool universalism of McDonalds stands in a productive dialectic with the hot politics of Islamic jihad, and yet at times they also interpenetrate each other. Jihad employs global technologies for its communication requirements and broadcasts its global message through modern media. Furthermore, Barber recognizes that American culture also produces jihadic politics in the form of radical Christian fundamentalism and militiamen. McWorld and jihad constantly intermingle and fuse with each other. He notes, for example, that Japan, in which national identity and national politics have been deeply preserved and fostered in the postwar period, has also embraced many components of Western consumerism. In 1992, the number one restaurant in Japan as measured by the volume of consumers was McDonalds. Finally, his argument is a defence of democratic politics against both McWorld and jihad. McDonalds undermines community and social capital, and thus erodes and corrodes the trust and communal membership that are essential foundations of secular democracy. The particularistic tribal mentality of jihad is difficult to reconcile with democratic politics that requires compromise and co-operation between groups and communities that do not share the same ethnic identities. It is important, therefore, to go beyond both McWorld and jihad.

Although Barber's analysis of fundamentalism has some merit in providing an understanding of the impact of the McDonald culture in international relations, it is misleading to regard Islamic fundamentalism as mere tribalism. Islamic fundamentalism strives for universalism, and is thus a modern social movement. Barber's thesis is useful, however, because it provides an account of how McDonalds is a cultural threat to Islamic authenticity. The postmodern consumer world has, however, a corrosive impact on every monotheistic religion in which a saviour God calls the guilty soul out of ignorance and damnation. The very notion of a salvation event is alien to the consumer world of the simulated self where many manifestations of subjectivity are possible. It is possible that this consumer self is the unintended consequence of Christian individualism, but the results are inevitably destructive of religious identities. The separation of these worlds is perhaps graphically illustrated by the fact that the Western press regarded the emancipation of the women of Kabul from the patriarchal oppression of the Taliban movement as illustrated decisively by the fact that Muslim women would be able to abandon their *burqas*, wear make-up and purchase the latest fashions. In the meantime, their men could visit the local barber's shop to have their beards cut. Emancipation from the discipline of the Taliban was marked by the early construction of the new Islamic identity, the consuming, post-jihadic Muslim.

## CONCLUSION

The political and economic world order has passed through a neo-liberal revolution between 1979 and 2001. We need to understand Islam and the Third World in the context of this neo-liberal global experiment, because it is this social and political revolution that has transformed modern Islam and created the foundation for Islamism and fundamentalism. The neo-liberal revolution was produced by the OPEC oil crisis when the cost of crude oil on world markets began to undermine the industrial economies, and made the funding of the welfare state impossible without increasing taxes. The Reagan and Thatcher years can be seen as attempts to revive the profitability of the Western economies by reducing personal taxation, cutting back state expenditure on health and welfare, reducing interest rates, and allowing currency exchange rates to float on a global market. It is possible to argue that the neo-liberal reforms did salvage the US and British economies, but the impact on Third World and developing economies was often catastrophic as the International Monetary Fund and the World Bank imposed neo-liberal economic arrangements. Islamic countries in Africa and Asia experienced massive social trauma as a consequence of economic restructuring.

Western economists argue that the Muslim societies, with the exception of the oil-rich Gulf States, Turkey and Malaysia, have failed to enter the economically developed world. If we take the average income of the advanced societies as a basic measure of economic success, the results show that the Islamic societies are economically backward. In 2000, World Bank figures show that the average income in the advanced societies was $27,450, with the US on $34,260. By contrast, in the Islamic countries from Morocco to Bangladesh the average was $3,700, and excluding the Gulf States, no Islamic society achieved incomes above the world average of $7,350. In terms of neo-liberal theory, economic liberalization is a cause of wealth creation, but it is also closely associated with political democratization. Political data on liberal freedoms also show that the Islamic societies are politically restrictive. The World Audit on economic controls showed that societies like Kuwait and Morocco were the most restrictive in the world. The Freedom House (2003) evaluation showed that Afghanistan, Iraq, Sudan, Somalia, Libya and Saudi Arabia were amongst the most politically repressive societies in the world.

Western imperialism can explain many aspects of this economic failure, but other societies that suffered from economic imperialism and political colonialism such as South Korea and India have, in fact, achieved remarkable economic growth. In terms of per capita incomes, the living standard in India is significantly higher than Pakistan. Whereas Egypt and South Korea had a similar standard of living in 1950, South Korea's standard is almost five times as high today. The principal attempts to reform the economies of Egypt and Syria were undertaken by socialist regimes, but those modernization experiments failed. Fundamentalism, as we have seen, has flourished in the political vacuum left by nationalist and socialist regimes.

With the end of the cold war and the collapse of organized communism, the second half of the twentieth century and beginning of the twenty-first century has been a period of increasing political tension between Islam and the West. This cultural and economic competition has often produced violent conflict in Afghanistan, Iran, Iraq and the Gulf, and political leaders such as Saddam Hussein, Chairman Arafat,

Colonel Gaddafi and Ayatollah Khomeini have been characterized by the Western press as evil figures. In 1998, the US Government offered $5 million for the capture of Osama bin Laden who was accused of embassy bombings in Kenya and Tanzania. In 2001, he was regarded as the evil figure who had orchestrated and partly financed the attack on the World Trade Organization building in New York. In former Yugoslavia, the ancient conflict between Christian Serbs and Muslims resulted in 'ethnic cleansing' in Kosovo and Bosnia (Sonyel, 1994). In the former Soviet Union, Muslims in Chechnya have become involved in a violent struggle for independence. As a result, Islamic culture came to be regarded as incompatible with Western values and perceived as a major political threat to the West.

These negative images of Islam can be interpreted as continuing aspects of classical orientalism in which the Islamic world is defined by its otherness, but the paradox of these negative images is that, as a result of expulsion, migration and globalization, Muslim communities have settled and evolved in most Western industrial societies, where they constitute an important element of the labour force. It is estimated that there are over 16 million Muslims in Europe, and as a faith, Islam is also well established in the USA (Smith, 1999). Western commentaries on fundamentalist Islam typically fail to consider the heterogeneity of contemporary Islamic belief and practice. For example, the apparent triumph of fundamentalism has been challenged by a number of prominent liberal intellectuals in Islam, and there is considerable opposition from radical Muslim women who reject the traditional seclusion of women, veiling and arranged marriages (Othman, 1999). The strength of democratic movements in contemporary Iran and Indonesia illustrate the resilience of intermediate associations and social movements within Islamic civil society.

## REFERENCES

Abercrombie, N. Hill, S. and Turner, B.S., *Sovereign individuals of capitalism*, Allen & Unwin, London, 1986.

Ahmed, Akbar S., *Postmodernism and Islam*, Routledge, London, 1992.

Barber, B. R., *Jihad vs McWorld. How globalism and tribalism are reshaping the world*, Ballantine Books, New York, 2001.

Derrida, J., 'Faith and Knowledge: the two sources of "religion" at the limits of reason alone' in Derrida, J. and Vattimo, G. (eds.), *Religion*, Polity Press, Cambridge, 1998: 1-78.

Featherstone, M., *Consumer Culture and Postmodernism*, Sage, London, 1991.

The Freedom House evaluation, 2003: http://www.freedomhouse.org/research/freeworld/2003/tables.htm.

Lechner, F.J., 'Global fundamentalism' in Benyon, J. and Dunkerley, D. (eds), *Globalization Reader*, Athlone Press, London, 2000: 155-59.

Grunebaum, G. von, *Medieval Islam*, University of Chicago Press, Chicago, 1953.

Huntington, Samuel P., *The Clash of Civilizations and the remaking of World Order*, Touchstone Books, London, 1998.

Ignatieff, M., *Virtual war: Kosovo and Beyond*, Vintage, London, 2001.

Matar, N., *Islam in Britain 1558-1685*, Cambridge University Press, Cambridge, 1998.

Othman, N., 'Grounding Human Rights Arguments in Non-Western Culture: Shari'a and the citizenship rights of women in a modern Islamic state' in Bauer, J.R. and Bell, D.A. (eds.), *The East Asian Challenge for Human Rights*, Cambridge University Press, Cambridge, 1999: 169-192.

Parson, T., 'Religion in Postindustrial America: the problem of secularization' in Turner B. S. (ed.), *The Talcott Parsons Reader*, Blackwell, Oxford, 1999: 300-320.

Robertson, R. *The Sociological Interpretation of Religion*, Basil Blackwell, Oxford, 1970).

Rojek, C., *Celebrity*, Reaktion Press, London, 2001.

Said, E.W., *Orientalism*, Routledge, London, 1978.

*Saint John of Damascus: Writings* translated by Frederic H. Chase, Jr, Father of the Church Inc., New York 1958.

Smith, J.I., *Islam in America*, Columbia University Press, New York, 1999.

Sonyel, S.R., *The Muslims of Bosnia: Genocide of a People*, the Islamic Foundation, Leicester, 1994.

Sweetman, J., *The Oriental Obsession. Islamic Inspiration in British and American Art and Architecture 1500-1920*, Cambridge University Press, Cambridge, 1988.

Tibi, B., *The Challenge of Fundamentalism. Political Islam and the New World Disorder*, University of California Press, Berkeley, 1998.

Thomas, S.M., 'Taking Religion and Cultural Pluralism Seriously', *Millennium: Journal of International Relations*, 29 (3), 2000: 815-843.

Touraine, A., *Can We Live Together? Equality and Difference*, Polity Press, Cambridge, 2000.

Turner, B.S., 'On the concept of axial space: Orientalism and the originary', *Journal of Social Archaeology* 1(1), 2001: 62-74.

The World Audit on democracy: http://www.worldaudit.org/democracy.htm

Yegenoglu, M., *Colonial Fantasies: Towards a feminist reading of Orientalism*, Cambridge University Press, Cambridge, 1998.

## NOTES

1. *De Daeresibus*, chapter 101, beginning in MPG, XCIV: 764-65. Cited in Grunebaum, 1953: 43-4, and for an English translation see *Saint John of Damascus: Writings* translated by Frederic H. Chase, Jr, Father of the Church Inc., New York 1958: 153.

2. Theophanes Confessor, *Chronographia*, ed. C. de Boor, Leipzig, 1883-5, I: 333-4; W. Grass, *Gennadius und Pletho*, Breslau, 1844, I: 116-17 (translates a small portion of the passage); Anastasius' *Historia Tripartia*, II: 208-10 (has a Latin version) cited in Grunebaum, 1953: 43-4.

3. See *Saint John of Damascus: Writings* translated by Frederic H. Chase, Jr, Father of the Church Inc., New York 1958: 153.

# SECTION 2

# Radicalism and Transnationalism

This section deals with a number of related themes that emerge out of the neo-orientalist paradigm of the 'clash of civilizations' where Islam and the West are represented as antithetical systems, locked into an opposition with each other and marked by a number of binaries. These chapters highlight the fact that globalization has intensified these tensions through the creation of 'transnational' networks that reproduce the 'clash of civilization' within Western society, representing Muslims as the enemy from within.

The four chapters in this section systematically challenge this pseudo-scientific paradigm. The chapters by Kamali and Talbot address the issue of radical Islam in Turkey, Iran, Pakistan and Afghanistan, producing evidence demonstrating that the radicalism of Islam did not arise out of a dichotomy between modernity and tradition but was a result of Western engagement with these societies. The radicalization of religion was a consequence of the interaction of the West with Islam rather than a product of the conflict of civilizations. The subsequent chapters focus on Muslim minorities in the West. Cesari's chapter shows that interpretations of Islam in the West, are not only subject to demands of co-existence with other faiths, but are invariably at variance with religious tradition and practice in countries of origin. This is reflected in debates challenging authoritarian tendencies coupled with a general attempt to translate Islam into more universalistic forms. The authors illustrate a form of hybridised Islam, which presents challenges not only to Western societies but also to the Muslim world.

The final chapter explores the impact of transnational networks among Muslim migrants, challenging long-standing views that strong networks result in poor integration. The evidence indicates that strong socio-economic integration reduces the impact of transnational influences; conversely poor integration, particularly, unemployment, results in strengthening transnational ties with the sending country. Engeberson shows that a vibrant ethnic identity is often a product of positive integration rather than a result of transnational influences, challenging recently established views that these are potential source for Islamic radicalism.

# 3

# Making of Islamic Radicalism: Iran and Turkey

*Masoud Kamali*

## SUMMARY

This chapter deals with the pathways of Iran and Turkey through modernity from the perspective of multiple modernities. The main assumption is that the modernizations of Iran and Turkey are largely formed by the two countries' particular historical and socio-cultural contexts. I reject the prevalent, dualistic analysis of modernity, and in particular its institutions that contrast 'occidental' and 'oriental' developments. The legacy of 'orientalism' has become an inseparable part of the social sciences, not only through the theories of Max Weber and Karl Marx, but those of Georg Wilhelm Hegel, John Locke, and others (Kamali, 2001). Among contemporary theorists, Ernest Gellner, Jeffrey Alexander and Samuel Huntington explain the failure of democratic development in Islamic countries as compared to those in 'the West' by the lack of 'civil society and individualism' in the 'Islamic world.' My approach rejects the simple formula of searching for and identifying selected differences between 'the West' and non-Western societies, e.g., 'differences in democratic development'. Such a formula serves to characterize 'the West' as all too unique, on the one hand, and the Islamic countries as a homogenous 'world'.

A central objective of the study is to argue that the modernizations of Iran and Turkey should be seen in the light of: (1) the multiplicity of modernizations in those countries and their particular socio-cultural properties, (2) the role of an indigenous Islamic civil society as the counterpart of authoritative secularization, and (3) the role of radical Islam in the democratization of those countries' polity.

## MULTIPLE MODERNITIES

The legacy of the modernization theory, which dominated American social sciences during the 1950s and 1960s, contributed to creating a tradition of thinking and speaking of modernity as a coherent and integrated whole (Yack, 1997: 57). This tradition follows the fact that those social theorists and philosophers who developed the idea of modernity viewed the modern age as a harmonious unity. Social theorists and philosophers believed that fundamental divisions, such as subject/object, public/private, inclination/duty, bourgeois/proletariat, structured modern life (Yack, 1997: 7–8). Others, such as Peter Taylor (1999), explore different modernities, which appeared almost simultaneously. He means that while Europeanization was occurring in the 'South', the Americanization of Europe was taking place in the 'North'. The twentieth century has been an era of Americanization, a projection of US power through both coercion and consensus. Taylor means that while consensus over Americanization was common in the 'North', the coercion side of Americanization was experienced by the 'South' (Taylor, 1999: 9–10). Both the Americanization and the Europeanization of the world were coupled with coercion and wars in the 'South' waged by colonial and imperialist powers engaged in direct fights, or using local surrogates to realise their ambitions (see Chomsky & Herman, 1979). 'American social scientists may have preferred to use the universal term 'modernization' at this time, but the popular descriptions of Coca-Colaization, Disneyfication, McWorld and the Levi generation leave no doubt as to its geographical provenance' (Taylor, 1999: 10).

Hence, the idea of modernity as a single and homogenous phenomenon has a strong Eurocentric assumption. Gerard Delanty (2003) suggests that 'the idea of an alternative modernity or alternative modernities is one of the most obvious solutions to the tendency to see modernity as uniformity'. Although there is an agreement that modernity does not take one form but many, there is little agreement on methodological implications or even clarity of the nature of the problem. Those social scientists who try to clarify and theorize 'alternative' modernities, such as the *Sonderweg* thesis of German modernity and 'American exceptionalism' (Lipset and Marks, 2000), seem to assume that there is a universal norm, and that everything that does not accord with it must be understood as aberrant (Delanty, 2003: 4). Delanty argues that even Soviet communism and fascism must be considered among the different societal paths to, and experiments with, modernity (see also Arnason, 1993; Yack, 1997).

The hegemonic understanding that modernity is a singular, universal process that started in north-western Europe and later spread all over the world is limited and Eurocentric. The 'genesis thinking' that has been widespread in the field of historical sociology is one of the main reasons behind the monological and Eurocentric understanding of modernity as a single, universal and homogeneous phenomenon. Paradoxically, such a tradition ignores the history of modernity in its global context and in particular the socio-cultural conditions. Modernity is pluralized into numerous socio-cultural forms (see Kaya, 2003; Taylor, 1999; *Daedalus*, 1998; *Daedalus*, 2000). This still seems to be a controversial claim even in the current global condition of the world. Singularity of modernity and universality of the 'Western experience' is still valid in many discussions of modernity and its European character (Giddens, 1990; Beck, Giddens and Lash, 1994). Although many scholars such as Hall et al. (1992: 2) mention that modernity is the sum of many different forces and processes, no single 'master process' was sufficient to produce it. They somehow believe in the pure Western roots and geography of modernity.

The singularization and harmonization of modernity has been, and still is, a part of the creation and recreation of established theoretical dualism in social sciences; for instance, the dualism of modern/traditional that is based on the Durkheimian 'structural differentiation' theory where societal transformations are conceptualized as a single movement from simple to complex, traditional to modern, community to society, sacred to secular and folk/rural to urban, among others. This natural/evolutionist bias has been based on the linearity of the historical developments that led to the displacement, for instance, of the traditional by the modern, or the irrational by the rational. However, recent research and available empirical evidence, based, for example, on the structural properties and social institutions of many non-Western, and in some cases even Western, countries, witness that such transformations are not happening. Furthermore, not everything that has replaced the old structures is rational. Militarism and the development of nuclear weapons, or according to Lawrence, 'preparing for Armageddon', are among the evidence for this.[1]

## MODERNITY AND WAR

Modernity is considered as a condition of self-confrontation, incompleteness and renewal, in which the past is reshaped by the present, and the future will be constructed by the present (Eisenstadt, 1966). Modernity expresses self-confidence in the transformative project of the present time as liberation from the past; modernity is the belief in the possibility of a new beginning based on human autonomy (Delanty, 2003: 3). As Heller argues, 'everything is open to query and to testing; everything is subject to rational scrutiny and refuted by argument' (1994: 41). Yet this rationality has proved to be both liberating and destructive. The rational organization of society by political means concentrated in the hands of modern states has resulted in disastrous wars, ethnic cleansing, and homogenization projects. Purification of modernity from its 'undesirable' consequences has occupied many social scientists. Many, such as Habermas, Beck and Lash, believe in the idealized ideas of Enlightenment, and have created a theoretical soup that tastes of progress and humanism. Others, such as Dahrendorf and Giddens, in close cooperation with neo-colonial political powers, such as the UK and the USA, legitimize the brutality of the modern world in the name of modernity.[2] They often draw a clean picture of modernity in which the modern economy and democracy appear together and as synonymous. And political modernity is considered as the rise of the secular state and a secular polity. In such theories the bloody history of nation states is missing or hardly mentioned. The very basis of the power of the modern state is not, in the pre-modern ones, based purely on military support or on religious legitimization, but rather on the scope of its political support that is managed by participation of the masses in political processes. However, political modernization is not to be understood as a process of democratization. 'The modern state is not necessarily democratic. A history of democratization, therefore, is not synonymous with one of state modernization' (Torstendahl, 1992; Therborn, 1992: 63).

Giddens (1990) stresses the industrialization of military power as one of the four most important properties of modernity (Hall et al.) and many other scholars of modernization and contemporary neo-modernization theories, such as Tiryakian (1991), purify modernization and make it an ideal type of what these theorists would like it to be, namely a process of unproblematic and evolutionary development towards welfare and democracy. Such an understanding of modernity as a process beginning in 'the West' and spreading all over the world is highly 'West-centric' and narrow-minded. 'In effect it is a theory of Westernization by another name, which replicated all the problems associated with Eurocentrism: a narrow window on the world, historically and culturally' (Pieterse, 1995: 47). In this sense, modernization and its 'natural consequence', globalization as a 'global order' are 'indicative of a Parsonian approach, transferred from an artificially isolated and unified society to the global condition' (Armason, 1990: 200). This is a kind of Occidental narcissism that ignores and omits the dark yet integrated sides of modernity, for example, the holocaust (Bauman), war (Joas), imperialism (Wallerstein), and orientalism (Edward Said). (See also Kaye & Stråth, 2000).

Giddens, though himself one of the most enthusiastic defenders of modernity as a continuous and global process, believes that the creation of a very effective surveillance system and the industrialization of military power are two of modernity's most important dimensions.[3] Monopoly over the means of violence has been of central importance for modern states (Giddens, 1990; see also Joas, 2000). However, the optimistic understanding of the modernization and Westernization of the world lost its validity in the face of the First World War (Gordon, 1989). The idea of a modern and peaceful world with its evolutionary progress was destroyed in the war's brutal slaughters. The war put an end to the widespread liberal optimism about the peaceful development of the modern world. The common understanding of a modern world was highly influenced by optimism in its rational and 'progressive' characteristics that make modernity and war two incompatible categories that exclude each other wherever they appear. Hence, a modern world was commonly assumed to be a peaceful world. Norman Angell in his work *The Great Illusion* (1910) was among many early scholars of the modernization theory who believed that the modern societies are so highly interconnected and bound to each other that war between them was unthinkable. Consequently, both the first World War and the emergence of the totalitarian regimes in Russia, Germany and Italy were seen as anti-modern reactions to modernity. However, this 'great illusion' came to an end very soon. Heidegger, among others, realized that Nazism, Soviet communism, and liberal democracy, all 'stand under the same reality'.[4]

The reflexive modernization so eagerly praised by Giddens and Beck has not been peaceful, or compatible with the prime ideas of Enlightenment philosophers. War, as Hans Joas argues, has always been a part of modernity and created problems for the 'positive' understanding of it. War and modernization are obviously, at least in modern times, two sides of the same coin. Joas points out that 'war demonstrates how inadequate it is to conceive modernization as a homogeneous whole with parallel developments in culture, economy and politics'. But, what catches the attention of Joas are the wars in the centre, namely in 'the west', and between Western nation-states. War has been among the most decisive factors behind the colonial and even post-colonial Western dominance.

War and its accompanying ideology constructing, disqualifying, de-legitimizing and demonizing 'the other', has been an inseparable part of modernity. Given the fact that for many Muslim countries such as Iran and Turkey, the modern world was revealed through war and the politics of contention, the exploration of war and the politics of enforcement by 'the West' are of great importance for understanding the specific forms of Iranian and Turkish modernizations. Modern wars and the mass mobilization of societies could not be successful without disqualifying, de-legitimizing and demonizing the 'other', who were the subject of military attacks, and with whom the invaders had a contradictory relationship. The invaders' military and economic superiority was prized and legitimized by the creation of a superior identity, which was highly dependent on the existence of inferiority among the invaded groups and nations. This condition can be compared to that of the Tower of Babel, in which the superiority of those on the top is based on the inferiority of lower status groups.

Wars, as many other political projects and actions, have to be legitimized, whether in the name of God, nation or morality. One of the most effective ways of legitimizing one's own righteous position in a conflict between two struggling actors is to demonize 'the other'. 'The other' has to be in many aspects different from 'us' and consequently has all the negative properties that make them different. One of the examples of such a mechanism that has been used by Western powers in demonizing 'the others' is the construction of 'the Orient' as the 'mirror image' of the West. The Orient and its 'scientific' legacy and discursive dominance came to play a crucial role in presenting Islam and Muslim countries as incompatible with modernity and democracy.

The established dualism of the paradigms of the Occident and the Orient is a manifestation of Western dominance, and colonial intentions and politics. Orientalism has been a discourse by which the inferiority of 'the Orient' has been constructed and maintained (Turner, 1994: 21). The discursive typologies of orientalism and occidentalism has been, and still is, used by 'the West' in order to legitimize its expansionist intentions and dominance in the modern world. By construction and reproduction of the concept and the discourse of orientalism, 'the West' reduced the complexity and heterogeneity of many countries and societies into a simple and definite order of patterns of behaviour, relations and structures. This has provided scientific legitimization for Western colonial policies in 'the Orient'. Although 'the Orient' had included some non-Muslim countries, it gradually came to mainly represent Muslim countries. The dominant position of the Ottoman Empire in the world reinforced the widespread and established 'Oriental discourse' in the West, in their competition and wars against the Muslim Ottomans.

The role of colonialists and imperial politics has been especially decisive in the constitution of the Western images of Islam and the analysis of 'Oriental societies' (Daniel, 1960; Southern, 1962). This has been one of the major obstacles to sociological studies of Muslim countries based on their real social forces and structures. In the examples given below of Iran and Turkey, it is clear indigenous forms of modernity were interrupted repeatedly by aggressive Western intervention.

## ISLAMIC CIVIL SOCIETY AND DEMOCRATIC DEVELOPMENTS IN IRAN AND TURKEY

The discussions about civil society have a long tradition in social sciences. Situated in historiographies of modernity, they are linked to the 'West/Europe' and not to the 'Orient'. The major concern of such discussions has been the role of civil society in democratic developments in many Western countries. The discussions on civil society from classics such as Locke, Tocqueville, Hegel, Marx, and Weber, to contemporary scholars such as Arato & Cohen and Alexander have had a very 'West-centred' theoretical bias. The classics believed in the European basis of both the concept and the phenomenon of civil society. Such understanding is still shared by contemporary scholars of civil society. The collapse of the Eastern Bloc and democratic changes in many Eastern European countries revitalized the political debates and theoretical discussions on democracy and civil society relations.

However, the resurgence of the discussions on civil society have been dominated by those who can not see any other form of civil societies other than a Western, theoretically and ideal-typically constructed one. Many of the discussions lack, on the one hand, an insight into the differences of civil societies between many countries in 'the West', and on the other hand, the awareness of a long tradition of the discussions of the concept of civil society and its real functions in non-Western countries. For instance, and as result of the dominating and theoretically taken-for-granted 'Oriental agenda' in the social sciences, there seems to be a consensus on the lack of civil society in Muslim countries among many scholars.

Historically, I contend that neither individualism nor Westernized democratic institutions have been, or are necessary for a civil society to exist. The basis of a civil society is the existence of influential civil groups and their institutions that can, through established mechanisms, counterbalance state power. In many Islamic countries, civil society is not directly conditioned by the existence of 'sovereign' and 'free' individuals, but by groups or communities and their institutions enjoying a significant degree of autonomy from the state. The autonomy of these civic society groups is based on social authority and legitimacy as well as socio-economic institutions. One of these groups was the *ulama*, which enjoyed a particular religious and legitimate basis to mobilize people and challenge the state. The *ulama's* economic independence from the state, which rested on such economic institutions as the *waqf* (religious endowments), religious taxes, *sahm-e Imam* (the share of the *imam* in Shia communities) and the bazaar's economic support, underpinned the *ulama's* autonomy from the state. *Ijtihad* has been another important source of the *ulama's* position and authority. *Ijtihad* is the preserve of *mujtahids* who possess proper knowledge and can provide Muslim individuals with guidance in matters of religion. The other main group of indigenous civil society, namely the *bazaris*, was also independent from the state in organizing their economic activities, and making and pursuing their social commitments.

The Islamic civil society was mainly based on the cooperation between two main urban groups, namely the *ulama* and the *bazaris*. Historically, the mutual needs and relationships between the two groups had institutionalized a civil authority that could, whenever necessary, influence state power. They had even controlled the public sphere of Islamic societies. The existence of the public sphere in Muslim countries and the prominent role of the *ulama* since the fourth century AH (tenth century AD) are well documented and elaborated (Hoexter et al., 2002).

Such conditions gave the *ulama* and also the *bazaris* the role of major promoters of social solidarity in Muslim countries. The moral basis of social solidarity (Durkheim) made the *ulama* the protectors of the 'have-nots' and had an effective role in promoting social justice. This was reinforced by the collection and redistributing of religious tax to 'have-nots' and creating the basis of an integrated society based on a sense of 'we-ness'.[5] Ibn Khaldun also discussed social complexity and the necessity of social solidarity in Muslim societies at the turn of the thirteenth century.

The power balance and institutionalized relationship between the indigenous Islamic civil society and the state in Muslim countries was challenged by new changes and transformations that were initiated by the state in order to reinforce state power through the creation of modern institutions. The state's authoritative efforts for modernizing Islamic societies could not happen without confrontation with the indigenous civil societies in those countries. This resulted in participation of the indigenous civil societies in the constitutional movements and revolutions in Persia (1905–1909) and in the Ottoman Empire (1876, 1907–1908), for instance. The idea of constitutionalism as a necessary means for the democratization of the Persian and Ottoman societies was adopted even by groups of indigenous civil societies, such as the *ulama* and the *bazaris*.

The constitutional revolutions in the Ottoman and the Persian empires followed specific paths based on the socio-economic and cultural settings of the two countries. The nineteenth century was a time of change in both Ottoman and Persian societies. Both the Ottomans and the Persians were faced with the rise of the new and powerful European powers. The three main foreign powers, which directly and indirectly played important roles in the two countries' modern history, were the UK, France and Russia. These countries' military and economic power forced both the Ottomans and the Persians into a state of dependency that highly influenced the course of modernization in both the countries. Military defeat, and the resultant political trauma of defeat, resulted in the adoption of Western models of modernization. The first reforms initiated by the state in both countries were aimed at reinforcing the military power and the centralization of the countries' power structures in order to survive growing external threat. As a survival strategy, the state was forced to seek foreign economic and military support, which resulted in the weakening of the bonds between the state and the indigenous groups of civil society. The states' authoritative modernization resulted also in the growing gap between the other groups of civil society, namely new Western-oriented intellectuals who advocated deeper socio-economic and political reforms, including exerting control over the sovereign and the state. The state's unwillingness to meet civil society's demand for change and their desire for participation in the destiny of the country resulted in confrontations and revolutionary movements, concluding in the political victory of constitutional revolutions in the Ottoman Empire in 1908 and in Persia in 1906.

Paradoxically, the constitutional revolutions resulted in the internal disintegration of Persia and of the Ottoman Empire. The post-revolutionary events witnessed a period of political attempts to create integration and political stability in those countries. The First World War, both for Persia, which officially stayed out of the war and for the Ottoman Empire, which participated, brought nothing but disaster. Gradually both Persia and the Ottoman Empire disappeared and were replaced by new, smaller nations, Iran and Turkey, in the early 1920s.

## Iranian and Turkish modernizations

The trauma of defeat and the weakness of the central governments in dealing with new challenges after the First World War resulted in many attempts to structurally change the Iranian and the Turkish political systems, and replace the traditional monarchy and caliphate systems with modern republicanism. This created revolutionary conditions that were skilfully used by the modern army officers and other Westernized groups led by Reza Khan in Iran and Mustafa Kemal in Turkey. In the early 1920s, the old monarchy was overthrown in Iran and a new, modernizing leader, Reza Shah, first claimed republicanism but later established a new monarchy, Pahlavi, in Iran in 1924. In Turkey, Mustafa Kemal abolished the system of caliphate and established the republic of Turkey in 1923. Thus, the two powerful leaders started projects of modernization in these two countries that each had a glorious past and a disastrous present. The new leaders' modernization programmes were both revolutionary and authoritative. One can summarize the primary goals of the Iranian, and the rapid modernizations, in the following terms: 1) authoritative political stability; 2) the creation of a strong national army; 3) economic development; 4) secularization.

Both Ataturk in Turkey and Reza Shah in Iran saw political stability, although authoritative and dictatorial, as a key means of introducing modern economic, social and cultural reforms, which they saw as necessary for the survival of the two countries in a world divided between the great powers. They sought alternative 'Wests' instead of the traditional 'liberal and unfriendly West' and found a 'new West' in Nazi Germany and Fascist Italy. This change was even supported by the Turkish and Iranian masses and many intellectuals who had experienced the disastrous imperialistic role of liberal Western countries. The 1930s' new authoritative ideologies and blueprints, such as Nazism and Fascism, provided alternative modernities for the Turkish and Iranian leaders. The 'radical and totalitarian West' was more compatible with the paternalistic ideologies of the leaders of the two countries and their authoritative political systems.

Political and military weakness had been disastrous for both countries. Therefore, the new leaders of modern Turkey and Iran were aware that the creation of a modern and powerful centralized state and a powerful national army would guarantee the state's stability and independence. One of the first tasks of the modern states in the two countries was to centralize and modernize the monopoly over the means of violence. Both leaders launched a lengthy programme for the creation of modern armies with modern training and equipment. The history of economic decline in both countries, which led to the disastrous economic dependency to the Western powers, convinced them of the necessity of a stable and continuous economic development to guarantee their independence and prosperity. As such, rapid industrialization and economic modernization were central priorities for both countries.

Both Reza Shah in Iran and Ataturk in Turkey saw the religious institutions as major obstacles to the modernization of their countries, and launched an authoritative vertical secularization programme which, together with other reforms, reduced and in some cases eliminated the socio-economic and cultural basis of the *ulama's* power and influence in both countries. The secularization and modernization programmes of Reza Shah and Ataturk had both intended and unintended consequences for their successors. Although they succeeded in modernizing their countries and reducing the power of the *ulama* and other religious groups and institutions, they also created new modern groups that came to challenge the very basis of their authoritative modernizations. Paradoxically, the modern middle classes and the working class created by the reform programmes from the 1920s to the 1940s in Iran and Turkey, together with the indigenous civil societies, came to challenge the dictatorship and to demand democratization of the polity.

Although Westernization and authoritative modernization had a long history in Iran and Turkey, the Second World War and its aftermath played a crucial role in further socio-political developments in the two countries. Both Iran and Turkey saw the Nazi regime in Germany, Soviet Bolsheviks and the Italian fascists as new alternatives to the traditional great powers of Europe, in particular the UK and Russia, whose imperialistic interventions in Iran and Turkey played a destructive role in the countries' economic and political development. They admired the disciplined society and the state of harmony in Italy, Russia and Nazi Germany compared to what they perceived to be the anarchy of the capitalist world. If these countries adopted such totalitarian modern models and methods they could create stronger and better societies.[6] The two countries saw in Germany an ally that could help them counterbalance the influence of the old great powers. However, Turkey's lack of oil, which was badly needed by both Germany and the Allies, helped that country to avoid direct confrontation with the Allies. Iranian oil, on the other hand, made Iran more important in a war in which oil resources were vital for the outcome. Although they had positive attitudes toward Germany, Iranian and Turkish leaders did not establish an open alliance with Germany. Using the pretext of a group of Germans residing in Iran, the allies, in particular the UK and Russia, attacked Iran and occupied the country in order to protect the important oil resources of Iran from being used by the Germans. This resulted in Reza Shah being sent into exile. His son, Muhammad Reza, became the new king. However, the occupation also brought about a period of democracy in Iran, which lasted more than ten years (1941–1953). The end of the Second World War was also the beginning of a democratic period in Turkey, which started in 1945 and was ended by the military coup of 1960. The temporary end of the political dictatorships in Iran and Turkey was coupled with revitalization of religious groups' participation in the political life of the two countries. In spite of several decades of authoritative modernization and secularization, and the reduction of the social power of the *ulama* and the religious groups, the democratic period marked the rise of religion in the two countries.

The appearance of moderate, modern and non-cleric religious groups in the two countries' civil societies, such as the Democrat Party in Turkey and the National Front of Iran (NFI) witnessed a change in the two countries' socio-political life. Decades of authoritative modernization and secularization had influenced the two societies, transforming and marginalizing the indigenous groups and creating new groups influenced by modern ideas, such as socialism and liberalism rather than the traditional religious ones. This forced many *ulama* and religious groups to change their traditional worldviews and political doctrines, and advocate the compatibility of Islam with modernity and progress. The post-war period was dominated by religious modernism as a way out of the crisis of the traditional religious groups' decline and marginalization.

Military interventions, which took place with the direct help of the new leader of the 'self-declared free world', namely the USA, put an end to the young democratic regimes in the both countries. The Iranian coup d'état of 1953 and the Turkish coup d'état of 1960 proved once more that 'the West' was not interested in democracy and development in these countries, and its primary concern was its own imperialist interests. This was partly the reason behind the radicalization of the political climate of the 1970s, with bloody confrontations between the oppositions and the regimes of the two countries. In Iran, the regime's violent confrontations with the opposition, the hardening of the political dictatorship, the rapid and selective modernization and the growing social problems in urban areas led to an uprising that was used effectively by the radical clergy and religious modernists to bring about the Islamic Revolution of Iran (1977–79).

Political turmoil and violence in Turkey during the 1970s did not end in a revolution, but in another military coup. The Iranian revolution made Turkey strategically very important for 'the West', in particular for NATO and the USA, which planned and conducted another military coup in 1980 (Birand, 1987).

## The crushing of democracy and radicalization of the polity

Both the Iranian and the Turkish democratic developments were brutally crushed by military means, and military governments systematically replaced democratic governments. In the Iranian case, the military coup of 1953 had a great impact on future political development in the country, the radicalization of contention politics and the progress of radical Islam. In May 1951, one of the best known and respected democratic leaders of the opposition and the leader of the National Front of Iran (NFI), Muhammad Mosaddeq, was elected prime minister. He was mostly known for his democratic background and his involvement in the nationalization of the oil industries in 1950, which was concluded in the Iranian parliament on 15 March 1951. At this time, religious leaders who were actively participating in opposition to the Shah, such as Ayatollah Kashani, were unwilling or unable to act as an alternative to the Shah, and were acting on behalf of the nationalists. The members of the NFI 'came from both the traditional, religious bazari and the modern, secular middle classes. This diversity of origins gave the groups in the NFI differences in political socialization that extended into all aspects of life' (Ghods, 1989: 182). More than two centuries of the Iranian people's bitter experience of the impact of the West culminated in massive support for the National Front. It is evident, too, that because of the structural setting of the society, Ayatollah Kashani's participation in the Front was important, and helped to gain the support of the traditional middle classes. One of the most important reforms pushed through by the National Front was the nationalization of the Iranian oil industries (Kamali, 1998). Because of this situation, the representative of the senate, General Sepahbod Fazlullah Zahedi, started a political campaign supported by the USA and the UK against Mosaddeq. Zahedi, in his numerous contacts with the USA through the American ambassador, Louis Henderson, mentioned the threat of 'the victory of communism in Iran' (Safai, 1373/1994: 104).

Mossadeq was a moderate, non-cleric Muslim, who, like Reza Shah, was a nationalist but, unlike him, was a highly committed democrat. He rejected both the pressures from the Left in the NFI to move towards republicanism, and the religious groups' demand for religious radicalism. On the other hand, Mossadeq rejected any cooperation with the communist Tudeh Party. Even when he was almost sure that an unholy alliance of the military, the Shah and the Western countries was about to overthrow him, he refused to give weapons to the Tudeh Party to counteract the coup.

The Western powers' economic and political interests were incompatible with the democratic government of Mossadeq, whose prime concern was the national benefit of the Iranian people. The summer of 1953 witnessed growing activity among military generals, security forces and the US Central Intelligence Agency to launch a coup and overthrow the national government of Mosaddeq. Western mass media, such as the BBC and the *Washington Post*, intensified their attacks on Mosaddeq and accused him of leading the country towards communism (Safari, 1373/1994: 123). On 6 August 1953, the American president, Eisenhower, in a conference on American foreign policy addressing the Iranian situation, said that, 'Mosaddeq, helped by communists, has closed the Iranian parliament and America cannot accept such a development and has decided to block the victory of communists in the Middle East and Iran' (Safari, 1373/1994: 125). Three days after Eisenhower's speech, in a secret meeting held in Switzerland, the decision was taken to launch the military coup in Iran and replace the democratic government of Mossadeq with a military government led by General Zahedi. Participating in that conspiracy meeting were Allen Dulles, the chief of the CIA; Henderson, the American ambassador to Tehran; Ashraf Pahlavi, Muhammad Reza Shah's sister; Kim Roosevelt, the deputy of CIA in the Middle East; and the former advisor to the Iranian gendarmerie, General Schwarzkopf (Safari, 1373/1994: 127).

On the morning of 15 August, the Shah, encouraged by the Americans, issued a secret decree dismissing Mossadeq and appointing General Zahedi as prime minister. A military coup was launched but it failed, thanks to a few generals who stayed loyal to Mossadeq, such as the Chief of Staff, General Riyahi. Some of the leaders of the coup, such as General Nasiri, were arrested. The Shah flew to Baghdad and later to Rome. Many of the NFI's leaders, such as Dr Fatemi, in demonstrations against the Shah, demanded the abolition of the monarchy and the establishment of a republican system in Iran (Safari, 1373/1994). Mossadeq would not accept any change in the constitution without democratic procedures. On 18 August 1953, the second and final military coup succeeded, and a military regime led by General Zahedi replaced the democratic government of Mosaddeq. Mosaddeq and many of his friends and ministers were arrested on 20 August. The Shah returned to Iran in August 1953, and thus put an end to almost ten years of democratic development in Iran. Once more, the democratic dreams of Iranians were crushed by the direct engagement of foreign powers protecting their own national interests.

Although the democratic period of 1941 to 1953 created plurality and competition in Iranian civil society, the post-coup d'état period forced many political groups and parties to cooperate against a brutal regime determined to carry out its economic reforms by political tyranny. This alliance was more visible in the national protest against the 'Oil Consortium Contract' between the government and American and British companies. Many religious and national leaders, such as Haj Firouzabadi, Haj Mosavi Zanjani, Haj Gharavi, Seyyed Mahmud Taleqani, Mehdi Bazargan, Dr Shahpour Bakhtiyar and Mohandes Entezam protested by issuing different announcements condemning the renewal of the destructive and imperialistic contract in favour of foreign companies (Safari, 1373/1994: 179). However, the contract was accepted by 'parliament' in November 1955. American and other Western powers' economic and strategic interests in Iran were the prime reason for them not to support any democratic development in the country. This left the people to fight the dictatorship of the Shah 'on their own'. Accordingly, the polity came to be dominated by radical Islamist and leftist groups who could easily recruit new members and gain popular support among intellectuals and the indigenous civil society groups such as the *ulama* and the *bazaris*.

The political situation in Turkey had many similarities to the Iranian one. During the post-Second World War period, Kemal Ataturk's heir, Ismet Inonu, who together with his government had sympathy for Fascist Italy, introduced democratic reforms to symbolize the distancing of himself from the losers of the war. However, Inonu presented other reasons for why he 'had to accept' democratic changes. He said, 'We trained everyone to be democrats, and then we find ourselves really having to accept it'.[7] However, the following years witnessed that the Ataturk view of 'teaching his folk to walk' by rapid modernization and authoritative secularization was not becoming a reality. On the contrary, both the established organ of secularization, the RPP and the new political parties had to reconsider the role of religion, and recognize the importance of Islam in Turkish civic society. Although removed from Turkish modern civil society during the Kemalist period, the *ulama* and other religious groups continued to play important roles in Turkish civic life. In other words, religion and its influence was pushed back from the public life of the republic, but not defeated and eliminated in the civic life of the masses. This became obvious in the electoral campaign of the election of 1950. Between 1945 and 1950, a number of parties emerged that sought to use religion in order to gain a foothold in electoral competition. Of the twenty-four parties founded during this time, at least eight had explicit references in their programmes to

Islamic themes (Toprak, 1981: 75). Some parties, such as the National Resurgence Party (Milli Kalkinma Partisi), founded in 1945, and the Social Justice Party (Sosyal Adalet Partisi), founded in 1946, had among their objectives the establishment of a world Islamic federation as well as a greater emphasis on traditional values in educational policy. Others, such as the Farmer's and Peasant's Party (Ciftci ve Koylu Partisi), the Purification and Protection Party (Antma Koruma Partisi) and Islamic Protection Party (Islam Koruma Partisi) had in the orientation of their programmes the protection of Islamic traditions and 'national' values (Toprak, 1981: 75).

The most important party reclaiming religious revival in Turkish society was the Nation Party, Millet Partisi, founded in 1948 by a group of dissidents from the Democrat Party. The Nation Party stressed the need for religious reforms, greater emphasis on Islamic values in social life, greater respect for Islamic institutions and the end of state control of religious organizations (Tunaya, 1962: 190–191). But the modern and rapid changes in Turkish society under the Kemalists created a society in which the traditional 'only religious' electoral promises were not successful in gaining the confidence of the voters. In other words, the Muslim voters needed more attractive programmes that were better adjusted to the new situation than mere religious propaganda. However, the Islamic revival was a crucial factor in the Turkish democratic election of 1950. Even the Kemalist party, the RPP, the motor of authoritative secularisation, showed its interest in Islamic issues and promised to remove the 'six principles of Kemalism' from the constitution if re-elected (Ahmad, 1993: 108). The party's electoral programme contained a range of promises of religious reforms, which were considered a retreat from its policy of strong secularization. It was, however, the Democrat Party that succeeded in combining religious messages with other reform programmes adjusted to the needs of the time, mobilizing the masses, and by gaining 53.38 per cent of the votes and 408 seats, win the election. Among one of the most symbolic reforms of the new government was the lifting of the ban on the recital of the *azan* in Arabic in the first month of Democrat Party rule and that of its prime minister, Adnan Menderes. It was quite effective in strengthening the party's popularity (Toprak, 1981: 79). A month later they permitted the broadcasting of Quran readings over the state radio (Toprak, 1981: 80). A range of religious reforms was launched by the Democrat government, and during the decade that the Democrat Party stayed in power, the religious groups and institutions were regaining their strength and influence in Turkey's authoritatively secularized civil society and its public sphere.

On 27 May 1960, the tank corps and the cadets, joined by the jet squadron, poured out of their barracks in Ankara, seized strategic points and occupied the Presidential Palace, the prime ministry and the parliament building. They apprehended President Celal Bayar, the prime minister, Adnan Menderes and his cabinet, jailed all Democratic members of the parliament and declared General Cemal Gursel the provisional head of state and of the government (Eren, 1963: 37-38). Many Democrats were put on trial for violating the constitution. Many were sent to prison, and 15 were sentenced to death, including the prime minister, Menderes, and his finance and foreign ministers, Hasan Polatkan and Fatin Rustu Zorlu. They were hanged on 16 and 17 September 1961.

The Turkish military, in the name of the restoration of the constitution and secularism, brought about a coup on 27 May 1960 and overthrew Menderes' democratic government. The coup, which set the stage for a disastrous political tradition in Turkish politics, was even supported by the RPP and groups from modern civil society, who saw Islam as being incompatible with modern politics. These groups received compensation after the coup through participation in a commission to prepare a new constitution, led by Professor Siddik Sami Onar, the rector of Istanbul University. The leader of the military coup, Colonel Alparslan Turkes, saw himself as the 'rescuer of the Republic'. The 'rescuer of the Republic' and his military collaborators had, of course, a particular interest in overthrowing the Democrats, since the latter were against any increase in the budget of the army. The government had joined NATO in the hope of reducing military costs, which were relatively higher in Turkey than in other NATO member states (Ahmad, 1993: 124).

In the name of saving 'secularism' and democracy, the democratic government and the Democrat Party were brutally overthrown and dissolved. But the legacy created by a decade of Democrat rule established a tradition of democratic governance without authoritative secularization. In other words, it showed that Turkey could continue its journey through modernization without Kemalism. The Democrat government proved the compatibility of Islam and modernity. One of the most important lessons of the elections of 1950, 1954 and 1957 was the fact that rulers could no longer ignore the desire of the Muslim masses and the influential groups for political participation. This became even more obvious in the decades following the *coup d'état* of 1960.

The Iranian regime during the 1960s and 1970s increased its brutal rule, and tightened its grip on the public sphere and the polity. In the name of struggling against 'red and the black reactionary groups', which meant the brutal arresting and killing of communists and Islamists, supported by the USA and its Western allies, the Shah continued his authoritative modernization without any sign of political democracy.

The dictatorship in Iran made the need for military intervention unnecessary. In Turkey, on the contrary, the periodic 'democratic reforms' made it possible for opposition leftists and Islamic groups to participate in democratic games, gain a foothold in the official polity. and in the case of Islamic parties, succeed in gaining popular support, enter parliament and form a government. This was unacceptable for the fundamentalist Kemalists and their Western supporters, in particular the USA. The army conducted several military *coup d'état* in order to crush the democratic parties and groups, and restore the republic without republicans.

During the 1970s, a period of intense terror was introduced both in Iran and in Turkey by their secular authoritative regimes. In Iran, the Shah's brutal attacks on all opposition groups, torture and execution of political dissidents increased drastically during the 1970s. This led to several bloody armed confrontations with opposition armed forces such as Fadaiyan-e Khalq and Mojahedin-e Khalq. The security forces tightened their grip on universities, and many people were arrested and executed. In 1976, the Carter administration came to power, and within an overall strategy, pressured the Shah to liberalize his regime. The liberalization encouraged some groups of liberals such as lawyers, human rights activists, poets and editors to organize themselves and begin to openly criticize the regime. Opposition groups who were under dictatorial pressure from the regime very soon dominated the political arena. The NFI and the LMI started their political activities by organizing meetings and gatherings, and claiming further democratization. But they were not alone in the new political scene. The radical religious groups, who were able to mobilize mass support in opposition to the Shah, emerged as a powerful political alternative to the Shah and to other opposition groups. Demonstrations against the Shah radicalized when the police and army started shooting at people and killing many demonstrators.

The first year of the popular uprising against the Shah, namely 1977, was marked by the Shah's efforts to suppress revolt and to re-establish his full control. During the second half of the revolution, 1977 to 1978, the Shah was no longer an alternative. Competition for state power went on between liberal loyalists, the army and a coalition of the NFI, the LMI and the clergy lead by Khomeini. The loyalists and the army lost their last chance to control or eventually build up a coalition. On 7 September 1977, more that 500,000 demonstrators protested at the imposition of martial law in Tehran. On Friday, 8 September, 75,000 protestors confronted the army in Zhaleh Square in Tehran, and were fired upon by the army on the ground and by helicopter gunships. Many were killed and injured on that Black Friday. 'Black Friday proved to be the turning point in the revolution, uniting the opposition and mobilising diverse sectors of the population under the banner of Islam' (Esposito, 1990: 25).

Once the Iranian political situation became highly uncertain and potentially revolutionary, important foreign powers not only articulated their policies toward the Iranian crisis, but also tried to influence it. The Soviet Union propagandized against the radical clergy and in favour of a constitutional monarchy; they feared the emergence of a powerful clergy and an Islamic republic.[8] Turkey also preferred a secular government. On the other hand, the USA preferred the clergy to the communists or other leftists. All, however, wanted the neutrality of the military and the emergence of a stable regime. Thus, there emerged a form of international consensus on a socio-political equilibrium based on the neutrality of the military, the avoidance of civil war and the establishment of a stable regime.

On the evening of 12 February 1979, Tehran Radio declared the defeat of the old regime and the establishment of a new Islamic regime. As a result of a compromise between Khomeini and the radical clergy with the liberals of the NFI and the LMI, which took place during the last months of the revolution, the new revolutionary regime had a dual structure from the beginning. It consisted of a liberal government on the one hand, and a revolutionary group led by Khomeini on the other. The revolutionary coalition started a turbulent period of rebuilding the state and the political leadership.

Turkey's political life in the 1970s began with the military coup d'état of 12 March 1971. The military junta appointed as prime minister the university professor, Nihat Erim (1912–1980).[9] In close connection with the army, Erim brought about a period of terror and political oppression.

The opposition was restricted, the press censored and the people arrested, jailed and killed. The outbreak of armed struggle against the state, and leftist and paramilitary activities, in particular those of the 'Turkish People's Liberation Army', made the chaotic political situation even worse.[10] The government announced martial law and became more oppressive to the opposition and the intelligentsia. As a result of an increase in guerrilla armed struggle, student revolts and the activities of the leftist Worker's Party against the government, the civilians lost control of the state and country to the military and the intelligence service. Thousands of students, leftist activists and members of the intelligentsia, including the famous authors, Yasar Kemal and Fakir Baykurt, were arrested, tortured and jailed.

A significant change was the establishment of a new party prior to the election of 1973, the National Salvation Party (Milli Selamet Partisi) that had an explicit Islamic identity. As a result of the election, the National Salvation Party (NSP) became the third major party in the country, and showed that Islam still played a significant role in Turkish society. The NSP was the heir of an Islamic party called the National Order Party (Milli Nizam Partisi), which was established in early 1970 by its influential leader, Necmettin Erbakan, who became leader of the NSP, and played a decisive role in Turkey's political future.[11] The NSP's programme was highly influenced by an old debate in Turkish society, an issue developed by many modern Muslim leaders from Young Ottomans to Erbakan. This century-old debate accused 'Westernization' of being a blind imitation of the West, and demanded the preservation of Turkish cultural heritage. They claimed that the best way to modernize the country was to preserve Islamic values and adopt the technical progress of the West. Erbakan and other leaders of the NSP criticized the backwardness of Turkey, and saw it as a result of the relationship between Turkey and 'the West'. According to Erbakan, Western countries had developed their technology at the expense of the Muslim world (Toprak, 1981: 100). Accordingly, one of the most important goals of the NSP was the creation of a powerful Muslim nation in Turkey (Toprak, 1981: 101). The election of 1974 in which the NSP gained 11.9 per cent of votes forced the RPP and its leader, Ecevit, to form an RPP–NSP coalition on 25 January 1974. Both Ecevit and Erbakan propagated radical programmes and changes, which were uncomfortable for the conservatives. The coalition promised to restore a democratic society, heal wounds left by the military regime, announce a general amnesty for those convicted of political offences and restore the rights taken away from the workers and the intelligentsia (Ahmad, 1993: 163). Militant groups from right wing parties and groups such as the 'commandos' or the 'Grey Wolves', who were the militants of the Action Party's youth movement, indulged in terror, kidnapping and murder, and created disorder and problems for the new government.

The government, however, started to realize its promises. In March, despite threats from Washington, poppy cultivation was restored in six provinces and a symbol of Turkey's subservience to America was removed. In May, the Assembly passed the Amnesty Bill after bitter debate and some amendments. Turkey's intervention in Cyprus, which led to the partition of the island between Greek and Turkish Cypriots, increased Ecevit's popularity, and created tensions between him and Erbakan. Ecevit decided to resign and force an early election, which could easily give him a majority. Ecevit failed, and Suleyman Demirel, leader of the JP, formed a new coalition with the NSP and other parties. The RPP was excluded from the new coalition, which came to be known as the 'Rightist Front'. Even the nationalist fascist party, the National Action Party (NAP) led by Alparslan Turkes, received ministerial posts in the new government. Using governmental instruments, the NAP created a situation of terror and violence against leftists, the RPP and other opposition groups. On the eve of the 1977 election, fascist and rightist groups attacked RPP meetings and the rallies of the leftist union, the Confederation of Revolutionary Workers Union (DISK), who decided to support RPP in the election (Ahmad, 1993: 169). In spite of violence and threats, the election was held. The RPP won 41.4 per cent of the ballot and the JP won 36.9 per cent. Even the NAP increased its share of the ballot and received 6.4 per cent. Again, the RPP failed to form the government and a new coalition of the JP, the NSP and the NAP formed the new government, which fell very soon and was replaced by Bulent Ecevit's new government. But Ecevit's government was confronted by increasing violence and terror organized by the NAP and other rightist groups unwilling to let a 'leftist' government rule. During the first fifteen days of Ecevit's rule, there were thirty political killings and over 200 people were wounded (Ahmad, 1993: 171). During the following months, many were assassinated by right-wing terror squads, among whom were university professors collaborating with the government and the editor of *Milliyet*, Abdi Ipekci, on 1 February 1979. Ecevit was forced to declare martial law in thirteen provinces and take some repressive action to control the devastating situation. These actions cost him his popularity, and in the partial senate election on 14

October, the RPP won only 29 per cent of the votes. The JP's votes had risen to 54 per cent, and Demirel succeeded in forming a new coalition with other parties, excluding the RPP.

The victory of the Iranian Islamic Revolution in February 1979, which led to the overthrow of the Westernizing regime of Muhammad Reza Shah, made the strategic position of Turkey very important for 'the West', in particular for NATO. Once more, 'the West's interest in the region changed Turkey's political map. The reason for the generals' intervention was their apprehension and sense of urgency regarding Turkey's instability now that she had suddenly become strategically important to 'the West' following the revolution in Iran. This was apparent to virtually anyone following events at the time, and may be confirmed by even a casual perusal of the contemporary Western press. As early as April 1979, *The Guardian's* Brussels correspondent wrote, 'Not surprisingly Turkey…is now seen as a zone of crucial strategic significance not only for the southern flank [of NATO] but for the West as a whole' (Ahmad, 1993: 174). 'The West' provided the opportunity and directly supported the Turkish military to take, once more, an active role in Turkey. The Chief of Staff, Kenan Evren, returning from consultations in Brussels with NATO, organized a meeting with other generals to discuss the timing for, and the forms of, their *coup d'état* (Birand, 1987).

'The West' needed a 'stable Turkey' in an unstable region, even if it would cost the destruction of Turkish democracy. In January 1980, the Americans forced Turkey to sign a new US–Turkish Defence and Cooperation Agreement. But Demirel refused to permit the use of bases in Turkey by the Rapid Deployment Force under consideration in Washington. Americans were sceptical of the Turkish government's loyalty to 'the West'. They were well aware of the hostility of Erbakan, Demirel's ally and leader of the NSP, towards Washington. The Americans concluded that the Turkish government was incapable of playing the regional role that Washington had assigned her (Birand, 1987). Finally, the Americans, through the Turkish army, brought about a military coup against the democratic Turkish government on 12 September 1980 in order to replace it with a more 'friendly' government capable of serving their policies.

## Authoritative secularism, modernization and radicalization of Islam

The authoritative modernization of Iran and Turkey by extremely secular regimes hostile to religious groups of both the countries' indigenous civil societies radicalized Islamic groups. In both Iran and Turkey the democratic periods resulted in the appearance of moderate, modern and non-cleric religious groups in the civil societies, such as the NFI in Iran and the Democrat Party in Turkey. This was partly a result of many decades of authoritative modernization and secularization in the two societies that transformed and marginalized the indigenous groups and created new groups influenced by modern ideas, such as socialism and liberalism, rather than traditional religious ones. This forced many *ulama* and religious groups to change their traditional worldviews and political doctrines, and advocate the compatibility of Islam with modernity and progress. The post-war period was dominated by religious modernism as a way out of the crisis of the traditional religious groups' decline and marginalization imposed on them by modern socio-economic transformations.

Military intervention, which took place with the direct help of the new leader of the 'self-declared free world', namely the USA, put an end to the young democratic regimes in both the countries. The Iranian *coup d'état* of 1953 and the Turkish *coup d'état* of 1960 proved once more that 'the West' was not interested in democracy and the development of those countries, but that its prime concern was its own imperialistic interests. This was partly the reason behind the radicalization of the political climate in the 1970s, with bloody confrontations between the opposition and the regime within the two countries. The regime's violent confrontations with the opposition in Iran and the hardening of the political dictatorship, the rapid and selective modernization, and the growing social problems in urban areas led to an uprising in Iran which was effectively used by the radical clergy and religious modernists to bring about the Islamic Revolution of Iran (1977–'79).

In Turkey, political turmoil and violence during the 1970s did not end in revolution, but in another military coup. The Iranian revolution made Turkey strategically very important for 'the West', in particular for NATO and the USA, which planned and conducted another military coup in 1980.

Iranian and Turkish experience of 'the West' was marked mainly by 'the West's' historical narcissism, which as part of modern culture dominated Western countries' policies towards the two countries.[12] On the other hand, the rapid modernizations of national governments left many groups behind, and reinforced popular support for religious groups in the societies. Although many moderate religious groups and parties did not want revolutionary changes in the two countries, and always advocated democratic change, dissatisfaction with the rapid and selective socio-economic modernization and the regimes' rejection of real democratization of the polity created more support for radical Islamists who propagated radical revolutionary changes. The Iranian Islamic revolution is proof of the claim that dictatorship and political tyranny are unable to create a secure modern and secular society.

The success of radical Islam in Iran and Islamist parties and groups in Turkey was due mainly to the monopoly of Iranian and Turkish polities by authoritative secularists who rejected any role for Islam in modern politics. Even today, the military *coup d'états* of the late 1990s and in early 2000 in Turkey, which excluded Islamic parties and groups from the Turkish polity, provide a strong argument for the claim that Islam is still a powerful ideology providing the moral basis of social solidarity, badly needed in many disintegrated Muslim societies.

Iranian and Turkish modern history witnesses the fact that as long as Islamic groups, both moderates and radicals, participated in modern democratic politics and alliance-making with other groups in civil society, they were successful. Such a policy helped them form governments in the military secularist republic of Turkey, and to seize political power in Iran in the 1976–79 revolution when revolutionary victory would not have been possible without their alliances with other non-cleric and nationalist groups. In Turkey, too, Islamist parties at best usually gained no more than 30 to 40 per cent of the vote.

Future democratic development in Iran and Turkey is thus dependent upon the willingness of the two parties, namely the secularists/modernists and the radical Islamists or religious modernists, to share political power and accept peaceful coexistence of the two civil societies in the country. Neither Islamist modernist parties nor secular modernists can be excluded from the polity. This must be understood by all parties involved, including Western powers and the USA. Western countries must change both their orientation and political narcissism, and social science has to search for a non-Eurocentric theory of modernity in which Islam and Islamists are included.

# REFERENCES

Ahmad, Feroz, *The Making of Modern Turkey*, Routledge, London, 1993.

Ahmad, Feroz, *The Turkish Experiment in Democracy 1950-1975*, London, 1977.

Alexander, Jeffrey (ed.), *Real Civil Societies: Dilemmas of Institutionalization*, Sage Publications, London, 1997.

Angell, Norman, *The Great Illusion*, Heinemann, London, 1910.

Arnason, Johan *The Future that Failed: Origins and Destinies of the Soviet Model*, Routledge, London, 1993.

Birand, Mehmed Ali, *The Generals' Coup in Turkey: An Inside Story of 12 September 1980*, Brassey's, London, 1987.

Beck, Ulrich, Giddens, Anthony & Lash, Scott, *Reflexive Modernization: Politics, Tradition and Aesthetics in the Modern Social Order*, Polity Press, Cambridge, 1994.

Chomsky, Noam & Herman, E. S., *The Washington Connection and Third World Fascism*, South End Press, Boston, 1979.

Daniel N. *Islam and the West: the Making of an Image*, Edinburgh University Press, Edinburgh, 1960.

*Daedalus*, Special Issue on Early Modernities, Vol. 127 (3), 1998.

*Daedalus*, Special Issue on Multiple Modernities, Vol. 129 (1), 2000.

Delanty, G., *Rethinking Europe and Modernity in Light of Global Transformations: The Making of a Post-Western Europe*, paper presented at Koc University, Istanbul, 2 May 2003.

Eisenstadt, Shmuel N., *Modernization: Protest and change*, Englewood Cliffs, New York, 1966.

Eren, Nuri, *Turkey Today and Tomorrow: An Experiment in Westernization*, Praeger, New York, 1963.

Esposito, John L., *The Iranian Revolution: Its Global Impact*, Florida International University Press, Miami, 1990.

Eze, Emanuel Chukwudi, *Race and Enlightenment*, Blackwell, Cambridge, Mass., 1997.

Ghods, M. Reza, *Iran in the Twentieth Century: A Political History*, Lynne Rienner Publishers, Boulder, Co., 1989.

Giddens, Anthony, *The Consequences of Modernity*, Polity Press, Cambridge, 1990.

Giddens, Anthony, 'The Third Way Can Beat the Far Right' in *The Independent*, 3 May 2002, London.

Gordon, David C. *Images of the West: A Third World Perspective*, Rowman & Littlefield Inc., New York, 1989.

Hall, Stuart, Held, David & McGrew, Tony, *Modernity and Its Future*, Polity Press, Cambridge, 1992.

Heller, A. *A Theory of History*, Blackwell, Oxford, 1994.

Hoexter, Miriam, Eisenstadt, Shmuel N. and Levtzion, Nehemia, *The Public Sphere in Muslim Societies*, State University of New York Press, New York, 2002.

Kaye, James & Stråth, Bo (eds.), *Enlightenment and Genocide, Contradictions of Modernity*, PIE-Peter Lang, Brussels, 2000.

Kamali, M., *Revolutionary Iran: Civil Society and State in the Modernization Process*, Ashgate, Aldershot, 1998.

Kamali, M., *Multiple Modernities: The case of Turkey and Iran*, Liverpool University Press, Liverpool, 2004.

Joas, Hans, 'The Modernity of War: Modernization Theory and the Problem of Violence', in *International Sociology*, Vol. 14, No. 4, 1999.

Kaya, I., *Social Theory and later Modernities: The Turkish Experience*, Liverpool University Press, Liverpool, 2003.

Lash, Scott, *Another modernity, a different rationality: space, society, experience, judgment, objects*, Blackwell, Oxford, 1999.

Lawrence, Philip K., *Preparing for Armageddon: a critique of western strategy*, Wheatsheaf, Brighton, 1988.

Lawrence, Philip K., *Modernity and War: The Creed of Absolute Violence*, Macmillan, New York, 1997.

Lewis, John, *Max Weber and value-free-sociology*, Lawrence and Wishart, London, 1975.

Lipset, S. M. & Marks, G., *It didn't happen here – Why Socialism failed in the United States*, WW Norton & Company, New York, 2000.

Morris, Jan & Raaflaub, Kurt A. (eds.), *Democracy 2500? Questions and Challenges*, 2000.

Nederveen Pieterse, Jan & Parekh, Bhikhu, (eds.), *Decolonization of the imagination: Culture, Knowledge and Power*, Zed, London, 1973.

Pippin, Robert, *Modernism as a Philosophical Problem*, Blackwell, Oxford, 1991.

Safai, Ebrahim, *Zendeginameh-ye sepahbod Zahedi* (The Biography of General Zahedi), Entesharat-e Elmi, Tehran, 1373/1994.

Safari, Muhammad Ali, *Qalam va siyasat*, Nashr-e Namak, Tehran, 1373/1994.

Southern, R. W., *Western Views of Islam in the Middle Ages*, Harvard University Press, Cambridge, Mass., 1962.

Taylor, Peter J., *Modernities: A Geohistorical Interpretation*, University of Minnesota Press, Minneapolis, 1999.

Therborn, Göran, 'The Right to Vote and the Four World Routes to/through Modernity', in Torstendahl, Rolf (ed.), *State Theory and State History*, Sage, London, 1992.

Tiryakian, Edward A., 'War: The Covered Side of Modernity', in *International Sociology*, Vol. 14, No. 4, 1999.

Torstendahl, Rolf (ed.), *State Theory and State History*, Sage, London, 1992.

Toprak, Binnaz, *Islam and Political Development in Turkey*, E. J. Brill, Leiden, 1981.

Tunaya, Tarik Zefer, *Islamcilik Cereyani*, Baha Matbaasi, Istanbul, 1962.

Turner, Bryan S., *Orientalism, Postmodernism and Globalism*, Routledge, London, 1994.

Weiker, Walter F., *Political Tutelage and Democracy in Turkey: The Free Party and its Aftermath*, E. J. Brill, Leiden, 1973: 219.

Wittrock, Björn, 'Modernity: One, None or Many? European Origins and Modernity as a Global Condition' in *Daedalus*, Winter, 2000: 31-60.

Yack, Bernard, *The Fetishism of Modernities: Epochal Self-Consciousness in Contemporary Social and Political Thought*, University of Notre Dame Press, Notre Dame, Indiana, 1997.

# NOTES

1. For more discussion see Lawrence, 1988.
2. Dahrendorf, a member of the House of Lords, has, after 11 September written several articles in which he claims the reunion of Europe and the USA to defend 'Western values' against terrorists. Giddens too in his article in *The Guardian* asks the authorities to be 'tougher on immigrants' in order to stop right wing parties and save Western democracy. He sees liberal immigration policy as a problem for the preservation of Western values.
3. The two other dimensions of modernity, according to Giddens (1990) are market economy and industrialization.
4. For more discussion, see Pippin, 1991.
5. See further discussion on 'a solidary sphere' and a sense of 'we-ness' identified by Jeffrey Alexander (1997) and discussed in this chapter.
6. In the case of Turkey see Ahmad, 1993: 62.
7. Cited on the opening page of Weiker, 1973.
8. Remember that a number of Soviet states in the south and south-east of the USSR were Islamic.
9. Erim's loyalty to the army and his brutal actions against the opposition cost him his life. A group calling themselves the 'Revolutionary Left' assassinated him on 19 July 1980.
10. The 'Turkish People's Liberation Army' was accused of being associated with the Turkish National Intelligence Organisation (MIT) and some factions of the army. For more discussion, see Ahmad, 1977: 293ff.
11. The NOP was dissolved by the military shortly after its establishment and declaration of its Islamic programmes.
12. For a discussion of narcissism as an inseparable part of the 'modern culture', see Philip Lawrence (1997).

# 4

# Afghanistan:
# Making of Transnational Jihad

*Ian Talbot*

Such varied writers as Edward Said (1981) and Akbar S. Ahmed (1992) have pointed out how the great faith tradition of Islam has been reduced in much popular representation to a monolithic hostile 'other' of the West. The events of 9/11 and their aftermath further reinforced media representations that linked Islam intrinsically with violence. While both Bush and Blair declared that the war on terrorism was not a war against Islam or Muslims, its main target was the 'fundamentalist' Taliban government of Afghanistan. Western governments' internal security pre-occupations post-9/11 were similarly focused on the threats posed by 'extremist' preachers and mosques, and by the need to police large immigrant Muslim populations. Nuanced portrayals of Islam's inherent pluralism and the Quranic[1] and Sufistic emphasis on peace and tolerance were overshadowed by populist reportage of 'Islam' being 'hijacked' by 'terror.'

In the fields of philosophy and religious studies, such works as Charles Kurzman's *Liberal Islam* (1998) have begun to question Western negative stereotypes. This chapter approaches the topic from the historical perspective. It seeks to contextualize the contemporary phenomenon of the transnational jihad movement that has in some portrayals become synonymous with Islam itself. By examining its roots planted in the Western response to the Soviet occupation of Afghanistan, this question can be addressed: is the militant jihad movement an integral part of Islam, or is it historically contingent and can thus in some respects be regarded as an aberration? The focus will be on the USA and Pakistan as the central players in the making of a transnational jihad movement. The latter country has received as negative a press in some quarters as Islam itself. There is no doubt there were other players involved such as the Arab states, but they did so at the behest of the USA. The question will be raised, however, whether Pakistan, despite its portrayal as a host of terrorism, has, in fact, recently been more its victim than propagator? Before turning to the consequences of the US response to the 1979 Soviet occupation of Afghanistan, it is necessary to briefly reflect on what is new about the transnational jihad movement.

Islam, from its birth, adopted a worldwide outlook expressed in the concept of the *Ummah*, the community of all believers. This was embodied in the office of the Caliph (Ahmed, 1998). The fate of the Turkish holder of this office so moved Indian Muslims that the largest scale political mobilization prior to the Pakistan movement took place in the Indian subcontinent in the period 1918–24 (Minault, 1998). Similarly, the concept of jihad has always been a central Islamic understanding. Holy war (jihad) or migration (*hijrat*) were the options open to Muslims living under infidel rule. To again take an example from colonial India, there were a series of jihads in the Frontier districts from the 1840s onwards. A spontaneous *hijrat* to the nearest abode of Islam in Afghanistan in July 1920 resulted in the temporary migration of 30,000 Muslims.

Nevertheless, in a number of respects the contemporary transnational jihad movement does involve a break with Islamic traditions. Jihad is a multifaceted phenomena that is historically contingent, and is an intensively moral struggle pertaining to the difficulty of leading a good life. Depending on the circumstances it can also mean fighting injustice, oppression and defending, militarily, Islam (Bonney, 2005). In contrast, Abdallah Azzam defined the avoidance of jihad as sinful and made it the only criteria on which a Muslim should judge his faith. This is a radical departure from past practices by making jihad, primarily, warfare. Furthermore, he legitimized martyrdom, thus allowing for the technique of suicide bombing, which was previously abhorrent to Islam, and ignored the classical understanding that the killing of non-combatants was forbidden (Cook 2005: 128-131). The final innovative practice was the issuing of *fatwas* in favour of jihad by those who were not the *ulama* such as Osama bin Laden. Indeed, as Yunas Samad has pointed out in an unpublished paper, the jihad movement must be recognized as a new social movement, in part because it is not led by *ulama*, who possess formal Islamic training.

It is also a new social movement in the sense that it is able to take advantage of globalized communication facilities and of the existence of Muslim diaspora communities. Nevertheless, the jihad movement should no more be regarded as an inevitable response to globalization, any more than it should be seen as totally espousing classical Islamic principles. Its development can be traced to the very specific circumstances of the Afghan War. In this respect the USA can be seen as bearing a heavy responsibility for the creation of a Frankenstein monster.

## THE AFGHAN WAR AND THE MAKING OF THE TRANSNATIONAL JIHAD MOVEMENT

The Soviet invasion of Afghanistan on 27 December 1979 both threatened US strategic interests and provided it with an opportunity to embroil Moscow in its own Vietnam. Zbigniew Brzezinski claims to have initiated the US intervention but it was under President Ronald Reagan that Washington involvement became significant. The Reagan administration increasingly linked the Afghan struggle with the wider strategy of economically crippling its cold war rival by raising missile deployment and technology. Support for the mujahedin went hand in hand with the deployment of cruise missiles and the Star Wars programme. While some US officials were aware of the dangers in arming and training radical Islamic groups, these concerns were set aside. The US sought not only to utilize the mujahedin on the ground in its proxy war, but also to demonstrate worldwide Muslim support for its cause. There were even short-lived plans in the mid-1980s to expand the jihad from Afghanistan to the Soviet Central Asian republics.

The CIA played a major role in providing weapons and training for the mujahedin. It has been estimated that up to 50,000 fighters were trained in camps run by the CIA and the intelligence wing of the Pakistan Army–ISI (Dorronsoro, 2002: 251-66). The mujahedin not only included so-called Arab Afghans, but radicals from as far afield as South-East Asia and the Muslim diaspora in the West. The Afghan struggle gave birth to a radicalized and romanticized view of jihad. The CIA can thus in a real sense be termed the creator of the transnational jihad movement that was to so dramatically take its revenge on its former US masters in 9/11.

Peshawar, in north-western Pakistan, became the staging post for the worldwide mujahedin effort. It was a cross between an arms bazaar and a university in jihad populated by Arabs, Bosnians, Chechens, Sudanese,

Indonesians, Malays and Muslims from the West. Much of the ideological and organizational drive was provided by the Jordanian Palestinian, Abdullah Azzam. He not only popularized the concept of jihad but also brought together the worlds of the Muslim Brotherhood, Saudi Wahhabism and Pukhtun Islamism. His Afghan Service Bureau (MAK) based in Peshawar was a forerunner of al-Qaeda. It disbursed huge sums of money from Islamic foundations, private donations and money raised in worldwide mosque collections. For a number of years, Azzam exerted a profound influence on Osama bin Laden. The parting of the ways between the two men came when, in the late 1980s, bin Laden sought to use the training, networks and resources that had been created during the Afghan struggle in the creation of a global jihadi force. Azzam, in contrast, remained focused on the Afghan conflict. With the collapse of the Soviet Union, the emerging transnational al-Qaeda organization was to turn its attention to the West and its 'apostate' Muslim allies. Within a decade, Osama bin Laden was to be transformed from a valuable Western ally to its major threat.

During the Afghan War, the CIA worked closely with the ISI and Istakhbarat, the Saudi Intelligence Agency. They together acted as a conduit for weapons and funds. The ISI developed a preference for working with favoured Islamist groups amongst the mujahadin (Hekmatyar's Hizb-i-Islami) in Afghanistan (Talbot, 1998: 317). It was to continue this approach during the Afghan civil war and later during the post-1989 Kashmir jihad. Indeed, the ISI under its head, General Hamid Gul, became so experienced in the manipulation of Afghan politics that it was seriously rivalling the Foreign Ministry with respect to policy influence by the 1990s.

The Saudis and Pakistanis worked alongside the USA during the Afghan war, but shared a different outlook. Reagan looked at the conflict from the cold war perspective, while Saudi Arabia viewed it as the struggle for worldwide Islamic leadership that had intensified since the Iranian Revolution. Pakistan's General Zia also harboured a desire to lead the Islamic world. But his primary focus was on the regional rivalry with India (Ziring, 1998: 490 & ff.). The latter's influence in Afghanistan had been feared throughout Pakistan's troubled post-independence relationship with its Muslim neighbour. The installation of a reliable ally in Kabul was seen as providing strategic depth in the struggle with India. The later collapse of the Soviet Union provided a further incentive for Pakistan to attempt to influence the course of the Afghan civil war. Stability in Afghanistan would enable a trade and energy supply route with Central Asia to be opened up. By this juncture, Gulbuddin Hekmatyar had proved to be a broken reed. Despite ISI support he had failed to dislodge Mahsud from Kabul. The Taliban were to become Pakistan's preferred means to stabilize Afghanistan.

The emergence of the Taliban[2] in the summer of 1994 was second only in importance to the Soviet invasion in creating the circumstances for the development of a transnational jihad movement. The USA was once again involved, albeit in a tacit way. The Taliban movement, as is well known, was the product of the mushrooming of Deobandi *madrassa* education during the Zia era. The greatest catchment area for the *madrassas* was formed by the Pukhtun areas of north-west Pakistan and the settlements of the three million Afghan refugees who had fled the Soviet occupation. Many of the *madrassas* propounded a narrow and intolerant version of Islam that was anti-Shia and jihad-centric. Maulana Sami ul Haq's Dar ulum Haqqania in Akora Khattak (NWFP), for example, supplied hundreds of recruits for the Afghan war. Many of the future leaders of the Taliban were trained there. The Taliban were to sweep to power in the mid-1990s in much of war-torn Afghanistan, aided and armed by the ISI. Pakistan's military assistance is well documented: it was far more effective than Russian and Iranian aid to their allies in Afghanistan. By September 1996, Kabul had fallen. While the Taliban were the protégés of Pakistan, the Americans had given tacit approval to the new Afghan policy emanating from Islamabad.

The US regarded the Taliban with favour because they were seen as both anti-Russian and anti-Iranian. Taliban rule also promised the possibility of ending the flood of opium into the West. Finally, the influential Unicol Company had administrative support in its plans to transport gas and oil from Turkmenistan through Afghanistan. Thus, Washington, like Islamabad, looked to the Taliban to end the chaos that had racked the country since the fall of the communist Najibullah regime in March 1992.

The Taliban were to prove a disappointment. They were never able to wrest control of the whole of the country from the Northern Alliance. The regime became embroiled with the UN and Western NGOs on human rights issues. Pakistan's ties with the Kabul government worsened its relations both with Iran and the Central Asian Republics. Nor were the Taliban the pliant junior partners hoped for by the Pakistan authorities. The difficult relations were symbolized by the public humiliation of head-shaving a Pakistan football team that had violated the Taliban dress code by wearing shorts in a match in Kandahar. In

February 2001, Pakistan appealed to the Taliban Information and Culture Minister, Mullah Qudratullah Jamal, over the fate of the Bamiyan Buddha statues. But the two-thousand-year-old artefacts were blasted from their cliff face. Nevertheless, Pakistan remained just one of three countries that recognized the Taliban regime. Even in January 2001, Pakistan artillery and commando units were assisting the Taliban in the fighting in the north-east of the country (*Dawn*, 2001).

The growing incidence of sectarian terrorism within Pakistan was another price to pay for this strategic and diplomatic support. The existence of the Taliban government in Kabul encouraged Sunni radicals in Pakistan. Zia's state-sponsored Islamization had left a legacy of heightened Sunni-Shia tension. Shias objected to the imposition of Sunni jurisprudence and of *zakat* (Islamic alms tax) that could be disbursed to Sunni institutions. It was in the context of Shia opposition to the Zakat Ordinance that the Tehrik-e-Nifaz-e-Fiqh-e-Jafria (TNJF) was founded in April 1979 to protect the Shias' separate religious identity. Shia protest forced the Zia regime to grant exemption from *zakat*. This enraged upholders of Sunni orthodoxy, some of whom began to deny that Shias were true Muslims. Increasingly, armed Sunni militants in such organizations as the Sipah-e-Sabha-e-Pakistan (Pakistan's Army of the Companions of the Prophet) and Lashkar-e-Jhangvi (Jhangvi's Army) trained alongside militant jihad groups in Afghanistan. Local sectarian organizations were penetrated by al-Qaeda following Osama bin Laden's return to Afghanistan from Sudan in May 1996. Clashes between Sunni militants and the Shia Sipah-e-Mohammad (Army of the Prophet) took an increasingly heavy toll within Pakistan. In all, bomb blasts, assassinations and machine gun attacks on rival sectarian places of worship resulted in 581 deaths and over 1,600 injuries in the period 1990–97 (Nasr, 2002: 85).

The Taliban and al-Qaeda ran the training camps in Khost, Afghanistan that had formerly been the preserve of the CIA, and indeed had been visited by William Casey when he was its director. Tomahawk cruise missiles were a less welcome US visitor in August 1998. They had been fired in retaliation for the al-Qaeda bombings of the US embassies in Nairobi and Dar es Salaam. Most of the Khost casualties came not from the Taliban, but the Kashmiri jihad organization, Harkat-ul-Ansar (Group of Helpers of the Prophet). HUA radicals were infiltrated into Indian Kashmir and fought alongside al-Qaeda's elite 055 Brigade against the Northern Alliance. Lashkar-e-Tayyaba (Pious Army)[3] was another group that trained and fought in Afghanistan as well as being involved in the Kashmir jihad.

General Pervez Musharraf's abandonment of the Taliban in the wake of 9/11 meant that Pakistan's long-established geopolitical strategy of close links with Pukhtun Islamist forces in Afghanistan was in ruins. The Muttahida Majlis-e-Amal's (United Council of Action) stunning success in the NWFP in the October 2002 national elections was, in part, a consequence of this (Talbot, 2003: 204 & ff.). Western institutions including churches, schools, hospitals and consulates became the target of terrorist attacks (Talbot, 2003: 201). These were carried out by jihad groups such as Jaish-e-Muhammad and Lashkar-e-Tayyaba that had been banned by Musharraf in the wake of 9/11 and the 13 December 2001 attack on the Indian Parliament building. The terrorist threat to Pakistan did not appear to be diminished in 2002–03 by the capture of a number of key al-Qaeda suspects.[4]

## CONCLUSION

In some Western reporting, Islam and terrorism have become synonymous. Leaving aside the issue of whether Islamic terrorism is contradictory in terms, it is important to understand how the transnational jihad movement that has perpetrated acts of violence came into being. This presentation has attempted to argue that its development was contingent on the Western response to the Soviet invasion of Afghanistan. The US strategy of training and arming militant Islamic groups was assisted by Pakistan, which had emerged as a 'frontline' state in the containment of communism. Pakistan, along with Saudi Arabia that funded many of the mujahedin, possessed profoundly different motives than the cold war perspective of the USA. Together, the three players helped weld together the previously disparate Islamist groups into a transnational movement. They also encouraged the popularization of the concept of offensive jihad. A prototype of al-Qaeda was developed. Anti-American sentiment was suppressed during the Afghan War, but surfaced with the basing of US troops in the Muslim holy land following the first Iraq War. The trail that leads from the CIA training camps in Khost to the Twin Towers of the World Trade Centre should not be obscured for political reasons.

# REFERENCES

Ahmed, Akbar S., Discovering Islam. Making Sense of Muslim History and Society, Routledge, 1998.

Ahmed, Akbar S., Postmodernism and Islam. Predicament and Promise, Routledge, 1992.

Bonney, Richard Jihad: *From Qur'an to bin Laden*, Palgrave Macmillan, Basingstoke, 2004.

Cook, David, *Understanding Jihad*, University of California Press, Berkeley, 2005.

*Dawn* (The Internet Edition), 22 January 2001.

Dorronsoro, G., 'Pakistan's Afghanistan Policy' in Mumtaz, S., Racine, Jean-Luc, Ali, Imran, Anwar (eds.), *Pakistan: The Contours of State and Society*, Oxford University Press, 2002,

Gohari, M.J., *The Taliban: Ascent to Power*, Oxford University Press, 2001.

Kurzman, Charles (ed.), *Liberal Islam: A Sourcebook*, Oxford University Press, 1998.

Matinuddin, K. *The Taliban Phenomenon: Afghanistan 1994-1997*, Oxford University Press, 1999.

Minault, G., *The Khilafat Movement. Religious Symbolism and Political Mobilisation in India*, Columbia University Press, 1982.

Nasr, S.V.R., 'Islam, the State and the Rise of Sectarian Militancy in Pakistan' in Jaffrelot, C. (ed.), *Pakistan. Nationalism Without a Nation?*, Manohar, 2002.

Said, E., *Covering Islam. How the Media and Experts Determine How We See the Rest of the World*, Pantheon Books, 1981.

Talbot, I., *Pakistan A Modern History*, Hurst, 1998.

Talbot, I., 'Pakistan in 2002: Democracy, Terrorism and Brinkmanship', *Asian Survey* xliii, 1 (January/February, 2003), 2003.

Ziring, L., *Pakistan in the Twentieth Century. A Political History*, Oxford University Press, 1998: 490 ff.

## NOTES

1. The Quran enjoins the repulsion of evil with goodness (41:34), of doing justice even to enemies (5:8) and of kindness to non-believers (60:8). None of these teachings provide a basis for the justification of terrorism.
2. For details on the Taliban see M.J. Gohari, *The Taliban: Ascent to Power*, Oxford University Press, 2001; K. Matinuddin, *The Taliban Phenomenon: Afghanistan 1994-1997*, Oxford University Press, 1999.
3. The Lashkar-e-Tayyaba is the militant arm of the Salafi (pious pioneers of Islam) movement. Markaz-a-Dawat-wal-Irshad organizational headquarters have been based since 1987 at Muridke. In December 2001, the Lashkar-e-Tayyaba moved its headquarters to Muzaffarabad in Azad ('free' i.e. Pakistani) Kashmir.
4. Ramzi bin Al-Shaiba, who was widely held responsible for coordinating financial transactions for 9/11 from Hamburg, was captured exactly a year later, after a dramatic gun battle in Karachi.

# 5

# The Hybrid and Globalized Islam of Western Europe

*Jocelyne Cesari*[1]

The planet's 'Coca-Colaization' is the most palpable facet of globalization. Another facet that receives less media attention but which is just as prevalent is cultural heterogenization, a phenomenon that becomes apparent not only in cultural crossbreeding, but also by the fact that different groups (communities, nations…) continue to survive and recreate themselves against the cultural imperialism of the West. The excessive homogenization of lifestyles can indeed be viewed as a danger, and in turn lead to all kinds of self-preservation and self-reconstruction, sometimes in the more excessive incarnations such as 'fundamentalism'. Planet 'Coca Cola', built around cultural products that have been standardized by the entertainment industries (music, television, cinema) and around communications industries, is a place where the search for true authenticity becomes difficult. 'Authenticity', this new buzzword to enter the international stage, refers to any movement that expresses within the political arena a need for specificity, whether in the form of Eastern nationalism, provincialism of Western democracies or religions.

The above ideas lead us directly to the following dilemma: is it impossible, as Samuel Huntington claims, to disassociate the quest for authenticity from all the varied forms of fundamentalism,[2] as well as from the notion of the clash of civilizations? Or, on the other hand, does this quest allow for the concept of individuality to be redefined (Lee: 3)? Certain people are inclined to favour the clash of civilizations hypothesis. According to this theory, Islam clearly becomes, in the period that follows the end of the cold war, the enemy of the West. Islam can only be considered a major cause of conflicts because of the supposed incompatibility between the Islamic value system and that of the West.[3] Other thinkers, such as Bryan Turner, prefer a postmodernist interpretation according to which the Islamic quest for authenticity confirms the defeat of the *Aufklarung*. According to this approach, it is understood that the anti-consumerist ethics, based on traditional Islamic doctrine (Turner, 1994: 4), are a response to the West's cultural domination; and it is posited that Muslims seek security (regarding their identity and authority) in a literal interpretation of the Islamic tradition, applicable to all areas of life.

My approach is not based on either of these interpretations. Neither religion in general nor Islam in particular will be considered merely as a cause of international conflict, or as a reaction against modernity (Halliday, 1994). I opt rather for a sociological investigation of Islamic religious identities and practices using analytic tools that have been applied to other religious groups in order to dissolve the artificial opposition between East and West (the 'Orient' and the 'Occident'), inside which the analysis of Muslim populations are still all too often enclosed, and that leads to Islam being considered as a 'special case exception'. This sociology of religious practices is based on the hypothesis that religions have the ability to accelerate the process of globalization by promoting the move from community ties to association-based ties. In other words, in the response to globalization, religions do not merely strengthen pre-existing identities (based on gender, family, or geography), but also offer resources for constructing new forms of individualization and globalization. The ideoscapes described by Arjun Appadurai are not exclusively tied to those promotions of Western culture such as Coca-Cola or McWorld.[4] Religious and cultural facts that spread the ideas of justice, morality, dignity and authenticity also play a crucial role in the shaping of ideoscapes in the same way that the Declaration of Human Rights, democracy, et cetera. In this respect, Muslim minorities within Western democracies come to be a very appropriate example of the complex relationships between modernity and globalization.

Western Muslims are faced with a radically new situation: the integration of the Islamic tradition at the heart of secularized democracies. Throughout this process, the compatibility of Islam with the notion of Western citizenship, the adaptation of tradition within a situation of pluralism, and the transmission of and education in Islam within a minority situation are topics that necessarily become of key importance. These questions are not only raised within the context of each national area, but echo and respond across national boundaries, an effect of cultural globalization. European Islam is connected with the stakes and political and cultural difficulties of the Muslim world, as demonstrated by the 11 September attacks. However, beyond sometimes-radical networks of political activism, it is a whole collection of doxa, debates, controversies and figures of authority that Western Muslims share with the *Ummah*. At the same time, they are far from being merely an echo chamber for the political and cultural issues that are taking place elsewhere, for they are, on the contrary, at the heart of religious and cultural innovations linked to their European context.

## MUSLIM MINORITIES IN THE WEST AS PART OF WORLDWIDE ISLAM

More than twelve million Muslims currently live in the main countries of Western Europe.[5] This Muslim presence is the consequence of immigration channels leading from the former colonial empires in Asia, Africa and the Caribbean to continental Europe, channels that grew to significant dimensions in the early 1960s. The official end to work-based immigration in 1974 meant that the taking-root of these populations has become irreversible, and is linked to the increase in policies regarding the reunion of dispersed families, thus leading to reshaping and increasing the size of families within Europe. Within such a context, an individual's belonging to the Islamic faith constitutes a major dimension of sedentarisation. It is thus around the visibility of Islam that inquiries, doubts, and sometimes violent oppositions connected with the integration of these 'new arrivals' within the different national collectivities will be crystallised.

The vast majority of immigrant Muslims come from countries where Islam is, if not a state religion, at least the religion of most people in the country. The transplanting of population, that implies interdependency with a majority non-Muslim environment, represents an unprecedented challenge to which Muslims are currently inventing responses that vary according to their competency in matters of Islam (in the sense Anthony Gidden gives to this concept). This competency is shaped in the first instance by the large variety of cultures, and the place given to Islam at the heart of the cultures and nations from which Muslims originate. However, this competency is also affected by the cultural traditions and national mindsets specific to each host society. Therefore, a double tropism is at the centre of the integration of Muslims in Europe: the first is oriented towards the *Dar-al-Islam* (the world of Islam); the second is anchored in the specificities of each host nation. In respect of the *Dar-al-Islam* we find solidarity networks and forms of mobility that form connections between European populations and the geographic and national spaces of the Muslim world. Regarding the host societies, the urban context is a determining factor because the global city is the privileged location for the settling and adaptation of Muslim immigrants to their new national and social contexts. Paris, Berlin, London, New York, and Los Angeles (amongst others) are henceforth Muslim capitals, given their high concentrations of Muslim immigrant populations.

Whereas an industrial city would be organized around groups whose defining lines do not coincide with ethnic and cultural borders (but rather along more universal aggregates: the proletariat, other employees, private sector versus the public, et cetera), the global city tends to give preference to, and to preserve, ethnic differences.[6] The development of 'ethnic business' as well as of all forms of self-employment within the service sector creates economic opportunities for the masses of new arrivals at the heart of the more larger cities. Given such circumstances, we have to wonder how Muslims can articulate their religious and spiritual needs in terms that take into account both the Islamic way of life and the host societies' dominant structures and systems, at the local and the national level.

In this process of accommodation, the role played by globalized forms of Islam is decisive. Over the past two decades, two different globalized forms of Islam have attracted more and more followers in different parts of the Muslim world and beyond. One form of global Islam refers to diasporic communities that develop solidarity beyond the boundaries of nations and culture, and that are often labelled 'transnational networks'. It refers to non-governmental participants such as religious leaders, immigrants, entrepreneurs, and intellectuals, who foster bonds and identities that transcend the borders of nation states. To achieve transnational status, a group must possess three main traits: (1) awareness of an ethnic or cultural identity, (2) existence of group organizations across different nations, (3) development of relations—whether monetary, political or even imaginary—linking people in different countries.[7] It is, in fact a double relationship to time (memory) and to space (networks of relationships, the construction of a mythical place) that is crystallized in the condition of Muslims living as a minority in the West. Certain Muslims preserve or even strengthen their links with their country of origin, which very often means the re-localization of local religious communities from Pakistan, Bangladesh, Lebanon, Algeria, Turkey or Egypt. This re-localization is sometimes accompanied by a rigidification/fossilization of Islamic references originating from the home countries, especially when the re-localization concerns rural groups. The relationship between men and women, as well as the status of women, are the most delicate questions of this eternalizing reproduction of traditionalist Islam.

The other form of global Islam refers to theological and political movements that emphasize the universal link to the Community of Believers (*Ummah*) such as the Muslim Brotherhood, the Tablighi Jamaat or the Wahabi doctrine. Today, the conditions for communication and the free movement of people/ideas make the *Ummah* all the more effective, without mentioning the fact that national ideologies have declined. Unlike Protestantism, where the diversification in interpretations of religious belief led to the founding of separate communities and the proliferation of different sects, the unity of the *Ummah* as an imagined and constantly renewed community based on an understanding of a shared fate is maintained. It is important to make a distinction at this juncture between radicalism and fundamentalism. It is the desire to believe in an Islam based on a direct relationship to the divinely revealed that is often the cause of people's decision to join Salafi or Wahabi movements.[8] They are thus fundamentalists, i.e. they refer back to the sources of the religion, the Quran and the *Hadith*. This return to the source texts can be conservative or puritan as is shown by the growing success of the Tablighi Jamaat, and by the fact that a part of the new generations find their source for inspiration in schools of thought such as the one built around Sheikh Al-Albani.[9]

However, this return to the divinely revealed sources can also give rise to more open-minded interpretations that are in touch with the social and political facts and contexts of various European contexts. Indeed, the global city liberates individuals and promotes the emergence of new ways of forming a Muslim identity that is not derived from ethnicity.

## INDIVIDUALIZATION AND SECULARIZATION OF ISLAM

The emergence of a minority of 'new Muslims', a minority that is growing in size, has been an unexpected consequence of Muslim settlement in the West. What is new to this group is their decision to separate religion and ethnicity. New Muslims have chosen to primarily anchor their identity within the transnational concept of the *Ummah* (the timeless community of believers), rather than in national culture. Their solidarity with their 'brothers' abroad was demonstrated by their protests against *The Satanic Verses,* their opposition to the Gulf War, and their support for peacekeeping efforts in Bosnia and Kosovo.

New Muslims exercise new levels of individual choice in the course of religious observance. Their encounter with democracy has fundamentally altered their relationship as individuals to Islamic tradition. Religion is experienced, first and foremost, as a matter of spirituality and personal ethics. In the Muslim world, where Islam is a part of the dominant social norms, as well as the religion of both state and the majority of citizens, the group—not the individual—serves as the vehicle for Islamic identification. New Muslims have not only adjusted to postmodernity, urbanity and globalization, but they have also adapted to a 'culture of separateness', one that presupposes autonomy and independence even in the religious realm (Myrdal, 2000). Consequently, identities that are integrated elements in Muslim countries are automatically deconstructed into their religious, social and ethnic components when transposed to a Western context.

Generally speaking, the increase in individual autonomy is weakening Muslim ethnic and family ties within the West. In Islamic countries, children are taught parental deference, especially toward their usually authoritarian fathers. Muslim children in the West are acculturated within a relatively permissive society that explicitly represents authoritarian parenting practices as outdated, if not damaging, and implicitly denigrates Muslim fathers on the basis of socio-economic status, educational background and ethnicity. A 'clash of civilizations' results within families where a generation gap separates fathers from children—one that is considerably wider among Muslims than amongst first generation non-Muslim immigrants. In extreme cases, children, generally adolescent males, develop adjustment difficulties when their efforts to reconcile incompatible values fail. Ironically enough, it is often new Muslims who heal rifts within their immigrant families by showing respect to their parents as a freely exercised religious choice.

Abandonment of both ancestral languages, such as Arabic, Turkish and Urdu, and cultural habits also weakens ethnic identification. Loss of cultural practices and of the ancestral language, however, has not signalled the end of religious observance. Rather, it has led to the growth of 'vernacular' forms of Islam in Europe and America, where sermons, religious literature and public discussions are increasingly in English, a language that is now becoming the second language of Muslims all over the *Ummah*.

When they don't identify with ethnic Islam, new Muslims in the West generally base their religious identities upon one of two foundations: either a secularized bond with Islam that relativizes its needs and requirements, or a fundamentalist attitude that demands respect for Islamic tradition in its totality, including the various minute details. Secularized Muslims resemble the 'pickers and choosers' of other religions in the West. Like 'consumers', they tailor their religious practice and tradition to their own subjective specifications.[10] The devout amongst New Muslims define Islam as a faith-based ethical system in which commitment of inner self takes precedence over rigid and public forms of observance. Even their fundamentalist practices are the result of individual choices, such as the decision of women to wear the *hijab*, independent of male pressure, as an expression of their spiritual self. Emphasis of true meaning over display affords new Muslims a universalistic perspective that enables their dialogue with non-Muslims. Such dialogue highlights shared values that are legitimizing Islam in Western eyes.

Many 'New Muslims' who are socio-economically disadvantaged or marginalized embrace Islam as a means to salvation. For these otherwise alienated groups within the global city, Islam facilitates integration into mainstream society. Islam has mistakenly been viewed as an obstacle to economic advancement, not only in Europe, but also in America, where a substantial Muslim presence is growing within the historically disenfranchised African–American community. The reality is that adherence to Islam can help protect the disadvantaged against the temptation of self-destructive activity (e.g. crime, delinquency, drugs, and promiscuity). As one young Muslim from a low-income suburb of Paris told me, 'We are not delinquents because we are Muslim. We are delinquents because we are not Muslim enough!' The importance of individual choice in religious practice is accelerating the pace of transnational Islamic developments. Firstly, 'small-scale, do-it-yourself societies of prayer and believers' (Hoeber Rudolph, 2000) that have always existed as amorphous forms of Islam today play an increasingly important role at the international level. As Dale Eickelman has noticed, mass education and mass communication are actually yielding self-trained religious micro-intellectuals, who are competing with formally trained *imams*. The unprecedented access that ordinary people have gained to sources of religious information and knowledge makes the creation of monopolies by official preachers more difficult, if not impossible. Secondly, 'electronic religiosity' is expanding Islam transnationally through the circulation of audio and videotapes, the broadcast of independent television satellite shows, and—most significant of all—the continuing birth of new websites. Bulletin boards, chat rooms and discussion forums on the internet are promoting alternative, even contradictory, understandings of Islam, where only nationally based ones previously existed. In so doing, they exert a moderating effect on Islamic discourse and break up the monopoly of traditional religious authorities over the management of the sacred.[11]

Global cities are thus veritable laboratories where we can see the renewal of Islamic religiosity that gives to European Islam its particularities. It is a notable fact that within such a context cosmopolitan Muslim elite is currently forming.

## CHARACTERISTICS OF THE COSMOPOLITAN MUSLIM ELITE

This elite is cosmopolitan not only because it is transnational, but especially because it mixes cultural references of different registers, which are often described as antagonistic, i.e., those of the Muslim world and those of European societies. It thus distinguishes itself from those leaders who have influence over Muslims at the level of the neighbourhood or housing project, and which seek to give new life within a European context to cultural models that originate from Islamic home countries. Such leaders (who might be described as 'parish' leaders) have often received little training, and are often bound directly to a specific ethnic group (e.g. from North Africa, Turkey, Pakistan) from which their authority derives. The cosmopolitan Muslim elite is also different from the official leaders sent to Europe by certain Muslim countries, and which have institutional authority and international connections.[12] The elite is currently creating a space for exchange at the heart of which ideas, controversy and slogans can circulate, at least in their English-language versions. This role of dispersing and transmitting information is probably the group's most manifest characteristic.

This cosmopolitan elite is composed of students and intellectuals, activists and converts. The university and intellectual milieu is particularly favourable to Islamic activism. A significant number of students pursuing higher education in Europe, and who were already politically involved while in their home country, come to re-focus their actions on the Muslim populations living in their newly adopted country. It is not rare to find at the head of major Islamic organizations leaders who arrived from their home country as students. For example, there is the case of the Union of Islamic Organizations in France (UOIF) that was founded in 1983 by Tunisian intellectuals having close ties with Ennahda.

It is the presence of new generations of intellectuals educated in Europe that is specific to the European element of this cosmopolitan elite. The associations, Young Muslims (UK), Young Muslims of France and the AGMT, founded in the 1980s and 1990s, illustrate this trend. Born in 1992, the Young Muslims of France association is lead by young men, either students or otherwise climbing the ladder towards middle class, who wish to 'wake up the minds' of Muslim youth in France. In the United Kingdom, it was in the 1980s that the first activism by generations educated in the country began: on 4 December 1984 Young Muslims (UK) was founded, and by 1993 it brought together more than 2,000 members, a number that keeps growing. In Germany, there are Avrupa Milli Gorus Teskilatari and Europaische Moscheebau und Unt erstutwungsgemeinschaft e.V. It is also important to mention the special place of converts within associations that work within the political and social sphere in Europe and America, even if this place is not always the most visible.

This cosmopolitan elite is not made up of clerics; it can be best described as being composed of independent entrepreneurs who, according to Weber's terminology, deal in salvation. Having continued their studies as far as higher education, their knowledge of Islam is either inherited from the family milieu, or acquired auto-didactically or in educational contexts that are separate from those connected directly with Islamic clerics. Members of this elite are distinct from Doctors of Law and from *ulama* whose authority is based on their knowledge and their ability to interpret divinely revealed texts. They are also distinct by their social origins: generally from the middle or upper classes of urban areas in the Maghreb, Egypt, Iraq, India or Pakistan, they are clearly distinct from 'parish' leaders who are, in general, less well educated and from the lower-middle or working classes of the same Muslim countries (Kepel et Richard, 1990). The cosmopolitan elite have a more personalized and more critical relationship to the Islamic tradition than the 'parish' leaders who have a greater tendency to reproduce the tradition—or Islamic competency, in Anthony Gidden's terminology—of the Muslim country they are from. This also separates them from the 'official' leaders who are in charge of upholding the doxa of the country of origin (like Algeria, Morocco, Turkey or Tunisia). This is, for example, the difference between, firstly, Bachir Dahmani, president of the Islamic Federation of Marseille, a first generation Muslim immigrant with a typical parish leader profile; secondly, Dalil Boubakeur, the current rector of the Paris Mosque and president of the new representative body of Islam (for which the elections took place in April 2003), is an example of an official leader; and finally, Tariq Ramadan, the cosmopolitan leader, grandson of Hassan El Banna and professor at the University of Fribourg. Charisma is often a supplementary resource that makes up for the shortcomings of social origin or cultural capital.

Members of the cosmopolitan elite who came to the West, in most cases, to pursue higher education in Europe, subsequently find there opportunities for employment and political expression that outstrip those available in their country of origin. For these intellectuals, the transmission of knowledge is no more institutionalized than the place of transmission. That places them in the same current as many members of the middle classes of the Arab–Muslim world who opted for the Salafi movement. Everyone is allowed to speak about Islam: their relationship to the texts and their ability to speak their opinion in complete freedom contributes to a democratization of the Islamic message in so far as the average believer can have a religious opinion, which constitutes a de-sacralization of interpretation within an Islam that becomes multiple and contradictory. Although this democratization of Islamic interpretation exists in the Muslim world, it is, in fact, exacerbated by the context of democracy and the condition of being a minority. What predominates at the heart of this cosmopolitan Muslim elite is its concern for preserving Islamic references within the European pluralist context and to make them coexist with other religious and philosophical systems. The main trends include a recognition of the dominant political institutions, a refusal to contest the regimes in place, and a search for systems that can explain life at the heart of secularism.

Although Europe has long been the Promised Land for the Westernized Muslim intellectual, it has also become, in a surprising move, a haven for the creativity and inventiveness of Islamic intellectuals. The fact of living alongside Muslims from different cultures and civilizations, as well as regular contact with non-Islamic religions, confer on Islamic intellectuals a cosmopolitan ideology and a sensitiveness to differences that has no comparable situation in the countries of origin. The conditions linked with one's role as citizen, inter-faith dialogue, the attempt to locate the borders between that which is open to negotiation and that which is not, the redefinition of orthopraxis—such are the favourite themes and the ways of approaching the Islamic tradition. Within such a context, democratization no longer means merely the extension and individualization of Islamic references but also a reflection about adapting to the 'other', including when this means tolerance for atheism.

## CONCLUSION

The condition of European and American Muslims brings to light the fact that the opposition between fundamentalism and universalism is insufficient in accounting for the complex relationship to religion that is generated by cultural globalization, a process that simultaneously promotes defensive reactions in the name of Islam; what Homi Bhabha (1994) calls forms of 'contra-modernity'. It is thus not difficult to understand how and why Islam can be called upon as a resource for fighting against a West that has been essentialized as destructive and oppressive. It is in such a context that the more conservative interpretations of the Islamic message (Wahabism and fixed forms of Salafism) have so many followers in all parts of the Muslim world.

At the same time, cultural globalization accelerates the crossbreeding or hybridization between the Islamic message and the European or American cultural context by generating an unprecedented reflection on the conditions necessary for tolerance and for proper respect of the Other. Islamic thought, which has long been primarily focused on governing Islam, is thus currently taking on a new dimension that emphasizes the terms of a co-existence between different religions at the heart of a shared national collectivity, and between religions and non-believers at the centre of a shared tradition. One of the unexpected consequences of 11 September has been the way this trend has moved towards the heart of the Muslim world, bringing to light for the first time an opposition between the 'local' and the 'foreign' Muslim. To this opposition can be added a further one, between fundamentalists and radicals in so far as a return to the fundamental texts of Islam, i.e. fundamentalism, need not automatically be a synonym for religious extremism, i.e. the shutting off of one's thoughts and the block rejection of other belief systems. It is important, however, not to make the hasty deduction that the trend of universalism is restricted to the western world alone. It is also present in many sectors of Muslim societies, even though the Western world functions as a kind of sound box for the ideas that are elsewhere silenced by authoritarian regimes.

As Humphrey (1998) has stated, 'The Western frontiers actually represented an opening which might engender scepticism about the authority of tradition; the possibility of challenging the World through the engagement of traditions in new spaces constructed by relations outside their control'. It is, therefore, not surprising to find that the emblematic figures of modernism nowadays live in Europe and America, where they are reconciling Islam and the West. Their presence alone constitutes a challenge to dominant historical narratives that continue to submit Muslims to the oppression of Western imperialism.

In addition, as interpretations of Islam become ever more numerous, debate intensifies over the use of Islamic symbols. 'Increasingly, discussions in newspapers, on the Internet, on pirated cassettes and on television cross cut and overlap, contributing to a common public space. New, accessible modes of communication have globalized these activities, so that even local issues take on a transnational dimension. The combination of new media and new contributors to religious and political debates fosters an awareness of the diverse ways in which Islam and Islamic values can be created. It feeds into a new sense of a public space that is discursive, performative and participative, and not confined to formal institutions recognized by state authorities' (Eikelman, 1999). However appealing they may be, romanticized visions of transnational religious networks as a pre-condition for democratization must be resisted. Authoritarian regimes can take control of or manipulate transnational groups, as the secular leader, Saddam Hussein, did when he invoked Islam in his media broadcasts during the Gulf War.

In a challenge to pluralistic democracy, transnational Islam is also raising questions about religious freedom and tolerance, as well as limits to public expressions of faith. Pluralism in Western secularized society no longer refers to the integration of socially subordinated groups or the representation of social diversity, but rather to the balance between cultural diversity and cohesion within the national community (Cesari, 2003). Democracies are thus forced to answer a number of questions regarding the possibility of reaching a collective agreement on cultural, political and religious values,[13] and on the possibility of evolving beyond shallow civility to genuine acceptance of the 'other'.

As a final conclusion, it is useful to recapitulate that in the global era, Muslims in the West are currently formulating new debates on Islam, democracy and modernization, and are involved in a process of translating Islam into more universalistic terms. Secularization is changing the meaning of Islamic observance, and altering the relationship between the individual and religious tradition. Western Islamic communities have become participants within transnational networks, and Western Muslims have become legitimate members of the *Ummah*. The ways Western Islam will challenge the Muslim world's regimes remains to be seen.

## REFERENCES

Appadurai, A., 'Disjuncture and Difference in the Global Cultural Economy' in Featherstone, M. (ed.), *Global Culture, Nationalism, Globalization and Modernity*, Sage Publications, London, 1990.

Bhabha, Homi, *The Location of Culture*, Routledge, London, 1994.

Cesari, Jocelyne, 'Intégrisme Islamique' and 'Sectes' in *Dictionnaire des Idées Rebelles*, Larousse, 1999 : 295-296 and 556-557.

Cesari, Jocelyne, 'Muslim Minorities in Europe: the Silent Revolution' in Burgat, F. & Esposito, J. (eds.), *Modernizing Islam: Religion in the Public Sphere in the Middle East and in Europe*, Rutgers University Press, London, 2003.

Cesari, Jocelyne (ed.), *Musulmans d'Europe*, Cemoti, Paris, 2002.

Cesari, Jocelyne, *Musulmans et republicains: Les jeunes, l'Islam et la France*, Complexe, Brussels, 1998.

Cohen, Robin, *Global Diasporas: An Introduction*, University of Washington Press, Seattle, 1997.

Dassetto, Felice, *La Construction de l'Islam Européen*, L'Harmattan, Paris, 1996.

Eickelman, Dale F., 'The Coming Transformation of the Muslim World' in: *Global Politics and Islam*, 1999: 1-5.

Halliday, Fred, 'The politics of Islamic fundamentalism, Iran, Tunisia and the Challenge to the Secular state' in Ahmed, Akbar S. and Donnan, Hastings (eds.), *Islam, Globalisation and Postmodernity*, Routledge, London, 1994: 91-113.

Hoeber-Rudolph, Susanne, 'Dissing the State? Religion and Transnational Civil Society', *International Political Science Association Congress*, Quebec City, 1-5 August 2000.

Humphrey, M., Islam, Multiculturalism and Transnationalism in *The Lebanese Diaspora*, IB Tauris, Oxford, 1998: 18.

Kepel, Gilles and Richard, Yann (eds.), *Intellectuels et militants de l'Islam contemporain*, Seuil, Paris, 1990.

Lee, Robert D., *Overcoming Tradition and Modernity, The Search for Islamic Authenticity*, Westview Press, Boulder, CO, 1997.

Mandaville, Peter, 'Information Technology and the Changing Boundaries of European Islam' in Dassetto, Felice (ed.), *Islamic Words, Individuals, Societies and Discourses in Contemporary European Islam*, Maisonneuve Larose, Paris, 2000: 281-297.

Myrdal, Gretty, 'The Construction of Muslim Identities in Contemporary Europe' in Dassetto, Felice, (ed.), *Islamic Words, Individuals, Societies and Discourses in Contemporary European Islam*, Maisonneuve Larose, Paris, 2000: 35-47.

Prévélakis, George (ed.), *The Networks of Diasporas*, L'Harmattan, Paris, pp. 37-46.

Sassen, Sasskia, 'La métropole: site stratégique et nouvelle frontière' in Cesari, Jocelyne (ed.), *Les anonymes de la mondialisation, Culture et Conflit*, Paris, no. 33/34, Summer 1999.

Turner, Bryan, *Orientalism, Postmodernism and Globalisation*, Routledge, London, 1994.

# NOTES

1. This chapter does not represent Professor Cesari's latest research on the topic.

2. I define fundamentalism as a shutting-off of thought (whether religious or not) that means one rejects all opinions and beliefs that are in contradiction with one's own convictions. See Cesari, J, 'Intégrisme Islamique' and 'Sectes' in *Dictionnaire des Idées rebelles*, Larousse, 1999 : 295-296 and 556-557.

3. Huntington's perception of Islam falls pray to the 'orientalist syndrome' in its use of an essentialist and fixist approach to the Islamic tradition. See Lee: 12. Unfortunately, the meta-narrative attached to the term 'Islam' too often provides the chief framework for coping with this unprecedented situation. The presence of Muslims in Europe is commonly perceived as a cultural or terrorist threat. With this reductive and biased point of departure, many reflections on Islam in Europe fail to reach any enlightening conclusion. The very question that many of these analyses seek to answer, 'Do Muslims fit into European societies?' presupposes a radical opposition between Islam and the West. This opposition formed the basis of Orientalism, which has implicitly informed many subsequent theories on Islam and politics, such as Samuel Huntington's theory of 'clash of civilizations'. Orientalism is primarily a tradition of knowledge on Islamic culture and civilisation. But it is also a set of representations on Islam and Muslims, characterized by an essentialist approach to religion and a linear vision of history that associates Islam, violence, and fanaticism. The meta-narrative based on the clash between Islam and Europe is continuously reactivated by political events such as the Islamic Revolution in Iran during the 1980s, the civil war in Algeria mid-1990 or the 11 September terrorist attacks on the World Trade Center and the Pentagon. It is shared by politicians and intellectuals as shown, for example, by declarations of Silvio Berlusconi in Italy, Pim Fortuyn in the Netherlands or the recent bestseller of Oriana Fallaci translated into French. See Jocelyne Cesari (ed), *Musulmans d'Europe*, Cemoti, Paris, 2002.

4. Appadurai, A, 'Disjuncture and Difference in the Global Cultural Economy' in Featherstone, M. (ed.), *Global Culture, Nationalism, Globalization and Modernity*, Sage, London, 1990: 295-311. Arjun Appadurai distinguishes five categories of cultural flux that he names ethnoscapes, mediascapes, technoscapes, finanscapes and ideoscapes, 'I use terms with the common suffix, -scape to indicate first of all that these are not objectively given relations which look the same from every angle of vision, but rather that they are deeply perspectival constructs, inflected very much

by the historical, linguistic and political situatedness of different sorts of actors: nation-states, multinationals, diasporic communities, as well as sub-national groupings and movements' (296). '...ideoscapes are composed of elements of the Enlightenment world-view, which consists of concatenations of ideas, terms and images, including freedom, welfare, rights, sovereignty, representation and the master-term, democracy.' (299).

5. The estimations vary according to the sources available in each country. According to Felice Dassetto, the number of Muslims currently living in Europe is approximately 11 million. (Cf. Dassetto, Felice, *La Construction de l'Islam européen*, L'Harmattan, Paris, 1996).

6. According to Sasskia Sassen's definition, the global city is, indeed, a 'dual' city in which the most developed segments of the world capitalist market live alongside and interact with the least qualified (possibly illegal) immigrant labourers. See, by Sassen, 'La métropole: site stratégique et nouvelle frontière ' in Cesari, Jocelyne (ed.), *Les anonymes de la mondialisation, Culture et Conflit*, Paris, no. 33/34, Summer, 1999: 123-140.

7. Diaspora is a form of deterritorialized identity that links dispersed populations with their countries of origin. In the case of Muslims, even if their bond with their country of origin is strong, it is challenged by a broader solidarity with the Muslim world at large. To understand how the term 'diaspora' is now used beyond its historical origin to designate transnational identities of immigrants see Gabi, Sheffer, (1996), 'Whither the study of ethnic Diasporas? Some theoretical, definitional, analytical and comparative considerations' in Prévélakis, George (ed.), *The networks of Diasporas*, L'Harmattan, Paris, pp. 37-46; Cohen, Robin, *Global Diasporas: An Introduction*, University of Washington Press, Seattle, 1997.

8. Historically the Muslim Brothers, founded in 1928, and the Wahabi movement, which is the foundation of the Saudi-Arabian monarchy, are part of the Salafist current. The institutional and political evolutions of these two trends have made the term 'Salafist', a synonym for conservatism, even for 'reactionary stance', notably within the context of Europe. Let us note that Wahabism is hostile to all forms of intellectualism, religious establishment, and even to mysticism. However, this is not true of all trends based on a return to the word of the religious texts. Not all Muslim Brothers, for example, were originally anti-modern or anti-intellectual.

9. A sheikh at the University of Medina, a specialist in *hadith*, who died several years ago.

10. For a longer explanation of this use of Islam, see Cesari, J, *Musulmans et republicains: Les jeunes, l'Islam et la France,* Complexe, Brussels, 1998.

11. Mandaville, Peter, 'Information Technology and the Changing Boundaries of European Islam' in Dassetto, F, op. cit., 2000: 281-297. It would be misleading, however, to consider on-line Islam as an exclusive indicator of a new democratic public space without paying attention to specific social changes within specific Muslim contexts. In other words, to assess accurately what Muslim websites are accomplishing in terms of knowledge, perspective and affiliation, sociologists must investigate how electronic religiosity is resonating with significant social changes in general.

12. I borrow this terminology from Dassetto, Felice, *La construction de l'islam européen*, op. cit.: 154.

13. This dilemma is illustrated by the opposition between liberals and communitarians in the USA.

# 6

## Transnationalism and Identities

*Godfried Engbersen*

## INTRODUCTION

Some qualitative changes have occurred in the nature of international migration and settlement patterns. I mention five of them (Castles and Miller, 1994; Koser and Lutz, 1998; Snel and Engbersen, 2002; Engbersen et al., 2002). First of all, the migrant population is becoming increasingly varied. Today's immigrants come from all parts of the world. Consequently, this migrant population is not only characterised by increasing ethnic heterogeneity, but also by growing social diversity: some of these immigrants are actually highly educated professionals.

Secondly, the migrant population is increasingly becoming a floating population. It is typical of this new type of immigrant that they often consider migration as merely a temporary phase. This is especially the case for highly educated professionals and commuting immigrants from Eastern and Central Europe, and probably also for the growing number of illegal immigrants in the Netherlands (including many asylum seekers who have exhausted all legal remedies).

Thirdly, there is increasing diversity in terms of the causes of migration. Whereas people mainly used to migrate because of decolonialization and a shortage of unskilled labour in Western countries, they now also do so because of war, violence, and oppression (refugees and asylum seekers), in order to start a family or be reunited with their family or because there is much demand for highly educated labour immigrants.

Fourth, an ethnic stratification on the basis of different resident statuses has become apparent. In the Netherlands, for example, three different resident statuses may be distinguished. Some groups have, or have acquired, Dutch nationality. They have all the rights pertaining to citizenship (citizens). Other immigrants have nearly full social rights and partial political rights: these are called denizens. Finally, there is a growing group of immigrants who are neither citizens nor denizens. They have a temporary or invalid resident status, and usually very limited social rights and no political rights at all (aliens or margizens). This group includes asylum seekers, immigrants with a temporary residency status and illegal immigrants (Engbersen and Van der Leun, 2001).

Fifth, a new type of migration is emerging, often referred to as transnational migration (cf. Faist, 2000a and 2000b). In the traditional view of migration, immigrants either settle permanently in the country of destination and are more or less assimilated, or remain there for a certain period of time before returning to their country of origin. The transmigrant, however, does not move from one society to another, but is someone who is part of both societies at the same time. The transmigrant is less assimilated by the country of destination, and becomes part of new, cross-border or transnational communities.

These trends in international migration force us to reconsider the premises of national immigration and integration policies. This involves fundamental questions surrounding admission, integration and identity formation. This chapter focuses on this fifth trend in order to analyze the meaning of transnational activities and identifications for the current groups of immigrants in the Netherlands. The empirical foundation is laid by a study conducted among 300 immigrants, 87 of whom were Muslim (Engbersen et al., 2003). Transnational activities relate to cross-border economic, political and socio-cultural actions of migrant groups. The notion of transnational identifications refers to immigrants in the Netherlands who strongly identify themselves with their compatriots outside the Netherlands (in their country of origin as well as in the international diaspora). It literally involves cross-border identifications with compatriots residing outside the Netherlands. Furthermore, this chapter analyzes the possible implications of transnational activities and identifications for the integration of immigrants into Dutch society. The position of Muslim immigrants in this respect will be discussed separately.

Two opposing assumptions served as guidelines in the analysis of the acquired material. The first was that a strong transnational orientation, possibly combined with a strong orientation towards compatriots in the host country, would not be conducive to socio-economic integration. The second assumption was that strong transnational identifications do not necessarily imply a weak identification with Dutch society (and therefore do not need to lead to poor integration into Dutch society).

## Transnational migration: exploration and delineation

Various authors argue that, in this era of globalization, the nature of international migration has changed (Bash et al., 1999; Faist, 2000a and 2000b; Portes et al., 1999). Whereas previously, immigrants used to settle in their country of destination, they nowadays maintain strong ties with their country of origin. They are now often referred to as 'transmigrants'. According to Portes et al. (1999), they lead a double life: they are at home in two countries, speak two languages and often earn their living by engaging in international activities such as the import and export trade. Others are involved in political or cultural transnational activities such as mobilizing support for certain political parties or promoting certain cultural activities from their country of origin. The term 'transnationalism' is used to emphasize the cross-border nature of these new migrants' activities, 'many immigrants today build social fields that cross geographic, cultural and political borders. Immigrants who develop and maintain multiple relationships—familial, economic, social, organizational, religious, and political—that span borders we call transmigrants' (Bash, Glick Schiller and Blanc-Szanton, 1999).

Given the large number of scientific treatises, studies and conferences dedicated to this topic, one may justifiably state that 'transnationalism' has become a central theme in the international migration literature of the past few years. Nevertheless, there is serious doubt as to the novelty of this phenomenon. According to some authors, it is an essentially new phenomenon in the global economy. Others are of the opinion that transnational relations have existed since the very beginning of labour migration. Labour migrants have always kept in touch with their families back home, whom they often supported financially, and visited whenever they could. The classic sociological study on Polish peasants in the USA from the beginning of the twentieth century was, for example, based on the letters these immigrants sent to their relatives back home (Thomas and Znaniecki, 1958). Portes et al. (1999) are right, though, by stating that transnational activities, although not new in principle, have acquired a different intensity and scale due to new communication and transport technologies. In the old days, it took months for a letter to reach Europe. Now, with e-mail and airmail, it is a matter of seconds or hours.

A second comment I would like to make concerns the question whether all current immigrants can be classified as transmigrants. Most authors agree that it does not make sense to call all immigrants 'transmigrants' from now on. Transmigrants constitute a select group among international migrants, namely of those who are actually involved in transnational activities. They are active in 'transnational social fields' and develop 'transnational activities'. According to Faist, these 'transnational social fields' are typified by the high frequency and intensity of cross-border ties, and the activities of people, networks and organizations. Portes et al. (1999) go one step further and propose to limit the label of transnationalism to those who have made transnational activities their trade. A Turkish labour migrant, who buys a house in Turkey, and goes on holiday there, is therefore not a transmigrant. But a merchant who sells products from Turkey in the Netherlands is. The same goes for an activist who is a member of a Turkish political movement and lives in the Netherlands.

Another way to further delineate the phenomenon of transnationalism is to investigate the transnational activities of migrants. Portes et al. emphasize that such an investigation should not merely concern the transnational activities of individual migrants. In his opinion, the emergence of transnational fields and activities is inherent to the logic of current capitalism, which is becoming increasingly global. This is particularly noticeable in the economic activities of multinationals, and in the emergence of international political institutions. Studies into transnational activities should, therefore, also include activities of institutionalized actors.

Portes et al. (1999) and a number of other authors distinguish between economic, political and cultural activities (cf. Faist, 2000b). Examples of transnational activities of individual migrants in the economic sphere are, among other things, the emergence of internationally oriented migrant entrepreneurs and of a new type of temporary long-distance labour migration. Transnational activities of individual migrants in the political sphere are, for example, political activities of migrants on behalf of organizations or political goals in their country of origin. And finally, transnational activities of individual migrants in the cultural sphere include, for example, Peruvian musicians who come to the Netherlands to play music in the streets, or *imams* from Egypt or Libya who come to instruct the Muslim flocks in the Netherlands.

This chapter will not discuss the institutionalized actors in detail, nor will it exclusively focus on migrants who made transnational activities their trade. The main focus will be on describing the relevance of transnational activities for six groups of immigrants. Subsequently, it will discuss the theme of transnational identifications and the question of social integration of different migrant groups.

## TRANSNATIONAL ACTIVITIES AND IDENTIFICATIONS

In this section, two central notions in empirical analysis are elaborated and operationalized: transnational activities and identities.

### Transnational activities

One way to make the phenomenon of transnationalism empirically researchable is by establishing to what extent immigrants are involved in various transnational activities. For this purpose, we more or less followed the typology of transnational activities as used by Al-Ali, Black and Koser (2001) in their study of Bosnian and Eritrean refugees in the United Kingdom, Germany and the Netherlands. This study comprised qualitative interviews with refugees, in which they were asked, among other things, about concrete activities relating to their country of origin. The main difference with the work of Portes et al. is that these questions did not only concern more or less professional activities, but also everyday activities such as keeping in touch with family and friends in the country of origin, transferring money or sending goods, visiting, et cetera.

In their typology of transnational activities, Al-Ali et al. (2001) make a relevant distinction between activities geared towards the country of origin and activities geared towards the host country. The former involve activities that actually cross borders such as transferring money, visiting the country of origin or voting in the elections in the country of origin. However, there may also be activities that are geared more towards the host country. Al-Ali et al. mention as an example mobilizing political support in the host country for a certain political party or movement in the country of origin. Another example is organizing or visiting cultural events in order to promote artists from the country of origin or participating in events that attract many compatriots in the host country. Using the above-mentioned typology of transnational activities, we asked our respondents a large number of questions on their involvement in various transnational activities.

## Typology of transnational activities

|  | Transnational activities geared towards the country of origin | Transnational activities geared towards the host country |
|---|---|---|
| Economic | Transferring money (q. 32)<br>Sending goods (q. 34)<br>Investing (q. 36)<br>Trading (q. 37)<br>Owning houses (q. 39)<br>Charity in country of origin (q. 40)<br>Business visits (q. 47d) |  |
| Political | Reading newspapers (q. 42)<br>Keeping in touch with politics (q. 43)<br>Membership of political party (q. 44)<br>Involvement in politics (q. 45) | Participating in demonstrations (q. 46) |
| Social | Visiting country of origin (q. 47)<br>Frequency of visits (q. 47)<br>Holiday trips (q. 47a)<br>Visits to family (q. 47c)<br>Visits to friends (q. 47c)<br>Keeping in touch with family (q. 50)<br>Frequency of family contacts (q. 51)<br>Membership of social organizations in country of origin | Membership of organizations from country of origin in the Netherlands (q. 66)<br>Attending meetings with compatriots in the Netherlands (q. 68) |
| Cultural |  | Attending meetings (q. 68)<br>Shows by artists from country of origin (q. 70) |

Figure 1
Adapted from Al-Ali et al., 2001: 619.

By asking our respondents concrete questions on all the above-mentioned transnational activities, we hoped to be able to ascertain per respondent to what extent they were involved in these activities, and more specifically, in what type of activities they were involved.

## Transnational identifications

Another key notion is transnational identifications. The question is, to what extent do transnational identifications play a role in migrant groups? To answer this question, we mainly based our research on Verkuyten's ideas on ethnic identities (Verkuyten, 1999). The starting point in his treatise is that people construct certain social identities. This social identity indicates how someone is defined in relation to his/her social environment. Social identity is closely connected with two basic questions in life: (1) who am I? and (2) how should I behave? The question, who am I? refers to the groups or social categories of which people are part or wish to be part. The question, how should I behave? refers to the normative or cultural component of social identities. The starting point here is that different social groups may have different opinions as to what is desirable behaviour and what is not. For the record, our study does not provide any answers with regard to the question of social identities. It is mainly meant to provide general insight into some basic social identifications of migrant groups (cf Verkuyten, 1999: 53-83). The sum total of the social identifications used by a person to define him/herself can be described as social identity. However, in this chapter we deal only with specific aspects or forms of ethnic identifications.

Three measuring tools were used to get a picture of the respondents' ethnic identifications. First of all, we asked the respondents how they would typify themselves. This question involved a number of different answer categories. They might, for example, consider themselves to be primarily a 'Dutchman/woman', 'American', or 'American Dutchman/woman' (depending on the respondents' country of origin). The underlying idea was to 'force' the respondents to decide whether they had fully adapted themselves emotionally to the host country (considered themselves to be Dutch), whether they still felt strongly connected with their own ethnic background (considered themselves, for example, Moroccan or American) or whether there is a possible mix of the new context in which they live (Netherlands) with their own ethnic background. In the latter case, one might speak of a multicultural or hybrid identity perception. In addition to these three outlined answer categories, respondents could also indicate that they considered themselves otherwise, for example, as 'immigrant' or 'world citizen'.

Secondly, we presented the respondents with fifty statements relating to those they felt close to, could relate to, felt proud of, felt ashamed of, whose moral values they took into consideration, and those with whom they agreed on matters such as 'important issues in life' or 'personal views on life' (raising children, husband–wife relations, et cetera). The statements were chosen in such a way that two central dimensions could be differentiated in the answers: on the one hand, solidarity with a certain group, and on the other, orientation towards the ideas and key values of a certain group. The answers showed that these two dimensions could indeed be differentiated quite well. Subsequently, two scales were constructed ('feeling of solidarity' and 'orientation towards key values').

Unfortunately, the above-mentioned method of measuring is partly dependent on the respondents' language proficiency (the questions were not always posed in the respondents' own language) and does not fully exclude the respondents' own interpretations of the questions (which might be culturally determined). In order to avoid this type of problem, we also used a third method to assess the respondents' ethnic identifications. We asked them to express by graphic means how they viewed their own relations with native Dutch people, compatriots in the Netherlands, compatriots in their country of origin and compatriots in other countries. The respondents could indicate per group whether or not they regarded their own relation with that group as two entirely separate circles, as two circles completely overlapping each other or as something in between these two representations. For example, we asked our American respondents how they viewed their relation with 'other Americans in the Netherlands'. They could tick one of the six boxes below the circles represented (see Figure 2).

**Example from the questionnaire (circle score)**

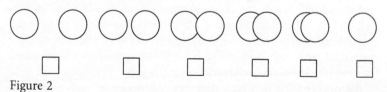

Figure 2

Finally, we also drew up a total score for the last three variables, indicating to what extent the respondents identified themselves with a social category.

## Social characteristics of the respondents

Our intention was to sketch a diverse picture of immigrants living in the Netherlands. In addition to the 'classic' minorities and 'new migrant groups' that usually arrive in the Netherlands through the asylum procedure, this study examined another category, namely that of the 'new labour migrants' (cf. Van den Tillaart et al., 2000). This category usually involves highly educated immigrants who have come to the Netherlands to fill very specific vacancies, some with foreign companies. As we examined two different specific migrant groups per type of migrant, this study covers a total of six migrant groups. In this study, Moroccans and Antilleans are examples of classic minorities in the Netherlands, Iraqis and people from former Yugoslavia represent asylum immigrants, and Americans and Japanese may be labelled as new labour immigrants.

Per separate migrant group, fifty people were interviewed, so that the total number of respondents participating in the study amounted to 300. Table 1 gives an overview.

Most of the Iraqi and Yugoslav respondents are male; in the other groups, the majority are female. Particularly striking is the large share of Japanese women interviewed (72 per cent). Although it was not difficult to get in touch with Japanese respondents at the time the data was collected, it proved far from easy to actually make an appointment with them for an interview. As typical examples of the new labour immigrants, the Japanese men we approached hardly ever had time for an interview due to their heavy workload. At some point in time we, therefore, decided to approach their wives for interviews. This explains why Japanese respondents comparatively often stated 'family reasons' as their motive for coming to the Netherlands (cf. Table 1).

Another difference between the groups is the unequal distribution of the number of the first and second generation immigrants. For four of the six groups, primarily first generation immigrants were interviewed (90 per cent or more). Only for Moroccans and Yugoslavs is the share of second generation immigrants among the respondents higher (26 and 20 per cent respectively).

## Social characteristics per ethnic group

|  | Morocco | Antilles | Iraq | Yugoslavia | Japan | U.S.A. |
|---|---|---|---|---|---|---|
| Sex (% male) | 46% | 42% | 54% | 62% | 28% | 40% |
| Age (average in years) | 31 | 35 | 36 | 39 | 41 | 45 |
| 1st generation (%) | 74% | 91% | 100% | 80% | 100% | 98% |
| Length of stay (average in years) | 20 | 14 | 8 | 17 | 10 | 17 |
| Age at time of migration | 12 | 21 | 29 | 24 | 30 | 33 |
| Dutch nationality | 74% | 100% | 68% | 86% | 12% | 22% |
| Dual nationality | 54% | 0% | 0% | 56% | 0% | 22% |
| Has a formal, paid job (%) | 36% | 64% | 48% | 62% | 86% | 80% |
| Receives benefit (%) | 20% | 10% | 30% | 28% | 8% | 16% |
| Registered as job seeker (%) | 23% | 44% | 50% | 50% | 8% | 7% |
| Education (% HBO or higher) | 14% | 24% | 44% | 28% | 74% | 86% |

Table 1

NB: HBO = Higher Vocational Education. The percentages for 'registered as job-seekers' relate to unemployed. For all respondents these percentages are 18, 20, 34, 24, 2 and 4 respectively.

A third remarkable difference concerns the number of respondents who have adopted Dutch nationality (as well). Also in this respect, there are very clear differences between the various types of migrant groups.

The fourth difference between the groups has to do with their socio-economic positions, measured according to labour market position and level of education. The Japanese and American respondents had generally high levels of education (74 per cent and 86 per cent respectively had completed a higher vocational or university education), and this is partly the reason why they occupy such a good position in the Dutch labour market, particularly when compared to the other respondents.

The fifth difference involves the age at which the immigrants came to the Netherlands. Moroccans in particular come to the Netherlands at a relatively young age. This is partly explained by the large share of second generation immigrants in this group (they were included in the calculation of the average as of age 0) and by the Moroccans' migration motive. Also, the first generation of immigrants from Morocco came to the Netherlands at a comparatively young age. This has to do with the rather large migration within the framework of family reunification and family creation in this group.

The last difference (not shown in the table) relates to the religious background. Given the commotion about Muslim extremism (alleged or actual), it was assessed which respondents were Muslim, and whether Muslims were more involved in political transnational activities (see next section). A total of 87 respondents were Muslim (all 50 Moroccans, 35 Iraqis and two Yugoslavs). Approximately half of them were younger than 25.

# Results

## Description of transnational activities

Table 2 offers a first overview of transnational activities reported by the respondents. Everyday economic activities between immigrants and their country of origin relate to such matters as transferring money, sending goods, owning houses or making contributions to charities in the country of origin. These are all transactions that occur relatively often, but there is a difference between the groups in this respect: Americans, Japanese and especially Antilleans are significantly less involved in these everyday economic activities than Moroccans and more particularly, Iraqis and Yugoslavs.

In addition, we differentiate professional economic activities, i.e. investing in, and doing business with, the country of origin, and as a result, making business trips to the country of origin. However, these professional activities—whereby immigrants actually earn an income thanks to the fact that they live in two worlds—occur considerably less often. In other words, the phenomenon of a rising class of immigrant transnational entrepreneurs as envisaged by Portes et al. (2002) has not yet really materialized in the Netherlands. In the groups that the Dutch consider new labour immigrants (Japanese, and especially Americans), this type of transnational activities occurs relatively more often, particularly among immigrants who are employed by multinational companies and therefore maintain business contacts with their country of origin.

Another question is, to what extent are immigrants involved in political activities that can be related to the country of origin? This particular aspect of transnational migration has received much political and public attention lately. Political involvement with the country of origin is, however, lowest among the group of Moroccan immigrants. Among the other migrant groups, political involvement is much stronger, particularly Americans, Yugoslavs and Iraqis. Americans generally keep in touch with American politics. A considerable number of members of this group (one respondent in five) are members of an American political party.

As far as social and cultural activities are concerned, a distinction is made between transnational activities in the country of origin and transnational activities in the host country. The former include such matters as paying visits to, and keeping in touch with, family and friends in the country of origin, and being a member of a social organization in the country of origin. As far as the latter is concerned, it should be noted that this only occurs frequently among the group of Iraqis. Sixty per cent of these respondents indicate that they are members of certain organizations in Iraq. Practically all respondents maintain contacts with family and friends in their country of origin, with the exception of the Iraqi respondents (probably due to the dangerous situation in their country). Furthermore, a large majority of respondents (varying per group from 70 to 100 per cent) have frequent contact with their country of origin. Moroccans have comparatively the least frequent contact with their country of origin. Three in ten Moroccan respondents do not have frequent contact. All in all, socio-cultural activities are the prevailing transnational activities among the respondents.

## Overview of transnational activities per migrant group (in %)

| | Morocco | Antilles | Iraq | Yugoslavia | Japan | USA |
|---|---|---|---|---|---|---|
| *Everyday economic activities* | | | | | | |
| Transfers money to family | 40 | 16 | 72 | 62 | 2 | 4 |
| Sends goods to country of origin | 28 | 14 | 4 | 54 | 12 | 14 |
| Owns house in country of origin | 16 | 8 | 14 | 46 | 24 | 14 |
| Contributions to charities in country of origin | 12 | 2 | 30 | 26 | 0 | 26 |
| Total (involved in at least one activity) | 54 | 28 | 78 | 82 | 32 | 42 |
| | | | | | | |
| *Professional/ economic activities* | | | | | | |
| Invests in companies in country of origin | 2 | 2 | 6 | 0 | 10 | 24 |
| Conducts trade with country of origin | 4 | 2 | 0 | 0 | 8 | 2 |
| Visits country of origin for business | 0 | 8 | 0 | 2 | 14 | 32 |
| Total (involved in at least one activity) | 4 | 10 | 6 | 2 | 22 | 50 |
| | | | | | | |
| *Political activities* | | | | | | |
| Reads newspapers from country of origin | 10 | 58 | 62 | 70 | 54 | 66 |
| Keeps in touch with politics in country of origin | 70 | 56 | 80 | 76 | 64 | 96 |
| Member of political party in country of origin | 2 | 6 | 24 | 0 | 6 | 20 |
| Participates in demonstrations related to country of origin | 4 | 6 | 52 | 58 | 4 | 6 |
| Total (involved in at least one activity) | 72 | 76 | 88 | 94 | 82 | 100 |
| | | | | | | |
| *Socio-cultural activities in country of origin* | | | | | | |
| Visits family/friends | 90 | 78 | 36 | 92 | 72 | 86 |
| Frequent contacts with family | 72 | 82 | 94 | 92 | 92 | 98 |
| Member of social organization | 2 | 4 | 22 | 0 | 6 | 16 |
| Total (involved in at least one activity) | 94 | 96 | 94 | 94 | 96 | 100 |
| | | | | | | |
| *Socio-cultural activities in the host country* | | | | | | |
| Member of organization related to country of origin | 16 | 16 | 62 | 8 | 18 | 16 |
| Attends meetings with primarily compatriots | 50 | 60 | 62 | 60 | 38 | 16 |
| Visits cultural events | 56 | 44 | 28 | 34 | 66 | 56 |
| Total (involved in at least one activity) | 86 | 90 | 96 | 84 | 88 | 68 |

Table 2
(The figures in this table indicate the percentage of respondents reporting the activity concerned)

Generally speaking, the respondents maintain very frequent contacts with their country of origin, which they often visit. The main exception has already been mentioned above. Two-thirds of the Iraqis hardly, if ever, visit their country of origin. As mentioned above, this is probably due to the dangerous situation there. Nonetheless, one in five Iraqis visits Iraq at least once a year. The number of frequent visitors among Antilleans is slightly higher: one in three Antillean respondents go home at least once a year. Two-thirds of the Moroccans and Americans, three-quarters of the Japanese and practically all Yugoslavs do the same. Worth mentioning in this respect is that one in three Americans go home several times a year. Moroccans have the least frequent contacts with family back home. One in ten Moroccan respondents contacts friends or family back home at least once a week. Among the other groups, the share of respondents who have such frequent contacts are as follows: Iraqis (25 per cent); Antilleans, Yugoslavs and Japanese (approximately 50 per cent); and Americans (almost 75 per cent). More than one in ten Americans even say they maintain contacts with family and friends back home on a daily basis. The conclusion must, therefore, be that there is intensive transnational social communication.

Finally, there are certain social and cultural transnational activities that primarily take place in the host country, for example, membership of organizations that in some way are connected with the country of origin, attending meetings with mainly compatriots, or visiting cultural events in the Netherlands where artists from the country of origin perform. The answers show that particularly Moroccans, Antilleans, Iraqis and Yugoslavs are transnationally active in this way. These groups indicate that more than half of them attend meetings that are mainly attended by their compatriots.

To summarize: a substantial number of immigrants in the Netherlands develop transnational activities; in most migrant groups, activities of a socio-cultural nature prevail; there are substantial differences between the groups with regard to the nature and scope of transnational activities. These differences are closely related to the nature of the migration to the Netherlands. For example, refugees develop relatively more political activities, and highly educated employees of multinationals are more involved in international trade; as for the involvement in transnational activities, considerable differences were found between the groups studied, which could not be reduced to differences in age at the time of migration or in the nature of the migration to the Netherlands. Apparently other factors, which have not been studied by us, also play a role in this, such as the cost and means of transnational activities. It may turn out, for example, that there is some relation between the high scores of Americans and Yugoslavs and the low costs of contacting the United States and (former) Yugoslavia.

## Description of transnational identifications

In this study, we tried in various ways to draw a picture of the respondents' social and ethnic identifications. The first question we posed concerned the respondents' ethnic self-identifications.

The first outcome is that assimilation in the sense that respondents like to define themselves as 'Dutchmen/women' does not occur very often. This occurs most frequently among Antilleans and Iraqis, and hardly, if ever, among the other groups (see Table 3).

**Ethnic self-identification (how do people classify themselves?) per group (in %)**

|  | Morocco | Antilles | Iraq | Yugoslavia | Japan | USA |
|---|---|---|---|---|---|---|
| As Dutchman/woman | 0 | 6 | 6 | 0 | 2 | 4 |
| As member of their own ethnic group | 20 | 42 | 46 | 40 | 82 | 44 |
| As both | 60 | 42 | 24 | 50 | 4 | 38 |
| Otherwise | 20 | 10 | 24 | 10 | 12 | 14 |
| i.e. as 'immigrant' | 6 | 2 | 12 | 4 | 0 | 0 |
| i.e. as 'world citizen | 4 | 4 | 2 | 2 | 0 | 10 |
| Total (N= 300) | 100 | 100 | 100 | 100 | 100 | 100 |

Table 3

A much larger section of the respondents define themselves primarily as members of their own ethnic group (as Moroccans, Yugoslavs, Americans, et cetera). This occurs most often among the Japanese group and least among Moroccans. The latter, on the other hand, most often indicate a mixed or hybrid identity. A large majority of the Moroccans interviewed define themselves as 'Moroccan Dutchmen/women'. This outcome can be explained by the fact that many of the Moroccan respondents were born in the Netherlands, or came to the Netherlands at a relatively young age.

However, the data on ethnic self-identification does not really tell us much about possible transnational identifications. People may primarily identify themselves with their own ethnic group, but this tells us very little about where they localize this ethnic group. This may be in the Netherlands, in the country of origin, or in 'transnational fields' that cannot be delineated as clearly (cf. Faist, 2000a). In the subsequent series of questions, the respondents were more specifically asked with whom they identified themselves. They could indicate whether they identified themselves to some extent with the native Dutch, compatriots in the Netherlands, compatriots in their country of origin or with compatriots living in other countries.

Table 4, below, presents the average scores per ethnic group on a scale from 1 to 5 (1 = minimum value; 5 = highest possible value). Each time, the relationship with one of the four social groups studied is described: with (1) the native Dutch, (2) their own ethnic group in the Netherlands, (3) their own ethnic group in their country of origin, and (4) their own ethnic group in other host countries (diaspora). The last two identifications may be called transnational: respondents identify themselves primarily with compatriots living outside the Netherlands (either in their country of origin or elsewhere). The central question in this study thus becomes whether strong transnational identifications in practice correspond with a strong identification with the ethnic group in the Netherlands or with a strong identification with the native Dutch. Finally, the last possibility is that immigrants who strongly identify themselves with compatriots outside the Netherlands do not identify themselves at all with groups in the Netherlands (neither with their own group in the Netherlands, nor with the native Dutch).

Table 4 represents the respondents' social identifications in various ways. 'Feels solidarity with' relates to the emotional bond between individual respondents and the social group. 'Is orientated towards values of' refers to a more cognitive component. This involves the extent to which respondents take the values of certain groups into account. Whereas the first two ways to identify the relationships with the social groups are based on the 40 statements that we presented to the respondents, the averages for 'Has a strong relationship with' result from the circle scores discussed above. These circle scores may be considered controls for the responses to the 40 statements. The total, each time, is the mean between the circle score, on the one hand, and the average score on the basis of the statements, on the other. This score probably best summarizes the strengths and weaknesses of the various group identifications.

## Ethnic and transnational identifications per group

|                                              | Morocco | Antilles | Iraq | Yugoslavia | Japan | USA |
|----------------------------------------------|---------|----------|------|------------|-------|-----|
| *Feels solidarity with:*                     |         |          |      |            |       |     |
|                                              |         |          |      |            |       |     |
| Native Dutch                                 | 3.0     | 2.9      | 3.1  | 3.2        | 2.9   | 3.4 |
| Own ethnic group in Netherlands              | 3.9     | 3.6      | 4.0  | 4.0        | 3.5   | 2.9 |
| Own ethnic group in country of origin        | 3.6     | 3.6      | 4.0  | 4.1        | 3.5   | 3.3 |
| Own ethnic group in other countries          | 3.5     | 3.5      | 3.6  | 3.9        | 3.4   | 3.2 |
|                                              |         |          |      |            |       |     |
| *Is orientated towards values of:*           |         |          |      |            |       |     |
| Native Dutch                                 | 2.6     | 2.7      | 2.4  | 2.8        | 2.9   | 3.2 |
| Own ethnic group in Netherlands              | 2.9     | 2.9      | 3.4  | 3.0        | 2.9   | 2.4 |
| Own ethnic group in country of origin        | 2.7     | 2.9      | 3.1  | 3.0        | 2.9   | 2.6 |
| Own ethnic group in other countries          | 2.6     | 2.8      | 2.9  | 3.0        | 2.9   | 2.5 |
|                                              |         |          |      |            |       |     |
| *Has a strong relationship with (circle score):* |     |          |      |            |       |     |
| Native Dutch                                 | 2.1     | 1.8      | 1.6  | 2.2        | 2.0   | 3.0 |
| Own ethnic group in Netherlands              | 3.1     | 2.3      | 2.1  | 2.9        | 2.4   | 2.6 |
| Own ethnic group in country of origin        | 2.3     | 2.6      | 2.4  | 3.1        | 2.6   | 2.6 |
| Own ethnic group in other countries          | 1.8     | 1.7      | 1.5  | 2.1        | 1.7   | 1.8 |
|                                              |         |          |      |            |       |     |
| *Total score:*                               |         |          |      |            |       |     |
| Native Dutch                                 | 2.5     | 2.3      | 2.2  | 2.6        | 2.5   | 3.2 |
| Own ethnic group in Netherlands              | 3.2     | 2.8      | 2.9  | 3.2        | 2.8   | 2.6 |
| Own ethnic group in country of origin        | 2.7     | 2.9      | 3.0  | 3.3        | 2.9   | 2.8 |
| Own ethnic group in other countries          | 2.4     | 2.4      | 2.4  | 2.8        | 2.4   | 2.3 |

Table 4
NB: The figures in this table are scores on a scale from 1 to 5.

What is striking is that the respondents from nearly all migrant groups feel more solidarity with people who are considered to belong to their own ethnic group than with the native Dutch. The American respondents are the only exception.

What is also particularly striking is that the respondents' emotional ties with their own ethnic group are the strongest. In the table, a distinction is made between two aspects of identification, namely, feeling emotional solidarity with a certain group and being orientated towards the values of a certain group. If you compare the scores for 'Is oriented towards the values of' with the scores for 'Feels solidarity with', you will see that the former show much smaller differences between the own ethnic group score and the score on the native Dutch. From this one might conclude that the respondents are not only oriented towards the values of their own ethnic group, but also towards those of the native Dutch—even though they indicate that they feel less solidarity with the native Dutch, a conclusion that is also very relevant to the current integration debate. A third outcome is the rather weak identification with the international diaspora. This becomes most clear from the data in the lower half of the table (data derived from the circle scores and total scores). These figures are significantly lower than the scores relating to the respondents' own ethnic group in the Netherlands and in their country of origin. Apparently, the transnational identifications of most respondents relate primarily to the country of origin. One might therefore conclude that 'bilateral' transnational identities prevail over 'multilateral' or 'cosmopolitan' ones.

The Americans distinguish themselves in two ways from the other respondents. First of all, they show on average a more pronounced tendency towards assimilation. They are the only ones who identify themselves significantly more strongly with the native Dutch than with their own ethnic group. It should be mentioned in this respect that the difference is primarily the result of their stronger cognitive orientation towards the values of the Dutch. Secondly, there are indications that the American respondents' group identification with other Americans in the Netherlands is relatively weak. This is particularly expressed by the relatively low scores on 'Feels solidarity with' and 'Is oriented towards values of'. Finally, Moroccans and Yugoslavs distinguish themselves by their strong orientation towards their own ethnic group in the Netherlands.

Further analysis shows that the chance of strong transnational identifications increases when immigrants (i) are more involved in transnational activities, (ii) have no formal paid job, (iii) have been in the Netherlands for a relatively short period, (iv) did not come to the Netherlands to start a family, and (v) did not migrate to the Netherlands at a young age (Engbersen et al., 2003). All in all, involvement in transnational activities seems to go hand in hand with stronger transnational identifications. The question is, however, to what extent this places constraints on the integration of immigrants into Dutch society. This question will be discussed in the final section.

## Transnationalism and social integration

At the beginning of this chapter, we formulated two opposite assumptions. The first is that a strong transnational orientation of immigrants, possibly in combination with a strong orientation towards their own ethnic group in the country of origin, will lead to poor socio-economic integration. The second assumption is that strong transnational identifications do not necessarily imply weak identification with Dutch society. Furthermore, such a transnational identification does not have to lead to poor integration in Dutch society.

The results of the present study amend both assumptions. Respondents who are closely involved in transnational activities do not run a greater risk of becoming unemployed. However, there does exist a negative relationship between identification with the country of origin and economic integration. This might imply that strong transnational identifications with the country of origin promote unemployment. It seems more likely, however, that not having a formal paid job reinforces this transnational identification with the country of origin. We also found that having a paid job correlates with weaker transnational identifications in so far as these relate to the country of origin.

As far as the position of respondents with an Islamic background is concerned (especially the relatively young Moroccan respondents), there are no large differences between this group and the other migrant groups. Many Moroccans typify themselves as 'Moroccan Dutchmen/ women' and show a relatively strong orientation towards their own ethnic group in Dutch society. A more detailed and qualitative analysis of the Moroccan group confirms some of the results put forward by Phalet, Van Lotringen and Entzinger in their report, *Islam in the Multicultural Society* (2001) (Engbersen et al., 2003). The second generation's attachment to their Muslim identity is undiminished, but their involvement with their country of origin diminishes the longer they stay in the Netherlands. Secondly, Moroccan youth draw a clear dividing line between cultural identifications and values in the private sphere (the family) and those in the public sphere. Thirdly, our analysis revealed that any fear for militant Muslim fundamentalism is without foundation. The Moroccan respondents showed, as we have seen, the least political involvement with the country of origin. Furthermore, we have not found any indication of new forms of political organization and mobilization of young Morrocans.

## REFERENCES

Al-Ali, Nadje, Black, Richard and Koser, Khalid, *Refugees and transnationalism: the experience of Bosnians and Eritreans in Europe*, Journal of Ethnic and Migration Studies, Vol. 27, No. 4, 2001: 615-634.

Bash, L., Glick Schiller, N. and Blanc-Szanton C., *Nations Unbound: Transnational Projects, Post-Colonial Predicaments and De-Territorialized Nation States*, Gordon and Breach, Amsterdam. 1999.

Castles, S. & Miller, M., *The Age of Migration: International Population Movements in the Modern world,* The Macmillan Press, Hampshire, 1994.

Engbersen, G. and van der Leun, J.P., 'The Social Construction of Illegality and Criminality' in *European Journal on Criminal Policy and Research,* jrg. 9, nr. 1, 2001: 51-70.

Engbersen, G., Snel, E., de Boom J. en Heyl, E., *Migration, Immigrants and Policy in the Netherlands. Report for the continuous Reporting System on Migration (SOPEMI) of the Organization of Economic Co-operation and Development (OECD),* Risbo, Rotterdam, 2002: 93.

Engbersen, G., Leerkes, A., Snel E. and van San, M., *Transnationale activiteiten en identiteiten,* Risbo/EUR, Rotterdam, 2003.

Faist, T., *The volume and dynamics of international migration and transnational spaces,* Oxford University Press, Oxford, 2000a.

Faist, T., 'Transnationalization in international migration: implications for the study of citizenship and culture', in: *Ethnic and Racial Studies, 23,* 2000b: 189-222.

Itzigsohn, J. and Saucedo, S., 'Immigrant Incorporation and Sociocultural Transnationalism', *The International Migration Review,* Vol. 36 (3), 2002: 766-798.

Koser, K. and Lutz, H. (eds.), *The new migration in Europe: Social constructions and social realities.* Macmillan Press, Houndmills, 1998: 185-198.

Portes, A., Guarnizo, L. and Landholt, P., 'The study of transnationalism: pitfalls and promise of an emergent research field', *Ethnic and Racial Studies,* Vol. 22 (3), 1999: 217- 237.

Portes, A., Haller, W. and Guarnizo, L., 'Transnational entrepreneurs: an alternative form of immigrant economic adaptation', *American Sociological Review,* Vol. 67, (4), 2002: 278-298.

Phalet, Karen, van Lotringen, Claudia and Entzinger, Han *Islam in de multiculturele samenleving: opvattingen van jongeren in Rotterdam,* Ercomer, Utrecht, 2001.

Snel. E. en Engbersen G., Op weg naar transnationaal burgerschap. De schuivende panelen van internationale migratie. In: F. Becker, W. van Hennekeler, M. Sie Dhian Ho en B. Tromp (red.), *Transnationaal Nederland. Het drieentwintigste jaarboek voor het democratisch socialisme,* Wiardi Beckman Stichting, Amsterdam, 2002: 23-48.

Thomas, William I. and Znaniecke, Florian, The Polish peasant in Europe and America, Dover Publications, New York, 1958.

Van den Tilaart, H. *Monitor Etnisch Ondernemerschap 2000. Zelstandig ondernemerschap van etnische minderheden in Nederland in de periode 1990-2000,* Instituut voor Sociale Wetenschappen, Nijmegen, 2001.

Verkuyten, M. *Etnische identiteit. Theoretische en empirische benaderingen,* Het Spinhuis, Amsterdam, 1999.

Vertovec, S. 'Conceiving and researching transnationalism', *Ethnic and Racial Studies,* 2 (2), 1999: 447-462.

Vertovec, S. Transnational challenges to the 'New Multiculturalism'. Working paper on Transnational Communities, Programme WPTC-01-06, 2001. www.transcomm. ox.uk/wwwroot/drsteve.htm

# SECTION 3

## Representation and Identities:
## Muslim Youth

This section deals with two interrelated themes, how Muslim youth are perceived by wider society and how the youth view themselves and construct their identity. Alexander's chapter skilfully lays bare the way in which the Muslim community, and young men in particular, are demonized by the media and the authorities as terrorists, rioters and militant clerics. This process has developed new momentum post-9/11 resulting in a moral panic which portrays young men of Muslim origin as the new 'folk devils'; a portrayal that resonates across most Western European countries.

In the aftermath of riots in the north of England, the UK Home Office argued that violence was underpinned by a 'self-perpetuating' cultural difference, resulting in self-segregation. The resulting 'community cohesion' strategy implemented by the authorities is viewed by many of its recipients as a 'one-way' process of assimilation. Cultural practices, especially among Muslims, are considered a negative factor, to be altered if necessary by legislation, thus ignoring the activities of the far right parties who reinforce social exclusion and encourage hatred.

The next two chapters examine the process of identity construction among youth in the diaspora. What attracts media attention is the emergence of Islamic symbols among the younger generation, which are viewed as evidence of increased religiosity and a potential breeding ground for religious militancy. This perspective is vigorously demolished in these chapters as one that ignores the internal reformulation and hybridization of identity among Muslim youth. Generational changes are resulting in the displacement of identification with country of origin as a primary factor with that of a 'Muslim' identity. Religion becomes the new ethnic identity of the young, with important gender variables, representing a shift from oral cultural-embedded Islam to a textual Islam espoused and articulated in a European language. Simultaneously, this hybridization process is being influenced by popular culture resulting in hybrid literary, musical and other cultural expressions. In Europe, the working class nature of the population results in greater integration with street culture and a cursory knowledge of Islam.

# 7

# Violence, Gender and Identity: Re-imagining 'the Asian Gang'

*Claire Alexander*

In the aftermath of the 'riots' that scarred the north and midlands of England in the spring and summer of 2001, and the events of 9/11, the profile of Muslim youth in Britain has scarcely been more significant, or more misinterpreted. These events have served to re-inscribe the position of Muslim youth as the foremost threat to British nationhood, fusing notions of religious, racial, gendered and generational dysfunction and marginalization. Bringing together the assumption of crime and conflict that underpins the racialized stereotype of 'the Asian gang' with the emergent spectre of religious 'fundamentalism' and the threat of terrorism, Muslim young men are now inseparable from the image of violence.

This chapter explores the formation of notions of 'violence' amongst Muslim young men, through the imagination of 'the Asian gang'. By exploring the intersection of current theoretical and policy approaches to ethnicity, masculinity and youth, the chapter critiques dominant problem-oriented accounts and offers an alternative approach to understanding Muslim youth identities.

## INTRODUCTION

On 1 May 2003, Asif Muhammed Hanif, a 21-year-old from Hounslow, killed himself and three other people in a suicide bomb attack in Tel Aviv. Along with a fellow 'British Muslim' (*The Guardian*, 9 May 2003), Omar Khan Sharif, aged 27 and from Derby, Hanif's actions have been met in Britain with a mixture of blank incomprehension and of almost gleeful fatalism in about equal measure. Descriptions of Sharif as 'a really nice kind boy' (*The Guardian*, 4 May 2003) and of Hanif's attraction to Sufism, of moderate, intelligent and 'Westernized' young men, vie with the 'told-you-so' pronouncements of the prophets of doom—who form an inclusive, somewhat eclectic mix of self-styled radical Muslim journalists, mainstream and right-of-centre pundits—on the fundamentalist/terrorist bandwagon. Without a doubt, the cheerleaders of the Islamic-apocalypse version of events will win the day—if only because an appeal to one young man's love of Eastern mysticism is unlikely to overturn the accumulating mountain of events and tales of terror in the 'It's a Muslim thing, you wouldn't understand' corner.

The linkages are seamless and almost incontrovertible. The actions of Hanif and Sharif are founded in the cultural incompatibilities of Britain's Muslim communities, evidenced in the explosion of the 'riots' of 2001, and fomented in the extremist Islamic schoolrooms of the preachers of racial hatred, such as Abdullah El-Faisal, jailed for nine years in March 2003.[1] It is this commonsense logic that brings together the actions of extremist individuals with the Muslim majority, and places the blame for the former squarely on the culturally dysfunctional shoulders of the latter. As Philip Johnston states in a recent 'Opinion' article in *The Daily Telegraph*, 2 May 2003, 'Home-grown fundamentalists pose a threat to Britain too', 'The fundamentalists need to be confronted directly in **their communities** by those who represent a law-abiding majority **largely cut off from the predominant culture**' (my emphasis). While I think the use of the term 'home-grown' is unintentionally double-edged (since it could refer equally to the structures and cultures of racism and discrimination in Britain that underpinned the 'riots' as to the 'Muslim-community-as-hotbeds-of-religious-fanaticism' imagery obviously intended) the message is unambiguous: the problem simply is 'the Muslim community'. The labelling of Hanif and Sharif as 'British Muslims' is thus more than a convenient description—it is a signpost to an established way of thinking, explaining and attributing responsibility. More than this, it is a trigger for a cascade of images that fuse violence, death, danger, anger and difference and which, in the wake of post-9/11 paranoia, increasingly define and engulf 'the Muslim presence' in Britain.

The conceptual mapping of 'the Muslim menace', which links suicide bombers with extremist Muslim clerics and the recent 'riots', articulates a very specific imagination of 'the Muslim community' in Britain—one which is marked by both gendered and generational difference. The focus of concern is, then, on young men, who are seen at once as vulnerable to the preaching of Islamist hardliners and as the embodiment of physical strength and threat. The 'riots' of 2001 were represented and understood as the result of a triple alienation—culture, masculinity and youth—and the harsh levels of social control enacted in their wake can be seen to reflect an extreme reaction to the personification of a national nightmare.[2] This demonization of Muslim young men fuses ideas of racial, religious and cultural difference with the spectre of social marginalization and urban deprivation—an evocation of violence that coalesces in the form of 'the Asian gang'.

As I have argued previously (2000, a, b), 'the Asian gang' represents the formation of a new British folk devil, reworking established notions of racial, cultural, gendered and generational dysfunction and threat. While public concerns around Muslim communities have been growing since the *Satanic Verses* affair in 1989 and Islamophobic sentiments were a growing feature of the 1990s, it is in the wake of post-9/11 paranoia that this particular folk devil has taken on a specifically religious costume. Fears around young black men, crime and violence are now inescapably fears around Muslim young men, crime and violence, with Islam adding a convenient additional explanatory pathology to the mix. Post-2001, photos of burnt-out BMWs and swaggering, masked young men with petrol bombs merge with half-remembered images of angry bearded crowds and book burnings to mark this new enemy within. The current study aims to explore this fundamentalist remix of 'the Asian gang', through its appearance in policy and political rhetoric after the 2001 'riots', and the academic assumptions that underpin its formation. The study also argues for a more nuanced and locally based analysis of Muslim youth identities and violence.

## ALIEN-NATION: CULTURING 'THE RIOTS'

On 7 March 2003, 'Britain's sheikh of race hate',[3] Abdullah El-Faisal, was jailed for nine years on convictions for soliciting murder and inciting racial hatred (*The Guardian*, 8 March 2003). The first Muslim cleric to be prosecuted in the UK for his preaching, and the first person to be charged with 'soliciting murder' in 100 years, El Faisal's sentence was described by Judge Beaumont as indicating 'society's abhorrence' of his teaching. He further stated, 'You had a responsibility to the young and impressionable of [the Muslim] community at times of conflict abroad and understandable tensions here. Instead of calming fears, you fanned the flames of hostility' (*The Guardian*, 7 March 2003). Beaumont's appeal to 'the Muslim community' in his statement makes an explicit link between El Faisal's preaching and a wider 'imagined community', and connects both to the ongoing 'war on terrorism' abroad and the threat of unrest at home. El Faisal is positioned as at once a foreign element exploiting Britain's 'tradition of free speech' to endanger others (a foreignness underscored by the deportation of El Faisal to Jamaica on serving his sentence), and as a potential agitator within the restless ranks of 'young and impressionable' Muslim men unsure of their relationship to the British nation.

It is significant that responses to El-Faisal's case drew parallels with the 'scorched earth'[4] sentences on the Bradford 'rioters', upheld only two months earlier (*The Guardian*, 31 January 2003). El-Faisal's defence counsel, Jerome Lynch QC, thus stated 'many Muslims will regard this as harsh... And will see it as **yet another attempt** to undermine the Muslim community' (*The Guardian*, 8 March 2003, my emphasis), while Trevor Hemmings of Statewatch was similarly quoted, 'The message that this sends out is that if you are black or Asian and say something out of order you get jailed for nine years and deported, but if you are on the right you can go out tooled up with knuckledusters and get half of that.'[5]

Since the summer of 2002, 282 individuals have been arrested in connection with the events in Bradford in 2001, with 134 people—overwhelmingly Asian young men—receiving sentences between 18 months and five years on a charge of 'rioting' (McGhee, forthcoming).[6] In August 2002, Amjid (sic) Rashid was given eight years for his involvement in the violence, while other young men were sentenced to between four and six and a half years for throwing stones at the police (*The Guardian*, 31 January 2003). In defending the sentences, Judge Stephen Gullick described the incidents as acts of 'wanton, vicious and prolonged violence' (*The Guardian*, 6 September 2002).

These two disparate events are linked not only in signalling a message, beyond the scope of the acts themselves, to the wider 'Muslim community' though the use of 'exemplary sentencing' (Hall et al., 1978), but in the positioning of Islam as a primary definitional framework for both cases. The 'rioters' become the embodiment of the 'young and impressionable' victims of El-Faisal's teachings, and the prosecution of war abroad becomes elided with the memory of civil unrest at home. The religious rantings of El-Faisal also function as a lens through which to retrospectively re-read the 'riots' as about religious antipathy, adding an additional global terror-gloss to the already culture-laden version in circulation: 'parallel lives' become transformed into segregated recruiting grounds for violence (*The Daily Telegraph*, 2 May 2003).

The 'riots' themselves have been largely understood in the media, and in the Home Office reports generated in their wake, as the outcome of cultural difference and processes of self-segregation, and have been wielded as a primary weapon in the government's resurgent assimilationist statements and policies—around language, marriage practices, citizenship education/tests and immigration. The Home Office reports on the 'riots' thus privilege a self-imposed and self-perpetuating 'cultural difference' as the key feature underpinning the violence, and in maintaining long-term conditions of social marginalization for both Asian and white communities—what has been captured in the notion of 'Parallel Lives' (Cantle, 2001). The Denham Report (2001), which maps out the government's blueprint on 'Building Cohesive Communities', thus points to, 'The fragmentation and polarization of communities—on economic, geographical, racial and cultural lines—on a scale which amounts to segregation, **albeit to an extent by choice**' (page 11, my emphasis). The report also cites Herman Ouseley's earlier observation that 'different ethnic groups (in Bradford) are increasingly **segregating themselves** from each other and retreating into 'comfort zones' **made up** of people like themselves' (ibid: 12, my emphasis).

Leaving aside here the disturbing echoes of New/Far Right discourses of naturalized notions of pseudo-familial/ethnic cultural preferences (CCCS, 1981, Back, 2002, a, b), the 'community cohesion' strategy takes as its central tenet the need to foster communication across these seemingly implacable cultural barriers. In his introduction, Lord Denham writes, 'We recognize that in many areas affected by disorder or community tensions there is little interchange between members of racial, cultural and religious communities and that proactive measures will have to be taken to promote dialogue and understanding. We also take on board the need to generate a widespread and open debate about identity, shared values and common citizenship as part of the process of building cohesive communities'.

In practice, however, the movement integral to the 'community cohesion' plan is strictly one-way—from 'immigrant'/foreign culture to 'host' centre, via a one-sided process of assimilation (and cultural eradication). Lest this be in doubt, it is worth linking the symbol of cultural 'dialogue' with the centrality of (English) language proficiency, or lack of it, in the reports as a key cause of social marginalization, or indeed to David Blunkett's widely reported views on 'mother tongue' usage.[7] In the aftermath of the riots, Blunkett's demands are, then, that ethnic minorities adopt British values and 'norms of acceptability' (*The Guardian*, 11 December 2001), which appears now in the guise of 'citizenship', and which explicitly questions the relationship between cultural plurality and nationhood. Blunkett, somewhat deceptively, asserts, 'There is no contradiction between retaining a distinct cultural identity and identifying with Britain. But our democracy must uphold fundamental rights and obligations to which all citizens and public authorities adhere. Citizenship means finding a common place for diverse cultures and beliefs, consistent with the core values we uphold' (2001, quoted in McGhee, forthcoming).

As Arun Kundnani (2002) has argued, the notion of 'community cohesion' and the privileging of discourses of citizenship signals 'the Death of Multiculturalism', in which cultural pluralism is forced to give way to the conformity of imagined core principles to which we all, as British citizens, adhere. The potential conflict between balancing a 'distinct cultural identity' and 'core values' is elided in Home Office rhetoric, though, ironically, a way forward is suggested by Bhikhu Parekh (1997) in the shape of the 'moral covenant'. Parekh states thus of ethnic minority (implicitly Muslim) cultures, 'Some of their values and practices might be unacceptable, and then they need to be changed by consensus when possible and **by law if necessary**' (1997: x, my emphasis).[8] It could be argued that the slew of Home Office interventions around 'backward' cultural practices, or indeed the prosecutions of the Bradford 'rioters' and Abdullah El Faisal, are the active implementation of Parekh's 'moral covenant', only bypassing consensus straight to legislation—the (sometimes literal) policy equivalent of a 'Go to jail' card.

If the actions of the Home Secretary represent the sharp, populist end of the move from 'celebrating difference' to 'managing diversity', it is also true that even the more apparently difference-friendly versions of 'community cohesion' carry with them at once the demand for cultural assimilation, and its impossibility. By establishing the 'riots' as generated from cultural difference rather than structural or socio-economic marginalization (or by subsuming the latter as the inevitable result of the former), the reports draw on a version of 'culture' which naturalizes and reifies ethnic boundaries as impermeable and unassailable. Not only does it render invisible additional factors, such as racism, Far Right activity,[9] police hostility and social exclusion, the effect is to reify cultural identity above any alternative identifications—gender, class, age, location—that cut within and across 'community' boundaries (Amin, 2002). 'Culture' thus becomes the prescribed catch-all explanation for all social ills, facilitating a convenient blame-the-victim approach and letting everyone else off the hook (or at least with reduced sentences). The violence of 'the riots' is then understood as the natural and inevitable result of antipathetic and irreconcilable cultural forces—Huntington's (1996) 'clash of civilizations' thesis writ small.

The conception of 'culture' that underpins the 'parallel lives' paradigm, and its remedial counterpart, 'community cohesion' reinscribes a version of cultural identity that has precedence not only in policy terms[10] but also in academic approaches to Asian communities in Britain. As I have argued elsewhere (2003), Asian communities have been consistently defined through recourse to an over-determined anthropological version of 'culture' whereby ethnicity—founded on conceptions of common origin, language, religion, descent and kinship, marriage patterns and shared values—is placed as the privileged site of identity formation. The Parekh report, for example, writes of Asian communities, 'Maintaining cultural and religious traditions is critical to their sense of identity... Traditions of origins are strongest in familial, personal and religious contexts, where there is a strong sense of extended kinship' (2000: 30).

It is important to note the conflation of personal, familial and cultural connections in this description, with the symbol of kinship marking out ethnic identity as a product of birth and blood, or what Tariq Modood has termed 'a mode of being' (1992). Also important is the way in which religion is now privileged as an integral, 'critical' part of this blood heritage, superseding allegiances of nation or neighbourhood, and which, of course, is the crux of the problem for those seeking the imagined security of absolute citizenship and nationhood. The emphasis on religion points to the central position of Islam in redefining the racial landscape, reinforcing the identification of Britain's Muslim communities with the unassimilable and antagonistic cultures at the heart of post-millennial paranoia.

This version of culture poses a logical impasse for the champions of 'community cohesion': if culture is part of one's 'mode of being', it becomes impossible to yield to the demands of an assimilative citizenship—to 'become' British. This cultural 'Catch 22' has strong resonances with the earlier pronouncements of Enoch Powell,[11] and effectively places Britain's Asian/Muslim communities outside of the possibilities of citizenship—an alien nation. And as the case of the Bradford 'rioters' makes clear, while becoming a citizen is not a possibility, the penalties for *not* becoming a citizen are swift and harsh.

## IMAGINING DYSTOPIC COMMUNITIES: CULTURE, MASCULINITY AND 'THE ASIAN GANG'

Mapping the terrain of the current discourses around culture and citizenship is crucial for understanding the construction of 'the Asian gang', because it is against the backdrop of cultural difference and pathology, and the threat that this carries with it, that the formations of gendered and generational identities take shape. Indeed, it is possible to argue that the idea of 'the Asian gang' crystallises a number of concerns about the limits of 'community'; in many ways, then, 'the gang' constitutes a dystopic imagination of Parekh's utopian vision of Britain as a 'community of communities' (2000). Thus, 'gangs' are seen to be bounded and highly localized, internally homogeneous and externally antagonistic entities, with clear group membership, shared traditions and values. In addition, the equation of 'gang' culture with criminality and violence only serves to render explicit the implicit assumptions of the 'culture of poverty' arguments that constitute 'the Muslim underclass'.

It is hardly surprising, then, that the highly gendered and generational boundaries of 'the gang' have come to stand for the wider ills of 'the Muslim community' before, during and after 'the riots'. The demonization of Muslim young men through the ongoing moral panics about 'Asian gangs' that dominated the 1990s ran alongside the pathologization of 'the Muslim underclass' and formed its most powerful symbol. Modood, for example, writes of 'a possible trend of criminalization among young Pakistanis and Bangladeshis' (1997: 147) as a facet of the 'ethnic penalties' experienced by Muslim communities—an integral part of the processes of social exclusion, cultural dysfunction and political marginality. Fears of an 'Asian crime time bomb' (Webster, 1997) linked to the younger age profile of Muslim communities have grown in recent years, and were a core feature of the reports on the 'riots' themselves. The Cantle Report thus stated, 'One activity which sadly seems to be present with all the communities we visited was drug dealing. There was even some suggestion that in Burnley some of the rioting... was in fact the result of a 'turf war' between drug gangs' (2001: 16). Similarly, the Burnley Task Force Summary Report described the events as 'disturbances [which] were caused originally by criminal acts involving both Asian and white criminal gangs, which were followed by deliberate attempts to turn the violent acts into racial confrontation' (cited in Farrar, 2002).

There is an unstated but obvious gendered dimension to these accounts, marked through the gender-specific mantra of drugs, crime and violence. This reflects a broader regendering of concerns around 'the Asian community' in recent years where the focus has shifted from the private plight of young women to the public dangers of young men (Alexander, 2000 a, b; Keith, 1995). This was clearly signalled in the move from 'victim' to 'aggressor' status in recent years (Goodey, 1999), which was particularly apparent in the run up to the Oldham events.[12] Fairly obviously, the 'riots' themselves were highly gendered clashes between Asian men and white men, or Asian men and the police; the Denham Report thus noted, 'the participants were overwhelmingly young men' (2001: 8).[13]

The 'riots' were read, at least partially, as the performance of a pathological masculinity, signalled through violence. This violence is anchored, crucially, not only in the living out of a racialized 'subordinated masculinity' (Connell, 1995) but also in the living through of a patriarchal cultural dysfunction. Asian masculinities are, then, constructed as doubly 'failing', firstly, because of a process of racialization which renders them incapable of succeeding in wider modern society (cf. hooks, 1992), and secondly, because of the inadequacies of their pre-modern, always already failing culture. The growth of concerns around religious 'fundamentalism' is, then, simultaneously a concern about a reconstituted hyper-masculinity, which sees the transformation of orientalist notions about feminised tyrants to a fear of 'martial men' (Said, 1978).

The conflation of religious militancy and cultural misogyny comes together with an all too secular version of the ghetto masculinity of 'the gang' to provide a convenient framework for the actions of Muslim young men. In her account of the 1995 Bradford 'riots' and crime (the link itself is suggestive), for example, Marie Macey (2002) argues that a culturally inflected Islamic identity is used to legitimize criminal behaviour (Macey even refers to 'Muslim crime' as a distinct category), most particularly in incidents of violence against women. Macey links routinized acts of aggression by Pakistani young men with organized criminal 'gangs' and a growing drug culture, and roots them in a 'religious and cultural tradition which militates against the progress of the Muslim community' (2002: 41). In an earlier study (1999), Macey also asserts, 'it is undoubtedly the case that in Bradford, young men have mobilized a particular Islamic code as a power resource against both women and the white establishment. **Public and private sector violence is implicated in each case.** In addition, a number of young men have been susceptible to the **influence of extremist variants of Islam which actively encourage violence**' (1999: 857, my emphasis).

The position of Asian youth in theory and policy practice has remained an ambiguous, if not contradictory, one. Where masculinity is seen to reinscribe and police the boundaries of community, generation is seen to at once lay bare the inadequacies of Asian cultures in British society and to represent the hopes for future integration. The Denham report thus points to intergenerational tension as a key factor in the violence, linking this to the emergence of militant religious and ethnic identities amongst young people, 'Disengagement of young people from the local decision making process, intergenerational tensions, and an increasingly territorial mentality in asserting different racial, cultural and religious identities in response to real or perceived attacks' (2001: 11).[14] However, the report also insists on the central role of young people in promoting community cohesion—they represent at once problem and solution.

This contradictory stance is compounded by its intersection with ethnicity. While youth in general can be argued to constitute a 'problem category' (particularly in its implicitly gendered and classed focus on working class young men), black youth have been traditionally understood in the academy as the product of social marginalization and alienation. Asian youth particularly have been represented as trapped 'Between Two Cultures' (Alexander, forthcoming), and this legacy is clearly traceable in the accounts of the 'riots' that see the breakdown of traditional authority and conflict with 'community elders' as a key feature of the violence (Denham, 2001)[15]. More generally, 'the gang' is usually placed within the narration of perceived cultural breakdown, where the peer group is embraced as a compensatory 'family', through which fictions of strength and success can be created; what Mac An Ghaill describes as 'the building of a defensive culture of masculine survival against social marginalization' (1994: 187). Asian youth are seen as simultaneously produced by backward, alien cultures

(Macey, 1999) and as outside these communities, adrift from any cultural mooring and out of control. The question arises then whether the problem for Asian youth lies in the possession of a backward culture, or in the absence of this culture—an issue that the culturalist bias of the post-riot reports leaves unresolved. Thus, the insistence on 'parallel lives' sits uneasily with the evocation of a trans-ethnic drug culture and associated violence, while the punitive measures exacted on the 'rioters' are clearly at odds with the inclusive 'why-can't-we-all-get-along' sentiments underpinning community cohesion (McGhee, forthcoming).

The search for simple categorizations and labels, which facilitate the triple demonization of Muslim youth, belies the more complex, often fraught, spaces of youth marginalization, interaction and acculturation. As Ash Amin has argued, 'There is a complexity to the cultural identity of the Asian youths that cannot be reduced to the stereotype of traditional Muslim, Hindu, Sikh lives, to the bad masculinities of gang life... to the all too frequently repeated idea of their entrapment between two cultures... Their frustration and public anger cannot be detached from their identities as a new generation of British Asians claiming in full the right to belong to Oldham or Burnley and the nation, but whose Britishness includes Islam, halal meat, family honour and cultural resources located in diaspora networks' (2002: 10).

Amin argues that the focus of 'community' building and citizenship needs to be shifted from the notion of shared values and civic responsibility towards issues of equality and discrimination. The 'riots' then move from being pathological acts of wanton and irrational violence to constituting 'disputed rights claims'. Although the Home Office reports acknowledge the role of Far Right groups, the failures of the police in tackling racial crime and violence and racialized inequalities in housing and employment as underlying causes of the 'riots', it is nevertheless the case that issues of racism and socio-economic marginalization have taken a back seat to questions of culture and identity.[16] This reflects a broader trend in studies of race and ethnicity in Britain in the past two decades, which have privileged ethnicity and difference over the social, historical and material conditions of their production (Alexander 2002). In particular, the focus on Islam, Islamophobia and 'the Muslim community' has served to separate out these phenomena from a wider racialized landscape and history of black and Asian struggle (Kundnani, 2001). It thus runs the risk of reinscribing essentialist and reductive culturalist analyses and hierarchies, which may facilitate social control but serve only to obscure understanding.

## REFLECTIONS: CULTURES OF VIOLENCE AND THE MYTH OF 'THE ASIAN GANG'

Amin's attempt to shift the discussion around Muslim youth from culture to 'rights' exemplifies one of the many silences that the current obsession with cultural difference and identity has generated. What the 'riots' clearly exemplify are both the ongoing processes of racial and social marginalization, and disadvantage experienced, however differentially, by ethnic minority communities in Britain, and the way in which culturalist discourses have served to obscure and exonerate these processes. The conflation of ethnicity with religion has led to the re-sanctification of cultural identity, so that it is increasingly difficult to imagine or define Muslim youth identities in any other terms. Religio-cultural categorizations become predefined and self-fulfilling, subsuming more secular, political, everyday or even (in the case of Hanif and Sharif) tragically bizarre events into the realm of the sacred, the pure and the defiantly unhybrid. Such identities become, then, outside of history, context, rationality, power—and even, it seems, outside of theory.

It becomes crucial, then, to place British Muslim youth identities back into context, and to challenge the common/nonsense pathologies that serve up stereotype and assumption as insight and understanding. This means recognizing that the resurgence of Islam, and Islamophobia, as the basis for identity construction in Europe has to be placed within the broader context of race and racialisation, and as part of specific historical and political (Halliday, 1999), national and even highly localised settings and processes (Samad, 1992). It also demands that even apparently essentialized identities have to be seen as part of the play of power, history and materiality—to replace structure as an integral part of cultural formation (Hall, 1992). Understanding the violence of 'the riots' involves a recognition of these structures and of the complex and multiple personalities and positionalities involved; it is clearly insufficient to dismiss these events as part and parcel of a cultural difference distilled through the filters of masculinist and generational conflict.

This is not to seek to simply replace the bad violence-as-culture version with a good violence-as-political-protest version of Muslim youth identities. Such over-simplifications, along with the desire to wholly reject or wholly celebrate the violence and its perpetrators, serve only to substitute polemic for understanding. It is perhaps worth observing that amidst the clamour of expert opinions, policy makers and ethnic/political opportunists seeking to voice their interpretations of the 2001 'riots', it is the young men themselves who remain silent[17] and invisible.

My own work on 'the Asian gang' (2000) suggests that even seemingly simple acts of violence are underpinned by a complex web of motivations, rationales and alliances. To retreat to essentialized notions of 'race', religion, ethnicity or masculinity to explain such events is to naturalize conflict and to abdicate responsibility in favour of socio-biological or genetic inevitabilities. It is imperative that we start to take ethnicized/racialized violence seriously as a social phenomenon that has roots and rationales that can be unearthed, and contours that can be mapped and engaged constructively. This means exploring first the discourses which frame and determine the interpretation of conflict, and second the complex matrices of personal, local, historical, gendered and generational factors that are played out in such encounters. This second element requires more than the view-from-a-safe-distance accounts which mark the dominant trend in racial and ethnic studies in Britain, and the willingness to get 'down and dirty' in the field, with all the ethical ambiguities and empirical messiness that this necessitates.

In the face of the re-emergence of global 'big picture' grand narratives that recent events have underscored, I want to make space for the local and the lived as significant points of reference and contestation. Otherwise we run the risk of mistaking myths for sociological reality, and accepting politically convenient and reactionary rhetoric as empirical fact. I want finally to suggest, then, that staking a claim for 'the little picture' demands a reconfiguration of the 'big picture' and a re-imagination of the limits of the current debates around Muslim youth identities.

# REFERENCES

Alexander, C., *The Asian Gang: ethnicity, identity, masculinity*, Berg, Oxford, 2000a.

Alexander, C., '[Dis]Entangling the Asian Gang' in Hesse B. (ed.), *Un/Settled Multiculturalisms*, Zed Press, London, 2000b.

Alexander, C., 'Beyond Black: rethinking the colour/culture divide', *Ethnic and Racial Studies*, Vol. 25, No. 4, 2003: 552-571.

Alexander, C., 'The Next Generation', in Ali, N., Kalra, V. & Sayyid, S. (eds.) *Asian Nation*, Christopher Hurst, London, forthcoming.

Amin, A., 'Ethnicity and the Multicultural City', Report for the Department of Transport, Local Government and the Regions, 2002.

Back, L., 'Aryans Reading Adorno: cyber-culture and 21st century racism', *Ethnic and Racial Studies*, Vol. 25, No. 4, 2002a: 628-651.

Back, L., 'Guess Who's Coming to Dinner? The political morality of investigating whiteness in the grey zone', in Ware, V. & Back, L., *Out of Whiteness*, University of Chicago, Chicago, 2002b.

Cantle, Ted, *Community Cohesion*, HMSO, London, 2001.

CCCS Collective, *The Empire Strikes Back*, Hutchinson, London, 1981.

Connell, R.W., *Masculinities*, Polity, London, 1995.

Denham, Lord, *Building Cohesive Communities*, HMSO, London, 2001.

Farrar, M., 'The Northern 'Race riots' of the summer of 2001 – were they riots, were they racial?', presentation to *Parallel Lives and Polarisation* workshop, BSA 'Race' Forum, City University, 2002.

Goodey, J., Victims of Racism and Racial Violence: experiences among boys and young men', *International Review of Victimology*, Vol. 5, No. 3, 1999.

Hall, S. et al., *Policing the Crisis*, Hutchinson, London, 1978.

Hall, S., 'New Ethnicities' in Donald, J. & Rattanis, A. (eds.), *'Race', Culture and Difference*, Sage, London, 1992.

Halliday, F., 'Islamophobia Reconsidered', *Ethnic and Racial Studies*, Vol. 22, No. 5, 1999: 892-902.

hooks, b., *Black Looks: Race and Representation*, Turnaround, London, 1992.

Huntington, S., *The Clash of Civilizations and the Remaking of the World Order*, Simon & Schuster, New York, 1996.

Keith, M., 'Making the Street Visible: placing racial violence in context', *New Community*, Vol. 21, No. 4, 1995: 551-565.

Kundnani, A., 'From Oldham to Bradford: the violence of the violated', *Race and Class*, Vol. 43, No. 2, 2001: 105-110.

Kundnani, A., 'The Death of Multiculturalism', Institute of Race Relations, (Online Resources), 2002.

Mac An Ghaill, M., 'The Making of Black English Masculinities' in Brod H. & Kaufmann, M. (eds.), *Theorising Masculinity*, Sage, London, 1994.

Macey, M., 'Gender, Class and Religious influences on changing patterns of Pakistani Muslim male violence in Bradford', *Ethnic and Racial Studies*, Vol. 22, No. 5, 1999: 845-866.

Macey, M., 'Interpreting Islam: young Muslim men's involvement in criminal activity in Bradford' in Spalek, B. (ed.), *Islam, Crime and Criminal Justice*, Willan Publishing, Cullompton, 2002.

McGhee, D., 'Moving to 'our' common ground – a critical examination of community cohesion discourse in 21st century Britain', *Sociological Review*, forthcoming.

Modood, T., *Not Easy Being British*, Trentham, Stoke on Trent, 1992.

Modood, T. et al, *Ethnic Minorities in Britain: Diversity and Disadvantage*, Policy Studies Institute, London, 1997.

Parekh, B., 'Foreword' in Modood, T. et al., *Ethnic Minorities in Britain: Diversity and Disadvantage*, Policy Studies Institute, London, 1997.

Parekh, B., *The Future of Multi-Ethnic Britain* (The Parekh Report), Profile Books, London, 2000.

Said, E., *Orientalism*, Routledge Kegan & Paul, London, 1978.

Samad, Y., 'Book Burning and Race Relations: the political mobilisation of Bradford Muslims', *New Community*, Vol. 18, No. 4, 1992: 507-519.

Webster, C., 'The construction of British 'Asian' criminality', *International Journal of the Sociology of Law*, Vol. 25, 1997: 65-86.

**Newspaper Articles**

11.12.2001, 'Race riots reports urge immigrant 'loyalty'', staff and agencies, *The Guardian*.

31.08.2002, '8 years for petrol bomber', Martin Wainwright, *The Guardian*.

06.09.2002, 'Anger at Blunkett's 'whining maniacs' attack', Alan Travis, *The Guardian*.

31.01.2003, 'Anger as court's stance on riot upheld', Vikram Dodd, *The Guardian*.

25.02.2003, 'Salvation Army boy who converted to campaign of hate', Tania Branigan, *The Guardian*.

07.03.2003, 'Cleric jailed for racial hatred offences', staff and agencies, *The Guardian*.

08.03.2003, 'Race hate cleric jailed for nine years', Tania Brannigan, *The Guardian*.

02.05.2003, 'Home-grown fundamentalists pose a threat to Britain too', Philip Johnston, *The Daily Telegraph*.

04.05.2003, 'Making of a martyr' Martin Bright & Fareena Alam, *The Guardian*.

09.05.03, 'Bomb suspect's relatives remanded in custody', agencies, *The Guardian*.

## NOTES

1. An article in *The Daily Telegraph* (2.5.03) makes precisely this conceptual journey, linking the suicide bombers to Muslim schools, the 'riots' and the Cantle Report, al-Qaeda and Richard Reid, El-Faisal and Abu Hamza, before laying the blame squarely at the feet of the Muslim community en masse.

2. There are interesting parallels to be drawn, for example, with the moral panics around black young men and 'mugging' through the 1970s and early 1980s (cf. Hall et al., *Policing the Crisis*, 1978).

3. El Faisal was labelled 'Britain's sheikh of race hate' by *The Times* in February 2002 (*The Guardian*, 25.2.03).

4. Derek McGhee (forthcoming) uses this phrase, taken from a letter from Nick Carter, one of the defence lawyers in the Bradford cases, to *the Guardian* (9.9.02).

5. Hemmings had been previously quoted as saying the case was 'part of the Islamophobia spreading across the country' (*The Guardian*, 25.2.03). The reference

to Far Right activities draws on the inequality of sentences handed out to white and Asian offenders in relation to the Bradford and other 'riots' of 2001.

6.  McGhee notes that the charge of 'riot' carries a heavier maximum sentence of ten years than the lesser charge of 'violent disorder' that was used to prosecute offenders in the Oldham and Burnley disturbances. The maximum sentences in Oldham and Burnley were two to three years, compared to an average of five years for those charged in Bradford (McGhee, forthcoming).

7.  In an essay on Britishness, Blunkett wrote, 'Speaking English enables parents to converse with their children in English at home and **participate in wider modern culture**, and it helps overcome the **schizophrenia which bedevils generational relationships**' (*The Daily Telegraph*, 17.9.02, my emphasis).

8.  It is interesting that the Parekh report (2000) has a greater concern with the problems of how to constitute core values than his earlier 'moral covenant' suggests, 'what values and loyalties must be shared by communities and individuals in One Nation... How is a balance to be struck between the need to treat people equally, the need to treat people differently, and the need to maintain shared values and social cohesion?' (2000: xv).

9.  It is significant that the role of the Far Right was taken into consideration during the appeal of the Bradford 'rioters' (*The Guardian* 31.1.03) although this did not affect the sentencing, which was largely upheld.

10. For example, the very early 'race relations' approaches to assimilation reflected in the work of the Community Relations Council (cf. CCCS, 1981, for a critique of this approach).

11. Enoch Powell stated in 1968, 'the West Indian does not, by being born in England, become an Englishman. In law, he becomes a UK citizen by birth; in fact he is a West Indian or Asian still'.

12. In April 2001, Chief Superintendent of the GMP, Eric Hewitt, claimed that 60 per cent of racial attacks in Oldham were by Asians on whites. This then led to the stepping-up of Far Right activities in the area prior to the outbreak of the unrest.

13. Interestingly, the Denham report played down the significance of drug-related crime.

14. The link between racialised identities and a 'territorial mentality' also conjures up the image of 'gangs', and is closely associated here with the inevitability of violence.

15. The press coverage of the case of Amjid (sic) Rashid, who was sentenced for eight years for his part in the Bradford violence, highlighted Rashid's lack of respect for community authority when, unlike other youths, he failed to turn himself in to the police.

16. Cf. the 'Fair Justice for All' campaign that has targeted police racism and Far Right activities as important trigger factors in the 'riots' in Bradford (McGhee, forthcoming).

17. Arun Kundnani thus writes, 'A generation of Asians, discarded for their class, excluded for their race, stigmatized for their religion, ghettoized and forgotten, has found its voice—but is yet to be heard' (2001: 110).

# 8

# Ethnicization of Religion

*Yunas Samad*

## INTRODUCTION

This chapter examines processes of identity construction among young Muslims. The empirical data is specifically related to Pakistanis in the United Kingdom. There are, however, some generalizations that are applicable to Muslim youth in the European Union, but with differences. It focuses on the context and parameters that lead to the reformulation of identification among young men and women.

## THEORY OF IDENTITIES

Contemporary understanding of community no longer accepts notions of identity as essentialist and unproblematic. Post-structural notions of identification see it as a dramaturugical process that is hybrid, and a complex social agency that varies over temporality, space and place: a process that is always 'becoming' but never arrives (Hall, 1996; Jackson and Penrose, 1993). Ethnic community, as many writers have argued, can be problematized with variations according to language, religion, gender, generation, social class, sexuality and political persuasion (Ranger, 1996). This ensemble of positions represents a much more mobile and subtle understanding of the complexity of the category community.

The modernization thesis in Western social science has argued that 'assimilation of cultural and religious identities into a national society was a necessary precondition for socio-economic and political development... it was assumed, that modernity had eroded communal identities in favour of citizenship and loyalty to the state'. Glavanis (1998) challenges social sciences to 'rethink the long-standing theoretical and conceptual models regarding the relationship between the 'new' ethnic (religious) identities and citizenship/nationhood.' He adopts Hall's argument that a new politics of representation has emerged which has to do with diasporic experiences 'and the consequences which this has for the process of unsettling, recombination, hybridization and cut-and-mix' (Hall, 1992). The strength of this approach, Eade (1996) argues, is that Hall's sensitivity to post-structuralist themes allows for the examination of new modes of representation to which anthropologists have paid little attention to date. Gilroy used this argument of hybrid identification as a way of levering open space for secular and radical politics. Several writers have challenged this assumption that new ethnicities are natural allies of the left. Both Van der Veer (1995) and Samad (1997, 1998) have argued that new ethnicities can be conservative as well as progressive. This does not mean that Muslim identification is necessarily 'fundamentalist' and that Muslims in the diaspora are hybrid and syncretic as cosmopolitan and secular intellectuals. Claire Alexander (2000) develops this argument further by introducing the concept of gender, specifically masculinity, in trying to understand new forms of representation among Bengali youth. Gender is used both by young men and women to lever open space as alternative strategies.

## GENERATION

Generation is an ambiguous and ambivalent social construction with no clear demarcation between the boundaries. There are two points that need to be considered, the first being that youth are active agents and not just victims. Amit-Talai and Wulff argue that young people negotiate cultural processes, are formed by them and are not simply reacting. They suggest that youth pick up what is around them to form their identity construct, and transform standard cultural artefacts into hybrid constructions (1995: 6-9). However, as much as youth try to lever open spaces to negotiate generational differences, there is a countervailing pull whereby adults try to re-enculturate them. Therefore, spaces that are levered open are being foreclosed, successfully and unsuccessfully, in a process that makes explicit hierarchy and claims to leadership.

## SOCIAL EXCLUSION AND RACISM

Two discourses intersect to produce the context that the Muslim communities are located in, and are external inputs that fuel social change. The first is the discourse of social exclusion, which impinges on the lives of the majority of the community. The working class characteristics of Muslim communities mean that social ills associated with de-industrialization have had a profound impact. Indices of social stress such as unemployment—in particular youth unemployment, health problems for the long-term unemployed, inadequate housing— both overcrowding and poor quality, low educational achievement and rising crime and drug abuse are an all too familiar pattern which can be found among the white working class located on housing estates in Britain and Europe. Like the white working class, Muslim youths are becoming a disarticulated, fractionalized and marginalized social formation, but so far are held back from going too far down that road by strong family and community ties. The boundary of social exclusion has a profound destabilizing effect on any community, and this disruptive input is compounded by the other discourse of exclusion based on race.

## SELF-IDENTIFICATION

There has been considerable discussion among academics on what categories of self-identification have been used by Muslim labour migrants in the UK. Historically, different categories of self-identification have become prominent at different times. Badhar Dahya's thesis, that a Pakistani community had established itself, was challenged by Verity Saifullah-Khan in the 1970s, when she argued that their primary identification was regional and *biraderi* based. Their citizenship and nationality were Pakistani but their identity was not (Dahya, 1974; Saifullah-Khan, 1976). She argued further that in due course they might become Pakistani, but that at the time they were Mirpuri. Anwar's (1979) research in Blackburn also showed the importance of clan network in the establishment and settlement of the community. Another micro-study by Werbner (1990) showed that *biraderis* are not static social relations and that they adapt in the diaspora. He argued persuasively that the rituals of *lena-dena* (taking and giving) incorporated friendship circles and created fictive relations and incorporated, in some cases, into the clan network. Allison Shaw's research work, conducted in the 1980s, also discusses the significance of *biraderi* but entitles her monograph *Pakistanis in Oxford,* suggesting that Saifullah-Khan's prognosis of becoming Pakistani had some substance (Shaw, 1988).

## LANGUAGE

A major driver for internal social change within the younger generations is education. The process of schooling has resulted in a different worldview as well as the nurturing of critical and rational thinking. The vehicle for this shift is indicated by the linguistic change that has taken place, as discussed earlier. While older generations speak in Urdu or regional languages such as Mirpuri, the younger generation consume media and primarily use English. They can articulate in a South Asian language but their proficiency is less than in English. This linguistic gap is reinforced by the fact that the majority of youth, those born or raised in the UK, are literate only in English, while their parents, if literate, would be mainly so in Urdu. These statements have validity only for the working class: middle class families are usually bi- if not tri-lingual and able to read and write in two languages. The fact that working class children are primarily English-speaking means that they access information primarily through this medium, which excludes them from the oral traditions of their parents' generation. Oral traditions, customs and religion are at best only partially transmitted, and this introduces generational differences in the understanding of Islam and in identification. The rational worldview cultivated by education is complemented by the rational character of modernist interpretations of Islam, which has a burgeoning body of literature in English. This is accessed through religious studies at school and from religious activists, and is freely available in some bookshops and supermarkets. This move away from orality as the prime source of religious information means that customary behaviours that regulate the lives of the older generations do not get effectively transferred. Complementing this development is the shift in identification away from Mirpuri or other regional identification, which is the dominant identification among the elder generation, towards Muslim identification among the younger generation. As linguistic skills are lost so does identification with Pakistan or a region of Pakistan, an area that at best they may have visited briefly, become less significant, and Muslim, as an identity, becomes more important. This is not related to an increase in religiosity or due to the rise of 'Islamic fundamentalism', but becomes prominent, paradoxically, as they become British. Muslim identification becomes dominant in the British context as other identifications have less significance or relevance. Again, it is suggested that middle class youth, because they develop greater linguistic skills and have a better familiarity with Pakistan due to having more opportunity to travel, have stronger identification with Pakistani identity. This does not mean that Islamic groups are not having an impact, but this must be qualified with the fact that most 'fundamentalist' groups are elitist in character and target the middle class, educated strata and their numbers are quite small. Musharaf Hussain's point should not be forgotten that 'most...young people (perhaps 90 per cent) have no links with any Islamic organization or mosque and no feeling of responsibility for the future of Islam in this country' (Lewis).

## GENERATION AND GENDER

Paradoxically, while elders of the community believe that the young are too Westernized, outsiders see them as becoming more Islamic. Here we are looking at the majority of young men from the working class, who are negotiating space for generation debates within a framework broadly defined by the older generations of the Pakistani community. It is about creating space from within. Youth draws upon a burgeoning body of literature in English to lever open space in generational issues. One of the consequences that emerges is that pernicious sectarian differences, even in pan-Islamic bodies such as the Bradford Council of Mosques, have less of an impact among the younger generation. They gravitate towards an ecumenical Islam and gloss over the differences that have been so divisive among the older generation. Among working class youth it was also noted that they were not well informed, and did not recognize major differences such as Shias. The more educated youth were aware of these differences.

Another major driver of social change on young people is the influence of popular culture. Much of the youth, particularly young men, are interacting with popular culture. Rap artists such as Fun-Da-Mental and Lala Man, some of whose members are or were from Bradford, are examples of how they are integrating in mainstream development. Paradoxically, members of Fun-Da-Mental declare that they are militant Muslims influenced by black nationalism and anti-racism, producing lyrics such as:

> I'm the soldier in the name of Allah
> So put down the cross and pick up the X...
> Louis Farrakhan, the Nation of Islam
> That's where I got my degree from
> So watch out now I'm comin' at ya

Their music is inextricably part of popular culture and yet exhibits their Islamic identification. What this shows is that there are no mutually exclusive categories of popular culture—Muslim, women—but rather overlapping and intertwining positions that eclectically select parts to create a hybridization of identification (Sharma, Hutnyk and Sharma 1996: 52). Identifications are not discrete and mutually exclusive categories but overlap, and this creates new forms of identification.

There is a conflation of rural Pakistani masculinity with northern English working class masculinity, which is more conservative than working class behaviour in the south of England (Ali, 1992). A major characteristic of young men is how they have adopted the behaviour and norms of the white working class. They spend a lot of their time 'hanging out' on the streets, this partly due to overcrowding at home, participate in various aspects of popular culture and are as quick to use violence as their white counterparts. Unlike their elder generation, Pakistani young men not only believe but also feel that they are British, and are not prepared to take abuse or be subject to violence in the meek manner of their elders, who are prepared to accept it because they feel they were interlopers who do not belong here. When compounded by frustration resulting from social and racial exclusion, we have, as one observer commented, 'angry, arrogant young men' with no idea why they are angry. In this context there is an overlapping of being 'hard' and 'izzat', as both are related to notions of masculinity. The propensity to violence becomes inherent in this situation, and in areas of high concentration such as Manningham, violence against white residents is rising and gives cause for concern. As we outlined earlier, Muslim identification has become prominent due to the linguistic shift taking place, and so it becomes understandable why young men have a propensity to use Islamic symbols and metaphors to justify their rebellious nature. Many are associated with various groups such as Ahle-e-Hadith, Tablighi Jamaat or Hizb-ut-Tahrir without showing signs of religiosity. In some cases, young men are far from being paragons of virtue, have so little knowledge of Islam that they do not know who or what Shias are, have criminal antecedents and yet identify with a religious organization. Rebellious young men either associate with a group because of the shock value or out of territorial loyalty. Working class men claim to be associated with Hizb-ut-Tahrir or daub wall with slogans such as 'Hamas Rules OK' because they know only that it is the most militant of the various organizations and has greater shock value (Samad, 1996, 1997).

Clearly the use of religious symbols and metaphors has entered the repertoire of young men who are using it to express their anger in the name of community that now is also being combined with notions of territoriality. This behaviour is similar to the trait found among equivalent groups in the white communities, and it is not surprising when large numbers of young men have nowhere to go except to hang around on streets in small groups. In this process these young men stake out territorial claims vis à vis each other. One respondent from West Bowling commented that 'you need a passport to go to Manningham' precisely because of territorial claims. There are occasions when these territorial differences are submerged because they become involved in a struggle against a common enemy (Samad, 1997). The vigilante campaign against sex workers is an example of this process. The Lumb Lane area of Bradford has traditionally been the red light district of the city, and for many years the activities of sex workers have been tolerated. Following a similar campaign in Birmingham, and the national attention received by the programme, 'Band of Gold', pickets and vigilantes were formed to encourage the sex workers to leave the area. The fact that some of the pimps were Pakistani and that many of the clients were from the community did not enter into the equation, and they were not harassed by the campaigners. The patrols began in mid-April 1995, and consisted mainly of young men who roamed the area theoretically to persuade the women to leave, but in practice they harassed the women in order to clear the area (Bradford Commission, 1996). This was an example of territorial control on a larger scale that was articulated on a much lower-key daily basis, and was justified in the name of the community.

The same argument of defending the community but in practice the articulation of territorial control was at the heart of the Manningham riots. The clear difference that emerges between Pakistani youth and their white counterparts is that while both present fractured and disarticulated politics of marginality, Pakistani youth still have some notion of community to mobilize around.

Generational differences become most explicit when cross-referenced with gender. Among young women brought up or born in Britain, understanding of Islam differs both from their elder generations and from their male counterparts. While young men tend to reproduce the patriarchal ethos of their elder generation (but with Bradfordian variations on this theme), young women are challenging this in a number of ways. The low status of women and patriarchal domination, in particular of family affairs, are challenged as not conforming to textual interpretations of women's status in Islam. Rather than challenging Islam, they are denigrating their community's cultural interpretation of Islam as non-Islamic. Some women argue that if their menfolk were more Islamic they could not continue to behave in such a macho manner. Women are given equality by Islam within a particular frame of reference, primarily that of modest behaviour and minimal sexual contact outside the framework of marriage. The diasporic context, however, challenges the subordinate position of women that was carefully cultivated in Pakistan.

The Commission on the Status of Women in Pakistan demonstrates vigorously that Pakistani women and girls are, from the earliest age, enculturated with the 'deification of a 'Devi' image of ancient India, which glorified a woman who was self-sacrificing, hard working, docile and subservient to the male' (1998: 29). Marriage outside of the *biraderi* is precisely an issue that explicitly counterpoises traditional androcentric notions with textual Islam. The former sees marriage as the perogative of the patriarch who looks at marriage as a means of keeping property within the clan and in terms of social obligations to the clan, of which a significant element is in Pakistan. These social obligations may be assistance received from other clan members to migrate, the reinforcing of clan ties through *lena-dena* of family members in marriage or contracting marriage with social superiors so that status is enhanced. Thus the arrangement of marriage can be motivated by a variety of reasons, all of which are based on traditions rather than on Islam. Young women in particular regard this as non-Islamic and patriarchal behaviour, which they counter with the citation of Islamic texts that give women the right to choose their own partner. Dress code is another issue with young women challenging the notion that *shalwar kameez* is the only form of dress they can wear. Young women argue that the Islamic text only stipulated that attire should be modest and that is interpreted to mean that if they wore long skirts or jeans with long-sleeved blouses, with or without a head scarf, that would fulfil the Islamic requirements.

## CONCLUSION

The evidence suggests that there are significant differences in the understanding of Islam along gender and generational lines. Young men and women are using Islam to lever open space for gender and generation negotiation. Islam has become an indicator that they are, or have become, more British/European and have reformulated differences in identification in relation to their parents. Islam is also used as a tool, in particular by women, to negotiate important life decisions such as marriage, continuing with education and working. It should not necessarily be seen as an indicator of increased devotion to faith or of religiosity.

## REFERENCES

Alexander, C., *The Asian Gang: ethnicity, identity, masculinity*, Berg, Oxford, 2000.

Ali, Y., 'Muslim Women and the Politics of Ethnicity and Culture in Northern England', in Sahgal, G. & Yuval-Davis, N. (eds.), *Refusing Holy Orders: Women and Fundamentalism in Britain*, Virago, London, 1992.

Amit-Talal, Vered and Wulff, Helena (eds.), *Youth Cultures: A Cross-Cultural Perspective*, Routledge, London, 1995.

Anwar, M., *Myth of Return: Pakistanis in Britain*, Heinemann, London, 1979.

The Bradford Commission Report, *The report of an inquiry into the wider implications of public disorders in Bradford which occurred on 9, 10 and 11 June 1995*, HMSO, London, 1996.

Dayha, B., 'The nature of Pakistani ethnicity in industrial cities in Britain', in Cohen, A. (ed.) *Urban Ethnicity*, Tavistock, London, 1974.

Eade, John, 'Ethnicity and the Politics of Cultural Difference: An Agenda for the 1990s' in Ranger, T., Samad, Y. and Stuart, O. (eds.), *Culture, Identity and Politics: Ethnic Minorities in Britain*, Avebury, Aldershot, 1996.

Glavanis, Pandelis M., 'Political Islam within Europe: A Contribution to an Analytical Framework', *Innovation*, Vol. 11, No. 4, 1998.

Hall, Stuart, 'New Ethnicities' in Donald, J. and Rattansi A. (eds.), *'Race' Culture and Difference*, Sage, London, 1992).

Hall, Stuart 'Politics of Identity' in Ranger, T., Samad, Y. and Stuart, O. (eds.), *Culture, Identity and Politics: Ethnic Minorities in Britain*, Avebury, Aldershot, 1996.

Jackson, Peter & Penrose, Jan (eds.), *Constructions of Race, Place and Nation*, UCL Press, London, 1993.

Lewis, Philip 'British Muslims and the Search for Religious Guidance', Conference paper, in 'From Generation to Generation: Religious Reconstruction in the South Asian Diaspora', at SOAS, London University, 1996.

Pakistan Commission on the Status of Women, *Report of the Pakistan Commission on the Status of Women*, 1989.

Saifullah-Khan, Verity, 'Pakistanis in Britain: Perceptions of a Population', *New Community*, 5 (3), 1976.

Samad, Y., 'The Politics of Islamic Identity among Bangladeshis and Pakistanis in Britain' in Ranger, T., Samad, Y. & Stuart, O. (eds.), *Culture, Identity and Politics: Ethnic minorities in Britain*, Avebury, Aldershot, 1996.

Samad, Yunas, 'Ethnicity, Racism and Islam: Identity and Gender and Generational Debates' in *Multiculturalism, Muslims and the Media: Pakistanis in Bradford*, unpublished manuscript produced as part of the research conducted for the ESRC (Award number L126251039), 1997.

Samad, Yunas, 'Media and Muslim Identity: Intersection of Generation and Gender', *Innovation*, Vol. 11, No. 4, 1998.

Sharma, A., Hutnyk J. & Sharma, S. (eds.), *Dis-Orienting Rhythms: the politics of the new Asian dance music*, Zed Press, London, 1996.

Shaw, A., *A Pakistani Community in Britain*, Blackwell, Oxford, 1988.

Van de Veer, Peter (ed.), Nation and Migration, University of Pennsylvania Press, Philadelphia, 1995.

Werbner, P., The Migration Process: Capital, Gifts and Offerings among British Pakistanis, Berg, Oxford, 1999.

# 9

# Young South Asian Muslims and Identity

*Aminah Mohammad-Arif*

## INTRODUCTION

The presence in the USA of South Asian Muslims goes back to the twentieth century, though it is only from 1965 onwards, when America liberalized its immigration policy, that this segment of the population migrated to the US in significant numbers. This minority group is characterized by a remarkable internal diversity at an economic and social level, as well as at a cultural and sectarian level. But more particularly, first and second generation South Asian Muslims provide, through their varied and complex nature, a wider perspective and understanding of the redefinition of Islamic traditions and the reinvention of collective identities. The focus of this study will be on the second generation whose experiences can be compared, if not contrasted (at least partially), with those of their peers in Europe, in the UK[1] and France[2] in particular.

After briefly presenting the demographic profile of South Asian Muslims in the United States, and discussing issues pertaining to the first generation, I will address in more detail the particular question of identity construction among the second generation.

## A DEMOGRAPHIC PROFILE

Since the census department does not ask people to state their religious affiliations, it is not easy to determine how many Muslims live in the USA. In the case of South Asians, a second difficulty arises due to the fact that while Indians are classified separately in the census under the category of 'Asian Indian', Pakistanis and Bangladeshis are still classified under the category of 'others', within the Asian sub-group. The distribution of Muslims per ethnic group is also not known. It is estimated that there are between five and seven million Muslims in the United States. They are reportedly divided in the following manner: between one-third to half, depending on the sources, are Afro-Americans; between a quarter to one-third are South Asians; between a quarter to one-third are Arabs; the rest being made up of Iranians, Afghans, Turks, et cetera (Mohammad-Arif, 2002a: 39). The South Asian Muslims would therefore constitute a population of 800,000 to one million, a large majority of them being Pakistani (between 500,000 and 700,000, according to the estimates of the Pakistani consulate in New York), followed by Indian Muslims (about 200,000 if we assume that they constitute, as in India, 12 per cent of the total Indian population, which, all religious affiliations taken together, reached the figure of around 1.7 million in the USA in 2000) and 100,000 Bangladeshis.

On the socio-economic level, in the USA, having encouraged the immigration of educated and qualified people during the 1960s and 1970s, particularly from the Indian subcontinent, the majority of the South Asians have a high level of education and are noticeably quite prosperous. Many among those who make up this population are doctors, engineers, scientists and computer specialists, whose success (especially that of the Indians) has become almost legendary. The second wave of immigrants (1980s and 1990s) comprises a fairly large number of less educated and underprivileged individuals (taxi drivers, newspaper vendors, petrol pump attendants, et cetera). The third wave (from the mid-1990s to the present) include a fairly high number of computer graduates, concentrated in the Silicon Valley, most being Hindus, but they include some Muslims as well. The South Asian population as a whole, Muslims included, continues to be made up mostly of immigrants occupying higher rungs of the social ladder. As a rough guide, according to an investigation conducted at Queens College in New York in 2001, 75 per cent of Muslim immigrants, whatever their ethnic origin, had completed university studies and earned salaries that were higher than the American average (*New York Times*, 2001). Likewise, South Asians from the second generation have been characterized by fairly good levels of academic performance. This success can be primarily attributed to their social background since many of them belong to educated and affluent families, and to the unconditional support that they receive from their parents, education-wise. The highly competitive atmosphere of the schools and colleges of South Asia, India in particular, to which most immigrants from the subcontinent have been exposed before migrating, is reproduced in the diaspora. South Asian first generation immigrants, very keen to see their children achieving the same, or even a higher, level of success, exert strong pressure on their children, this becoming increasingly, it should be noted, a source of tension between generations (Mohammad-Arif, 2002b).

## IDENTITY ISSUES AND THE PLACE OF RELIGION AMONG THE FIRST GENERATION

Needless to say, identity is a subjective and fluid concept, fluctuating in space and time, according to circumstances. Affiliations based on nation, ethnicity and language remain of utmost importance in diaspora. But like other South Asians, many Muslims in the USA have tended to accord a significant place to religion as well in the construction of their identity. Among the reasons that can be given is the American context itself. Compared to Europe, and to France in particular, the USA is characterized by the highest degree of religiosity among all the so-called industrialized countries (Japan excepted). Besides, most ethnic minorities in the USA (Irish, Greek, Jewish) have traditionally seen in religion an efficient vehicle in their community formation and identity recomposition.

The USA offers Muslims a freedom that may be very difficult to find elsewhere (including in Muslim countries). The way religious freedom is defined in the USA is fairly comparable to how India addresses the issue: the treatment of all religions on an equal footing. But at the same time, Muslims suffer from a sentiment of discrimination against Islam in the USA. Hence the paradox of the situation: on the one hand, American relative tolerance in the religious field allows Muslims to practice their religion openly (as testified by the tremendous increase in the number of Islamic institutions all over the US); on the other hand, the anti-Islamic prejudice of the population (even before 9/11), strong enough in many ways to be called Islamophobia, perpetuated by the media and reinforced by events in the Middle East and in other parts of the Muslim world, has contributed to the nurturing of religious sentiment among Muslims: reacting to what is perceived as discrimination, they claim their identification to Islam even more intensively.

It should also be observed that an enhanced sense of religiosity does not necessarily exclude for all identification with America, even after 11 September. The Muslims in the USA have obviously been traumatized by the events, and in many ways perhaps even more so than (other) Americans. As a number of them have admitted to me, particularly those immigrants who have been settled in the US for a long time, they feel they have been 'double victims' of the attacks, 'We are victims as Americans and victims as Muslims.' The price paid by the Muslims of the USA, who as a community are on the whole well integrated and eager, like all the other minorities, to share in the American dream, has been fairly high. The attacks have represented a setback for them in their process of integration, not to mention the discrimination many of them have been the victims of in various forms and to various extents. But many among them still like to call themselves American Muslims, or even Muslim Americans. It should be noted that this attitude of the Muslims of the USA puts them in an odd position in relation to the rest of their compatriots and co-religionists around the world. Anyway, as far as I can tell, the present crisis does not seem to have undermined the feelings of the immigrants in terms of their affiliation with America, at least among those who have been settled in the USA for some time, especially in cities like New York. However, the current crisis does raise in the minds of many Muslims questions concerning their identity, such as, 'Can one be both a Muslim and a patriotic American?' Many still answer in the affirmative (Mohammad-Arif, 2002a: 55).

To come back to the issue of an enhanced religiosity, a dialectical link can also be observed between migration and nation, as underlined by Peter van der Veer (1995), which in the case of Muslims, and also of other South Asians, expresses itself through religion: in other words, Muslims become more Muslim in the diaspora (Mohammad-Arif, 2002b), while Hindus become more Hindu. Neither Islam nor Hinduism are 'taken for granted' anymore, and Muslims discover their 'Islam-ness' in diaspora while Hindus discover their 'Hindu-ness', this in turn having political implications extending as far as the home countries.

The influence of some Islamic movements, like the Jamaat-i Islami,[3] on the immigrants, as indirect as it might be, should not be neglected either to explain this heightened religiosity. The Jamaat-i Islami has played a significant role in setting up a number of organizations in the US, such as the Muslim Student Association, and has therefore been able to exert a certain impact on students and immigrants (Mohammad Arif, 2002c: 175-203).

But one of the major reasons for this 'rediscovery' of the Islamic roots of the immigrants clearly lies in their concern for the transmission of their cultural heritage to their offspring. Religion is seen as a prime instrument for curbing the (inevitable) process leading towards Americanization. It remains to be seen how young South Asian Muslims respond to these pressures that come along with other (conflicting) demands from the host society.

## THE SECOND GENERATION: BETWEEN COMPARTMENTALIZATION AND IDENTITY MALAISE

Young South Asian Muslims often have to face, on the one hand, the aspirations, full of paradoxes, of their parents, and on the other hand the contradictory injunctions of the host society (through school, media and so on) that call for emancipation, especially for women. As opposed to South Asia and countries like the UK, where parents do not attach tremendous importance to the education of girls, many parents in the US encourage their daughters to pursue higher studies, including at university level. But this openness towards education does not allay their anxiety that the more the children are educated, the more they are exposed to the risk of acculturation and especially of the questioning of their parent's authority. They fear in particular that an exacerbated Westernization might cause the youngsters to break with their families and/or even encourage them to enter marital alliances that may not conform to the parents' expectations (who usually are in favour of arranged marriage or, at least, of endogamous marriage). That is why parents spare no effort in ensuring that their cultural and religious heritage is transmitted to their children. The latter are inculcated from an early age with the idea that they will have an arranged marriage, and that any free mixing of genders beyond the immediate family goes against Indo-Islamic values (Mohammad-Arif, 2002c: 107-114). But above all, parents exert strict control over their offspring, especially girls.

Considering the level of conservatism of parents, the propensity to rebel is relatively low and the degree of internalization of the values inculcated by the parents is fairly high, and this at whatever the level of education achieved. This concern to satisfy their parents may culminate later, for some at least, in their acceptance of arranged marriages. This low propensity for rebellion observed in the analysis of the relationships between generations in the diasporic context testifies to the acceptance by young South Asians of family authority. Family is invested without much resistance with its traditional role of socialization.

But at the same time, young South Asian Muslims are prey to an identity 'malaise' that is nurtured by a relative absence of communication with their parents and by the difficulty to choose between a plethora of references, this being a characteristic of the diasporic context. This identity confusion can take several forms. For the majority of youngsters, this situation leads to a compartmentalization of their lives, sometimes resulting in quasi-schizophrenic behaviour. Often it is the only alternative for young people, who are willing both to give satisfaction to their parents and to please their peers in the host society.

For a few young South Asians (who are in a minority), this situation could create grounds for a calling-into-question of traditional schemas and the search of vectors of expression. Particularly concerned are those young girls whose sexuality has been oppressed, even suppressed, under the cover of a culturo-religious preservation (Mohammad-Arif, 2000: 84).

For some youngsters, both men and women, this work of reflection translates into an exploration of their sexuality. This can sometimes lead to behaviour perceived by the community as deviant or even sometimes totally un-Islamic. Homosexuality is an example. Since the 1980s, there has been a burgeoning of Indo-Pakistani associations representing homosexuals. Interestingly, homosexuality represents a powerful means of integration as it breaks down social, ethnic and religious barriers, bringing together individuals only linked by 'common' sexual behaviour. It should be also noted that the constitution of progressive groups in the USA, whether they are in defence of the rights of homosexuals, battered women or taxi-drivers, has partially resulted in the promotion of a 'South Asian' identity, especially within the second generation. This would mean that whereas in the subcontinent the concept of South Asia merely refers to geographical boundaries, in the diaspora this could take on a more extended meaning, implying even the erasure of the borders created during Partition (Mohammad-Arif, 2002b: 225).

The identity malaise can also lead to creativity, this being symptomatic of a dynamic and individual identity construction. This is notably expressed through music (neo-*bhangra* groups) and literature, as shown by the mushrooming of literary works produced by South Asian women in particular (whether Hindu or Muslim).

But the identity malaise can also be expressed, in an almost reverse logic, through religion (a phenomenon also observed in the first generation). Religion does not necessarily become an instrument of contest, and in fact Islam, as stated earlier, is usually perceived by parents as the most efficient vector used to perpetuate traditional values and to curb the effects of Americanization. Besides, the majority of young Muslims in the US are willing to keep their religious heritage without seeing in it a potential instrument for contest. These youngsters do not necessarily indulge themselves in a rigid and traditionalist reading of Islam: Islam, on their initiative, is subjected to recomposition, even to rehabilitation, as well as to questioning (for instance, on the relationship between Islam and democracy, Islam and secularism, and so on). But these youngsters express at the same time the will to relegate religion into the private sphere.

A small minority, on the contrary, sees in Islam an 'efficient' instrument in externalizing their identity malaise and asserting their individual identity. This phenomenon is particularly observed among girls wearing the veil. Of all the 'neo-religious' youngsters I met, most had at least one parent who was very religious. As opposed to North African families in France where, according to Farhad Khosrokhavar (1995-96: 68-84), children suffer from the inability of their parents to inculcate an identity connected with their past or their country of origin, young South Asians seem to be finding in the family sphere the necessary references for identity construction. However, the explanation for this asserted religiosity cannot simply be explained by the continuation of family tradition.

It should be also noted that, unlike France, the veil has not aroused any spectacular hue and cry in the USA. If sporadic opposition is expressed, in schools in particular, it has not become a 'national issue'. Conflicts, in the majority of cases, are settled in favour of the veiled person (Mohammad-Arif, 2002b: 102).

Yet we cannot systematically compare the young Muslims of New York to their peers in Europe. Young South Asian Muslims in the USA on the one hand and young Arabs in France, and young South Asian Muslims in Britain on the other, do not usually have the same social backgrounds, the former belonging in most cases to the middle class, or even the upper-middle class, while the latter tend to belong to underprivileged classes. But they all share the experience of an identity malaise, even though it acquires a less poignant dimension in the case of South Asians in the US. The exacerbated religiosity constitutes in most cases the ultimate expression of an identity crisis, and lies within the scope of the emergence of the Islamic phenomenon throughout the world. It should also be noted that if most young South Asians have not suffered much from discrimination at a personal level (or at least did not suffer much post-11 September), what is perceived as an ambient hostility against Islam in the USA (as exemplified in the association of Islam with fundamentalism and terrorism) exerts a definite impact on their identity construction, some of them seeing in Islam the ultimate instrument to recover a dignity that has been flouted (Mohammad-Arif, 2002b: 102).

The redefinition of Islam, whether it is in a more rigorous fashion or not, also stems from the educational background of young South Asian Muslims in the US. The youngsters have been educated in an American system that encourages questioning and reasoning as opposed to memorizing lessons without much reflection. Even in most mosques, teachers, aligning themselves to the American model, try to set up courses that encourage reflection and participation by their students. This schema offers a contrast with traditional methods of teaching in the subcontinent, religious teaching in particular, which are still largely based on memorizing texts without making much effort at comprehension, if not rationally, at least through some intellectual questioning.

This tendency to understand religion in a more rational way in migration, as opposed to the mechanical practices of Islamic religion in the country of origin, is also observed within the first generation. Interestingly, the so-called rationalization is used by parents, not only in the logic of the quest for the self but also, and perhaps above all, in the hope that a religion transmitted with explanation and commentary rather than mechanically will have a greater effect on their children, who will then be more willing to keep their religious heritage. In any case, the concern for rationality, which is also symptomatic of the logic of the individualization of religion, urges young Muslims to get interested in religion not so much through the intermediary of rites borrowed from South Asian tradition but rather through the (re)reading of religious texts (Quran and *Hadith* in particular), (re)interpreted in the light of their needs.

The second generation expresses at best a limited interest, if not indifference, or even expresses in some cases open criticism of rituals that it does not understand the significance of: young Muslims aspire to rationalism, and are not inclined to perpetuate religion through socio-cultural traditions directly inherited from the country of origin. Such an attitude leads to a distinct vision of Islam that not only widens the gap between generations in their respective perceptions of religion, but also creates the conditions for the emergence of a redefinition of Islam. This process of redefinition engenders in some cases, still very much in the minority, an attraction for a way of life close to that advocated by fundamentalist groups throughout the world, or at least for an activism that seeks a revaluation of Islam. Some, by indulging themselves in comprehensive studies, are inspired to push the logic of the quest for sense and rationality to its extreme, opting for a lifestyle in accordance with their own interpretation of Islam. A common will seems to characterize the youngsters of the USA or of France and the UK who aspire to revive an internal purity in reference to an Islamic past that has been altered by previous generations. This notion of purity takes on a double meaning because it not only refers to a desire for internal purification, but also to a 'pure' way of practising religion, as testified by the following remark (Mohammad-Arif, 2002b), 'What I love in the US is that we can practice the Islamic religion in the purest way, without all the cultural stuff of the first generation.'

But beyond these aspects of 'inner pride' and spiritual quest, the phenomenon is also symptomatic of the impact exerted on South Asian Muslims by movements like the Salafis, the Tablighi Jamaat, and especially in the case of the USA, the Jamaat-i Islami that can be observed within the first generation, and is making headway within the second generation, as testified by this whole rhetoric of purity and purification.

However, this avowed Islam-ness is not always the result of a thorough reflection on religion, of a spiritual quest or even of the sheer impact of fundamentalist movements, but occasionally reveals identity crises that are sometimes taken to an extreme.

Interestingly, it should also be noted that outfits, notably the *hijab*, often worn with jeans and in some cases with (outrageous) make-up, suggest not only a certain Americanization of Muslim girls, but also a homogenization, with physical appearance as a first step. Let us bear in mind that traditionally, women in the subcontinent do not wear the *hijab* like their Muslim peers in Europe or the Middle East: either they cover their heads with their *saris* or their *duppatas*, or they wear the *burqa* that covers them from head to foot. If in some regions of the subcontinent, the *burqa* is still frequently worn, it increasingly tends to disappear in urban areas where the families of young South Asian Muslims hail from: their families usually belong to the Westernized elite rather than to the traditional elite that is still keen to maintain the system of the *purdah* as a sign of respectability. But in the United States, most Muslim women, whether they belong to the first or to the second generation, cover their heads with a *hijab* (meaning here a scarf that fully covers the hair), thus opting for a way of veiling themselves which does not derive from South Asian culture, but which has been adopted throughout the world (including now in the subcontinent) by followers of militant Islam. The word '*hijab*' then takes on a kind of generic meaning as the female covering cloth worn in accordance with Islamic principles, independent of the ethnic and national origins of the wearer (Weibel, 1996: 136). It should also be recalled that the wearing of the veil falls within the logic of the re-appropriation of Islam vis-à-vis the parents, who will fear less the 'harmful' consequences on their daughters of an American-style emancipation, and vis-à-vis the self: the veil offers young Muslim girls a form of protection that allows them in return to occupy sectors traditionally reserved for males, without fearing a violation of Islamic law. The wearing of the veil offers an internal pride, and in some cases, a feeling of superiority in front of other non-veiled Muslims threatened, according to the veiled girls, by the risk of 'disintegration' into the host society.

The combination of the *hijab* worn with a pair of jeans or a long skirt seems to constitute the uniform of a youth that are prey to doubt in a materialistic and individualistic society. This uniform, a visible symbol of a quest for identity, creates at the same time a bond between these girls, and by standardizing their physical appearance, reinforces their efforts to break the ethnic barriers between Muslims experienced by their immigrant parents. But nothing in the behaviour of these girls suggests submission to any particular authority: they are characterized by independent, sometimes even provocative manners. Whereas in the subcontinent, the behaviour of an individual, of a woman in particular, often depends on the judgement of society, this concern disappears in the USA, among the veiled girls at least. By not caring about the way the society considers them, the veiled girls demonstrate their independence, and almost paradoxically become closer to a certain form of American ideal that encourages autonomy of the mind. To be precise, I am referring here to the cases of girls who wear the veil of their own free will and not in response to parental pressure. It could be argued that this indifferent attitude vis-à-vis the opinion of the host society implies sentiments of non-belonging of these girls to this society. But in fact interviews reveal that most of these girls consider the USA as the ideal country to live in and to practice their religion because of the freedom it offers (this particular point has been observed during a research conducted before 11 September). Furthermore, this deliberate identification with Islam is not necessarily the logical consequence of identity anxiety vis-à-vis the host society since, unlike the situation of Muslims in Europe, that of the Muslims in the US, in particular those from the subcontinent, is neither to their disadvantage on the economic level, nor definitely confrontational on the cultural or political level. As for the community's opinion, which is mostly concerned with the issue of social integration and economic success, and hence does not necessarily approve of the wearing of ostensible religious symbols, this does not influence the behaviour of the veiled girls either. In some cases, the wearing of the veil can provoke, if not a confrontation, at least dissension within a family whose opposition to the veil can be a matter of principle; but it can also betray an anxiety because of the potential repercussions of this visible sign on the children in their relationship to the host society, today more than ever (Mohammad-Arif, 2002b: 106).

We have so far mostly underlined the case of the female population by raising the question of the *hijab*. Males show strong similarities in their behaviour as well as in their motivation for (re)Islamization. The phenomenon answers the same quest for sense and identity, engendered and reinforced at the same time by the ambient hostility, or at least felt as such, against Islam in American society, by the education in the American system which calls for questioning of the self and of the surrounding milieu, and by the impact of movements like the Jamaat-i Islami. Above all, Islamization is perceived as an attempt to fill the void created by what is perceived as the failure of secular ideologies.

The religious conduct described above involves only a minority of Muslims in the USA. However, if religion often remains confined to the private sphere, it does have a determining importance in the construction of the identity of young Muslims, and in their will either to perpetuate their heritage or to blend into the dominant culture.

## CONCLUSION

Young South Asian Muslims are characterized by a fairly high level of education, and are thus structurally integrated into American society, like the first generation. In that sense, they differentiate themselves from many of their peers in the UK or from North African Muslims in France. They retain nonetheless an attachment to their so-called traditional values, as reflected in the importance given to family, an essential point of reference. However, the conciliatory attitude of the youngsters towards their family (reflected notably in their acceptance of endogamous, and even of arranged, marriages) does not imply an absence of internal conflict among children: they are often the victims of misunderstanding by their parents, while submitted to contradictory pressures from the family and the host society. This conflict frequently fosters an attitude of schizophrenia and a compartmentalization of life, in particular during the teenage years. This phenomenon puts young Muslims in the USA closer to their peers in Europe, who basically share the same type of experience in terms of identity construction and relationships vis-à-vis their parents, and this in spite of differences in social class.

Islam occupies a notable place in their identity construction but apparently more in response to a quest for understanding in a materialistic society than as a result of a social rejection that could lead to a logic of confrontation, as is the case with many of their peers in the UK and with North Africans in France. The discrimination that nevertheless affects some young Muslims in the USA contributes to the reinforcement of their identity assertion, but does not necessarily represent the main reason for this assertion. However, a distinction should be made between youngsters for whom Islam represents one element, even though a potentially essential one, of their identity, but who will not necessarily follow rigorously the precepts of Islam, and those (in the minority) who will not only call into question traditional teachings but also pursue the logic of their quest to the point of trying to adopt a way of life that is as Islamic as possible in a non-Muslim society. The effects of migration and education in the USA cause many youngsters to reject rituals whose significance they do not understand, and to favour a certain rationalization. It is not Islam *per se* which is rationalized, but religion is learnt in a more rational way in migration, unlike the mechanical practice of religion that is still observed in South Asia. Finally, the impact of fundamentalist groups, like the

Jamaat-i Islami, noticeable within the first generation, affects the second generation as well. The very redefinition of Islam in diaspora in a more rigid form testifies to it. But anyway, beyond the slight influence of particular fundamentalist groups, the diasporic situation favours the emergence of an Islam that is redefined in a more 'sober'[4] but also more rigorous way, this being more suitable to the needs of migrants (c.f. Roy, 2002).

The importance given to Islam does not exclude an identification with the 'ethnic' kin group. In other words, some young Muslims from the subcontinent may also stress their affiliation with other South Asians, beyond the religious connection.

The question of the attitude vis-à-vis American society now remains. First of all, the above analysis suggests a close link between the latter and the way identity is constructed: the otherness is expressed vis-à-vis, even in reaction to, American society; but the intellectual progress leading to a certain form of identity construction, as well as to the setting up of organizations of a religious or cultural type, seems to result from the migration process, although this process took place a generation ago.

But most important, the vast majority of youngsters, whatever the degree of their religiosity, strongly identify themselves with America. Interestingly, their approach in matters relating to discrimination, especially when it is contrasted with the attitude of their parents in this matter, is a good indicator of their level of Americanization. Many immigrants tend to adopt a fatalist attitude, considering as inevitable, even normal, the discrimination they are subjected to. The second generation, on the other hand, which quickly absorbs American identity, does not feel foreign in the USA and is even more aware of its rights than the elders. It, therefore, denounces with greater virulence discrimination (whatever the target or form it takes), even after 11 September. The kind of queries and questions Muslims have been submitted to after the attacks have also generated different kinds of reaction in the first and second generations. The latter indeed, while acknowledging the importance of denouncing the attacks and of making Islam better known in the USA, expresses its exasperation in a more pronounced manner than their elders. 'Why should I have to justify myself in relation to these attacks, to constantly state my position on the matter, to repeat that Islam and terrorism are incompatible, as if it was not obvious! People ask me why Muslims have committed an act of this kind. Simply because I am a Muslim, I am supposed to know what it is that has motivated these people. Did all the Christians in the USA have to justify themselves after the action of Timothy McVeigh?'[5] exclaims, for instance, the president of the Muslim Students' Association at Columbia University, a young Indian Muslim born in the USA (Mohammad-Arif, 2002a: 63-64). It is too early to determine what kind of impact the current crisis will have on young Muslims in terms of their identification with America. What is certain, however, is that this crisis has aroused an awakening of identity in a number of young people. Many of them have suddenly become aware of their affiliation with Islam. If we are to believe an article from the *Houston Chronicle*, the number of veiled women might even have increased one year after 9/11 (whereas immediately after the events many women had temporarily removed the veil). This piece of information, is of course, difficult to prove, but in such a situation that is favourable to identity reactions, some people, youngsters in particular, might be tempted to draw on Islam as a source of dignity in the face of the humiliations of which they are victims.

## REFERENCES

*Houston Chronicle*, 'More women of Islamic faith opting to wear traditional veils', 8 September, 2002.

Khosrokhavar, Farhad, 'L'identité voilée', *Confluences – Méditerranée*, L'Harmattan, Paris, 16, Winter, 1995-1996.

Khosrokhavar, Farhad, *L'islam des jeunes*, Flammarion, Paris, 1997.

Lewis, Philip, *Islamic Britain*, I.B. Tauris, London, 1994.

Mohammad-Arif, Aminah, 'A Masala Identity: Young South Asian Muslims in the US', *Comparative Studies of South Asia, Africa and the Middle East*, XX (1 & 2), 2000: 84.

Mohammad-Arif, Aminah, 'The Impact of September 11 on the Muslims from the Indian Subcontinent in New York', in Grare, Frédéric (ed.), *The Muslims of the Indian Subcontinent after the 11th September Attacks*, India Research Press, Delhi, 2002a.

Mohammad-Arif, Aminah, *Salam America: L'islam indien en diaspora*, CNRS Editions Paris, 2000. Translated into English as *Salaam America: South Muslims in New York*, Anthem Press, London, 2002b.

Mohammad-Arif, Aminah, 'Ilyâs et Maudûdî au pays des yankees', *Archives de Sciences Sociales des Religions*, EHESS, Paris, 117, janvier-mars, 2002c.

*New York Times*, 14 November, 2001.

Roy, Olivier, *L'islam mondialisé*, Seuil, Paris, 2002.

Vali Reza Nasr, Seyyed, *The Vanguard of the Islamic Revolution: the Jama'at-i Islami of Pakistan*, I.B. Tauris, London/New York, 1994.

van der Veer, Peter (ed.), *Nation and Migration: The Politics of Space in the South Asian Diaspora*, University of Pennsylvania Press, Philadelphia, 1995.

Weibel, Nadine, 'Islamité, égalité et complémentarité: vers une nouvelle approche de l'identité féminine', *Archives de sciences sociales des Religions*, n°19, July-September, 1996.

# NOTES

1. For Muslims in Britain, see in particular Philip Lewis, *Islamic Britain*, I.B. Tauris, London, 1994.
2. For young Muslims in France, see in particular Farhad Khosrokhavar, *L'islam des jeunes*, Flammarion, Paris, 1997.
3. The Jamaat-i Islami was created in 1941 in pre-partitioned India by Abul Ala Mawdudi. It is considered to be one of the major fundamentalist movements in the Indian subcontinent. Cf. Seyyed Vali Reza Nasr, *The Vanguard of the Islamic Revolution: the Jamaʿat-i Islami of Pakistan*, I.B. Tauris, London/New York, 1994.
4. All the elaborate rituals connected with Sufi shrines, for instance, are increasingly on the decline in the diaspora, while in most cases they have been purely and simply suppressed, especially in the USA.
5. Main author of the attack against the FBI building in Oklahoma.

# SECTION 4

# Discrimination, Legalization and the War on Terror

The first chapter of this section deals with the contradictions inherent in legislative systems in many countries of Europe, notably France and Britain, in providing equality for religious minorities. Whereas the French system only recognizes citizenship as the basis for equality, it does not deal with the inherent inequalities in the real world of work and welfare, in particular for Muslim minorities. In Britain, on the other hand, while (in theory) equality legislation is intended to protect all minorities, in reality, as in France, economic and social disparities are wide between different communities and there is little monitoring of this process. While Choudhury argues for specific legislation to protect religious minorities, the subsequent chapters in this section, notably those by Levidow and Khan, illustrate that current global politics, and in particular, the 'war on terror' are rapidly eroding many established civil liberties which affect minority Muslim communities disproportionately. Khan, in particular, assesses issues of identity and ethnicization, which act in his view as a cover for growing inequality of access and opportunity and a pandemic of race discrimination despite the fanfare of multiculturalism and diversity. Together, these studies contribute to a lively discussion of the current debates in Europe over Islam, citizenship and inclusion.

# 10

## Comparative Perspectives on Discrimination Law

*Tufyal Choudhury*

This chapter is based largely upon the work of the Open Society Institute reports into the situation of Muslims in the United Kingdom, France and Italy.[1] The reports were published at the end of 2002 and were part of the OSI monitoring programme looking at minority protection in the EU.

From the case studies of the UK and France it is clear that, in both countries, demands for equality and protection from discrimination by Muslims provide significant challenges to the existing frameworks for the promotion of equality and protection against discrimination. In the UK, the assertion of Muslim identities presents a challenge to the pre-existing legal and institutional framework that views minority communities in terms of race and ethnic background. In France, the assertion of Muslim identities challenges a framework that is reluctant to acknowledge the existence of minorities and the notion of a secular state. Furthermore, the claims for equality by Muslims raise important questions about the understanding of equality and the aim of anti-discrimination legislation.

## THE RECOGNITION OF A MUSLIM MINORITY AND THE COLLECTION OF DATA

In the UK, the assertion of Muslim identities presents a challenge to the pre-existing legal and institutional framework that views minority communities in terms of race and ethnic background. The large-scale immigration of Muslim communities from the 1950s onwards was a part of a wider process of post-war migration. During the early period of migration, state policy operated under a laissez-faire assumption of assimilation. It was thought that the black and Asian immigrants would adapt quickly to the cultural, life style and attitudinal norms of the host community. However, social tensions soon began to emerge, particularly in relation to housing. Successive governments failed to meet post-war demands for housing, and 'the arrival of large numbers of immigrants, particularly in the inner city areas with the most acute housing problems, inevitably exacerbated already serious shortages and supplied ready-made scapegoats on whom already extant problems could be blamed' (Mason, 2000: 26).

The initial policy response linked control of immigration to good race relations. The need for successful integration was used to justify restrictions on immigration from the new Commonwealth. The legislative support for integration included the enactment of the Race Relations Acts in 1965, 1968, 1976 and 2000. The creation of the Commission for Racial Equality in 1976 was an acknowledgement that the problems faced by minority ethnic communities were of covert and structural racism. This is strengthened by the Race Relations Amendment Act 2000, which creates a duty on public authorities to eliminate racial discrimination and to promote equal opportunities and good relations between persons belonging to different racial groups.

The primacy given to racial and ethnic community formations has meant that, until recently, religion has largely been missing from the discourse on minority protection. There are differences in the treatment of different religious groups. Jewish and Sikh communities are recognized as ethnic groups and so receive the full protection of the Race Relations Act. The Act does not provide the same protection to Muslims. For Muslim groups 'the effect of the Race Relations Act 1976 has been to make race the most powerful and all-pervasive keyhole through which to perceive society...the implication of this on the Muslim community—ironically the most multi-racial and biggest within the ethnic community—has been disastrous' (An-Nisa Society, 1992: 4).

Professor Tariq Modood (1992: 33) pointed out the limitations of viewing social exclusion purely through the lens of race, by showing that disaggregating groups in different ways leads to new perspectives on advantage and disadvantage. He found that 'by most socio-economic measures there is a major divide between Sunni Muslims on the one hand and the other Asians, and that this divide is as great as between Asians and whites, or between Asians and Blacks.' A study by the Cabinet Office (2003: 26) found that 'unemployment does vary significantly by religion. Even after controlling for a range of factors, [Indian] Sikhs and Indian Muslims remain almost twice as likely to be unemployed as [Indian] Hindus' (Cabinet Office Strategy Unit, 2003: 26).

In the UK, comprehensive ethnic statistics have proven a valuable tool for the development of differentiated policies to improve the quality of public services offered to racial and ethnic minority groups. The statistics have revealed that in the areas of education, healthcare, social protection, housing, public service provision, employment and criminal justice, the Pakistani and Bangladeshi communities (which are overwhelmingly Muslim) experience particularly high levels of disadvantage, deprivation and discrimination even in comparison to other minority ethnic communities.

However, the focus on ethnic identities has meant that there are no statistics to identify the level of disadvantage experienced by Muslim communities. While statistics collected on the basis of ethnic origin show high levels of disadvantage amongst the overwhelmingly Muslim Pakistani and Bangladeshi communities, they cannot be used to identify the experience of Muslims from other communities. The utility of ethnic data more generally is limited. The census category 'Black African', for example, 'covers such a wide range in terms of culture, socio-economic situations and migration experience that it is almost entirely unhelpful' (The Runnymede Trust, 2000: 144). Similarly, 'the term 'Indian' fails to distinguish between the large Punjabi and Gujarati communities, and does not take account of certain smaller communities with roots in India which are culturally, religiously and socio-economically different from the larger group' (The Runnymede Trust, 2000: 145). Muslims from the Balkans, Ghana, India, Iran, Iraq, Malaysia, Nigeria, Turkey, Somalia, South Africa, Sudan, Yemen and North African countries remain invisible, hidden behind figures for white, black or other. There is little empirical data to say if these Muslim communities suffer the same level of disadvantages experienced by the Pakistani and Bangladeshi communities. However, Muslim organizations report plenty of anecdotal evidence to suggest that Muslims other than Pakistanis and Bangladeshis also suffer severe disadvantage.

The prison service is one of the few areas where statistics are collected on the basis of religion. If the prison service had collected data on the basis of ethnicity only, this would have hidden the size of the Muslim prison population. 'South Asians' only constituted 3 per cent of the male and 1 per cent of the female prison population (Home Office, 2001: 108). Muslims account for 7 per cent of male and 3 per cent of female inmates (Guessous, Hooper and Moorthy, 2001: 6). The statistics show that Muslims form a majority with a recorded religion among the 'South Asian category' (86 per cent), the largest faith community in the 'Chinese and other ethnicity' group (47 per cent) and the second largest group among 'black' prisoners (19 per cent) (Home Office, 2001: 115).

The 2001 census for the first time will provide data on the basis of religion, although, in England and Wales, religious affiliation was an optional question.[2] Muslim organizations and community leaders campaigned for and welcomed the inclusion of a question on religion in the census (The Runnymede Trust, 1997, p. 32). The Office of National Statistics (ONS) is considering producing a multi-source topic report on religion. This will pull together information from the 2001 census and other sources to provide a comprehensive and authoritative overview of key topics (Office of National Statistics, 2002).

The extent of discrimination against Muslims in France and Italy is also obscured by the unavailability of comprehensive statistics or other reliable data. As decisions about how to categorize people reflect political decisions about which patterns are likely to be important, and which groups deserve protection, launching research initiatives on the Muslim communities and collection of data would send a strong signal that states are committed to the protection of Muslim communities along with racial and ethnic communities.

The lack of data is often justified by concerns for privacy and protection of personal information. Ironically, some states used the lack of reliable data as grounds for dismissing critiques of their record on providing adequate protection to minority groups against discrimination and violence. Italy objected to ECRI findings that the number of racist acts in Italy was higher than the number of criminal proceedings before the court, on the grounds that this conclusion was 'not enough supported by factual elements, or statistical data' though such data was not officially available.[3]

## Challenging notions of equality and non-discrimination

In France since the 1970s, a series of laws have been adopted to facilitate the fight against discrimination, culminating with the adoption of comprehensive anti-discrimination legislation in November 2001. In the face of growing evidence of discrimination against minority groups, including Muslims, there has been increasing recognition from officials and the public that there is need for State-supported action to ensure that these laws are respected in practice. However, the need for anti-discrimination policies and programmes is always balanced against and placed within the republican principle of equality.

In France, racial, ethnic, national or religious discrimination was first prohibited in relation to provision of goods and services and employment in 1972.[4] Discrimination on the basis of gender and family circumstances was prohibited in 1975,[5] customs in 1985,[6] and disabilities and health status in 1989.[7] The 1992 Penal Code prohibits discrimination on grounds of 'real or supposed membership or non-membership of an ethnicity, nation, race or religion,'[8] *inter alia*, and prohibits direct discrimination by public authorities on these grounds.[9] Legislation adopted in November 2001 establishes a general framework for fighting discrimination.

In France, claims for equality and protection from discrimination by Muslims challenge the existing understanding of equality. The traditional approach has been to promote the assumption of a single, national public French identity for those immigrants who attain their citizenship—an ideal of national integration that is difficult to reconcile with cultural linguistic or other affiliations that do not accord with those of the majority. For example, while France is a signatory and has ratified the major international human rights instruments on discrimination, it has always entered reservations on articles that relate to the rights of individuals belonging to ethnic, religious and linguistic minorities. These reservations deny the existence of minorities in France. France has also refused to ratify the Council of Europe's Framework Convention for the Protection of National Minorities. In this context, the claim for special rights by any minority group are perceived as a threat to the Republic's citizenship structure in the long term (Audrad, 2001: 227-243). As one expert has noted, in this way 'the immigrant problem has been quickly transformed into a reflection on the development of French society and its capacity for integration' (see Maschino, 2002).

The cultural difference of Muslim French citizens is regarded as particularly unfavourable, as adherence to Islam is considered to be at odds with republican values, especially *'laicité* (secularism). A rigid interpretation of *'laicité* makes it difficult to embrace multiculturalism, as culturally and religiously specific characteristics are considered secondary to the concept of equality for all individuals.

Thus the notion of equality in France is focused on formal equality. This is based on the Aristotelian notion that likes should be treated alike, and that fairness requires consistency of treatment. But this conceals assumptions that underline decisions about when two individuals are relevantly alike and about distinctions that are legitimate and can be taken into account in making people not alike. Equality as consistency of treatment is problematic in its treatment of difference. Cultural and religious differences can require positive measures that value difference to achieve equality. Equality as consistency of treatment requires people to be treated the same irrespective of their group identity. It ignores or denies the importance that group identity may play. Cultural, religious and ethnic group membership is an important aspect of an individual's identity. To abstract the individual from their context is to clothe them in the attributes of the dominant culture or ethnicity (see Fredman, 2001).

One of the innovations of the legislation adopted in 2001 in France was the inclusion of the notion of indirect discrimination. This is a move away from equality as consistency of treatment and towards substantive equality. It looks at the disparate impact of equal treatment and creates room for developing a notion of equality that can accommodate diversity. Indirect discrimination allows for an examination of what appear to be neutral provisions or criterion, and shows the extent to which the dominant culture or religion is favoured. Proof of indirect discrimination requires evidence that a particular requirement has a disparate impact not on the individual alone but on the individual as a member of a protected group. Here the difficulties of collecting ethnic and religious data will be a significant weakness for indirect discrimination cases. While the legislation covers indirect discrimination it does not provide a clear definition; according to one expert, doing so 'would imply referring to [special] categories of the population (which is prohibited by the French Constitution)' (Borillo: 126).

Attempts to tackle indirect and structural discrimination are more developed in the UK. But here again the focus is on ethnic and racial discrimination rather than on religious discrimination. The UK does not have comprehensive anti-discrimination legislation. Northern Ireland is the only region to have anti-discrimination laws that prohibit discrimination on the grounds of religious belief. There it is illegal for public bodies[10] as well as for employers and providers of goods, services and facilities to discriminate on such grounds.[11] Public authorities are required not merely to refrain from discriminating but, in carrying out their functions, must also 'have due regard to the need to promote equality of opportunity between persons of different religious belief' and 'have regard to the desirability for promoting goods relations between persons of different religious belief, political opinion or racial group.'[12] This legislation is plainly influenced by the particular sectarian issues within Northern Ireland and is focused on the Protestant and Roman Catholic communities. This is clear, for example, from the definition of 'affirmative action' as 'action designed to secure fair participation in employment by members of the Protestant, or members of the Roman Catholic community, in Northern Ireland.'[13]

Although there is no express reference to religious discrimination in the RRA, several ways have been found to extend protection under the Act to some religious groups. Some religious communities, such as the Sikh[14] and Jewish communities,[15] have won protection against direct and indirect discrimination by emphasizing the extent to which they also constitute ethnic groups. Muslims,[16] Rastafarians[17] and Jehovah's Witnesses[18] have been held not to constitute racial or ethnic groups. The development of the law in this way has created a hierarchy of protection. Muslim communities feel particularly aggrieved that they are not offered the same level of protection that is given to other minority religious communities that are able to bring themselves within the definition of an ethnic group. The development of the case law in this way has resulted in 'inconsistency, inequity and a hierarchy of protection and provisions afforded to different ethnic minorities' (FAIR, 2002: 13).

Members of some Muslim communities have pursued the strategy of obtaining protection under the RRA through the concept of indirect discrimination. For example, actions taken by an employer causing detriment to Muslims as a class, such as refusal to allow time off work for religious holidays, might be held to constitute indirect racial discrimination against those from an ethnic or national origin that is predominantly Muslim, such as Pakistani and Bangladeshi Muslims.[19] However, a European, Afro-Caribbean or Chinese Muslim cannot use this strategy as they come from ethnic communities where Muslims are a minority (see Franks, 2000: 917-929).

The Report on the death of black teenager Stephen Lawrence was a major impetus for changes in race equality laws (Stephen Lawrence Inquiry, 1999). It recognized the existence of 'institutional racism' in the Police Services and in other institutions countrywide (Stephen Lawrence Inquiry, 1999, para. 6.39). It defined 'institutional racism' as,

> the collective failure of an organization to provide an appropriate and professional service to people because of their colour, culture or ethnic origin. It can be seen or detected in processes, attitudes and behaviour which amounted to discrimination through unwitting prejudice, ignorance, thoughtlessness and racist stereotyping which disadvantages minority ethnic people. It persists because of the failure of the organization openly and adequately to recognise and address the existence and causes by policy, example and leadership. Without recognition and action to eliminate such racism it can prevail as part of the ethos or culture of the organization. It is a corrosive disease. (Stephen Lawrence Inquiry, 1999, para. 6.34)

Muslims argue that where there is institutional racism there is institutional anti-Muslim discrimination which manifests itself in,

> [S]topping and searching Muslim youths because they look like 'fundamentalists'; when a social worker assesses a Muslim couple for adoption and judges them to be unsuitable as 'fundamentalists' because they pray five times a day; when Muslim children in care get placed in non-Muslim homes because the authorities insist on placing a child in a racially matching family regardless of the child's religious heritage, when agencies only advertise in the 'ethnic' press for job vacancies thereby excluding potential Muslim applicants for jobs, when the only system for obtaining promotion is by hobnobbing with colleagues in the pub which would exclude, for example, alcohol-unfriendly Muslims for promotion (Khan, 1999: 26).

One consequence of the Report is the RRAA 2000, which requires that public bodies eliminate unlawful racial discrimination, promote equality of opportunity and promote good race relations between people of different racial groups. However, the new legislation works within the framework of existing race legislation, and in doing so reproduces its defects. Namely, the protection and provisions of the Act, too, are extended to ethnic-religious minority communities but not to non-ethnic religious communities, a fact which has come in for criticism from Muslim organizations:

> There are no moral or legal justifications for giving more comprehensive protection against discrimination to some religious minorities, (e.g., Sikh and Jews), whilst denying them to others (e.g., Muslims) who are clearly at risk of discrimination on the grounds of their religion (FAIR, 2002: 13).

## THE LIMITS OF PROHIBITING DISCRIMINATION

Pressure for amendments to existing legislation and policy for tackling discrimination on the grounds of religion or belief comes from the European Union and the need for implementation of the Employment Directive, (DTI, 2000) which covers discrimination on the grounds of religion or belief; new legislation must be in place by December 2003. However, the Directive only covers discrimination in employment; it does not cover areas outside employment, for example, in the provision of goods, services, facilities, housing or education. The OSI research indicated that there was significant discrimination in all these areas in the UK, France and Italy.

The approach to discrimination under the EC Directive can also be criticized for focusing on a negative prohibition on discrimination rather than a positive duty to promote equality. Critics have called for the development of a new generation of equality legislation, which would require promotion of equality of opportunity for all. The new legislation would create a positive duty on public authorities to promote equality and eliminate unlawful discrimination. This duty would apply to their procurement, grant and subsidy, licensing and franchising functions. It would require employers to take responsibility for achieving equality through developing equal employment and pay equity plans. Professor Sandra Fredman (2000: 145-168 at 164) has made the argument for this proactive approach persuasively:

> At the root of the positive duty is a recognition that societal discrimination extends well beyond individual acts of prejudice. Equality can only be meaningfully advanced if practices and structures are altered proactively by those in a position to bring about real change, regardless of fault or original responsibility. Positive duties are, therefore, proactive rather than reactive, aiming to introduce equality measures rather than to respond to complaints by individuals...in order to trigger the duty, there is no need to prove

individual prejudice, or to link disparate impact to an unjustifiable practice or condition. Instead, it is sufficient to show a pattern of under-representation or other evidence of structural discrimination. Correspondingly, the duty bearer is identified as the body in the best position to perform this duty. Even though not responsible for creating the problem in the first place, such duty bearers become responsible for participating in its eradication. A key aspect of positive duties, therefore, is that they harness the energies of employers and public bodies. Nor is the duty limited to providing compensation for an individual victim. Instead, positive action is required to achieve change, whether by encouragement, accommodation, or structural change.'

For over two decades the European Union has been a key driver for tackling discrimination. For much of this time its focus has been on sex discrimination. Through the introduction of Article 13 in the Amsterdam treaty the EU has taken a welcome first step in addressing issues of discrimination in other areas. At the time there was great scepticism as to whether the Member States would ever agree on a Directive. The Directives should only be the start point for implementing Article 13. In its next steps the EU needs to ensure an equal level of protection for all forms of discrimination. Furthermore, it needs to move beyond its negative prohibitions on discrimination to positive duties on states to tackle discrimination and promote equality.

Finally, it is important to place discrimination in the wider policy context. Legal protection from discrimination is only one tool for addressing Islamophobia and anti-Muslim prejudice. Effectively tackling discrimination requires using all available policy tools. Discrimination can be the result of treating Muslims on the basis of Islamophobic stereotypes, rather than on evidence about the particular individual. For example, people may assume that a Muslim woman wearing a *hijab* is oppressed and has no choice in her mode of dress, or a Muslim man with a beard may be viewed as threatening: 'a fundamentalist'. These stereotypes are sources of discrimination but tackling them requires policies beyond a legal prohibition on discrimination. Islamophobic discourses that generate such stereotypes should be countered by support for challenging alterative voices. There is a role here for arts, media and cultural policies that encourage and support Muslim participation in all areas of cultural life from film, television and music to art and journalism.

## REFERENCES

An-Nisa Society, *Second* Review *of the Race Relations Act 1976—A Response*, Wembley.

Audrad, C., 'Multiculturalisme et tranformation de la citoyennete' (Multiculturalism and the transformation of citizenship), *Archives de philosophie du droit*, 2001: 45.

Borillo, D., *Les instruments juridique francais et europeens dans la mise en place du principe d'egalite et de non-discrimination*m (French and European legal tools in the implementation of the principle of equality and non-discrimination).

Cabinet Office Strategy Unit, *Ethnic Minorities and the Labour Market: final report*, Cabinet Office, London, 2003.

DTI (Department of Trade and Industry), *Towards Equality and Diversity: Implementing the Employment and Race Directives*, London, 2002.

FAIR (Forum Against Islamophobia and Racism), *Towards Equality and Diversity— Implementing the Employment and Race Directives: Response from the Forum Against Islamophobia and Racism*, London, 2002.

Franks, M., 'Crossing the borders of whiteness? White Muslim women who wear the *hijab* in Britain today,' *Ethnic and Racial Studies*, Vol. 23 (5), 2000.

Fredman, S., 'Equality: A New Generation?' *Industrial Law Journal*, Vol. 30, No. 2, 2000.

Fredman, S., *Discrimination Law*, Oxford University Press, Oxford, 2001.

Guessous, F., Hooper N. and Moorthy, U., *Religion in Prisons 1999 and 2000*, Home Office, London, 2001.

Home Office, *Prison Statistics England and Wales* 2000, Cm. 5250, London, 2001.

Khan, K., 'Where's the Muslim in MacPherson's Black and White Britain?' *Q-News*, March 1999.

Maschino, M., 'Liberty, Equality, Identity: Do you eat couscous at home?' *Le Monde diplomatique*, June, 2002.

Mason, D., *Race and Ethnicity in Modern Britain*, Oxford University Press, Oxford, 2000.

Modood, T., *Not Easy Being British*, Trentham Books, Stoke on Trent, 1992.

Office of National Statistics, *Religion: Scoping Report*, London, 2002.

The Runnymede Trust Commission on British Muslims and Islamophobia, *Islamophobia— a challenge for us all*, London, 1997.

The Runnymede Trust Commission on the Future of Multi-Ethnic Britain, *The Future of Multi-ethnic Britain—The Parekh Report*, Profile Books, London, 2000.

'*Stephen Lawrence Inquiry*', Report of an Inquiry by Sir William MacPherson of Cluny, Cm. 4262-I, London: HMSO, 1999.

## NOTES

1. *Monitoring the EU Accession Process: Minority Protection Volume II—Case Studies in Selected Member States*, (Open Society Institute, Budapest): Tufyal Choudhury is the author of the United Kingdom report, the authors of the France report were Valerie Amiraux and Nardissa Leghmizi, and for the Italy report, Silvio Ferrari, Filippo Corbetta and Gianluca Parolin.

2. In England and Wales the census form asked the optional question: 'What is your religion?' In Scotland and Northern Ireland there were two non-optional questions: 'What religion, religious denomination or body do you belong to?' and 'What religion, religious denomination or body were you brought up in?'

3. European Commission Against Racism and Intolerance, Second report on Italy, adopted on 22 June 2000 and made public on 23 April 2002.

4. Law 72-546 of 1 July 1972. Sanctions were outlined in the Penal Code, Art. 415 (amended as Art. 225-1).

5. Law 85-772 (1975).

6. Law 89-18 (January 1989).

7. Law 90-602 (July 1990).

8. Penal Codes of 22 July 1992, amended 1 March 1994, Art. 225-1 to 225-4.

9. Penal Codes of 22 July 1992, amended 1 March 1994, Art. 432-7.

10. Northern Ireland Act 1998 (hereafter NIA), s. 76.

11. Fair Employment and Treatment (Northern Ireland) Order 1998 SI No. 3162, (hereafter FETO).

12. NIA, s. 75.

13. FETO, Art. 4.

14. *Mandla v Dowell Lee* [1983] 2 AC 548.

15. *Seide v Gillette Industries Ltd* [1980] IRLR 427.

16. *Tariq v Young* Case 247738/88, EOR Discrimination Case Law Digest No. 2.

17. *Crown Suppliers (Property Services Agency) v Dawkins* [1993] ICR 517.

18. *Lovell-Badge v Norwich City College of Further and Higher Education*, Case No: 1502237/97, (Spring 1999) 39 EOR Discrimination Case Law Digest, 4.

20. *J H Walker Ltd v Hussain* [1996] IRLR 11 EAT. Other cases where the indirect discrimination provisions have been used include: *CRE v. Precision Manufacturing Services Ltd.*, 10 October 1991, Case No 4106/91, (Summer 1992) 12 EOR Case Law Digest, 8; *Yassin v. Northwest Homecare* (Spring 1994) 19 EOR Case Law Digest 2.

# 11

## Terrorizing Communities:
## the so-called 'War on Terror' in the UK
### *Les Levidow*[1]

> 'My name is Shazia Mirza. At
> least that is what it says on
> my pilot's licence.'
>
> Female, Muslim, stand-up
> comic (Bedell, 2003).

## INTRODUCTION

In the so-called 'war on terror', migrant communities hear contradictory messages. They are told that this is 'not a war on Islam', but rather an essential effort to pre-empt threats of violence. Yet the supposed threat is linked largely with communities originating from Muslim countries. Their social networks and cultural practices are treated as 'suspicion' of terrorist links. Indeed, public anxieties are projected onto entire migrant communities. The above quote illustrates a Muslim response, using conventions of British humour to subvert racist fears and stereotypes.

This chapter will sketch how migrant communities have become terrorized (mainly in the UK), some effects on Muslims in particular and the Europe-wide dynamics.

## 'TERRORISM' SCARES

In the UK, the public has been encouraged to fear foreigners, especially those from Muslim countries. As in George Orwell's novel *1984*, permanent propaganda campaigns continually invent enemies to justify a perpetual war. Imaginary links are drawn between Iraq, al-Qaeda, refugees, Muslim networks and organized violence.

The supposed need for special powers has been justified by high-profile police actions, especially by using 'anti-terrorist' powers to arrest people who could have been held instead under immigration law or under the ordinary criminal law. In the run-up to the US–UK military invasion of Iraq, the government attempted to make Britons fear violent attacks from Islamic fundamentalists. For example, it sent tanks to Heathrow airport, branded refugee circles as an 'al-Qaeda cell', spread fears about a cyanide attack in the London tube and linked detainees with the poison, ricin.

Despite all the scares, no prosecution case has presented clear evidence of plans for organized violence. For example, ricin 'traces' found were no greater than those which naturally occur in castor oil beans. Apparently these were being used for quite different purposes: to extract a substance useful as an ink remover, e.g. for forging travel documents. Yet the mass media has encouraged public fears about mass poisoning and 'chemical weapons factories'. Such stories appear not only in the tabloid newspapers but also in *The Financial Times*. Later, the US government claimed to find ricin at an Iraqi factory, while implying a link to those found in London.

In such ways, malicious rumours about detainees have been spread by government sources and reproduced by the mass media—even before criminal trials. Ordinarily, such character assassination would be treated as contempt of court. Yet this practice has been tolerated and has become routine. Consequently, 'The legal procedures have been atrophied and are by now merely a charade of in-built protections which do not really exist', argues a leading solicitor for some defendants (Peirce, 2003).

## NEW POLICE POWERS

How did this happen? Long before the 11 September attacks on the Twin Towers, the Terrorism Act 2000 broadened the definition of terrorism to encompass ordinary political activities. It includes simply 'the threat' of 'serious damage to property', in ways 'designed to influence the government' for a 'political cause'. Organizations can be banned on the basis that their activities in other countries fit this broad definition. This law creates new crimes of association, e.g. with banned organizations, and with property or funds that may be used for 'terrorism'. This framework potentially stigmatizes a wide range of community networks and political activity as 'terrorism'.

Soon after 9/11, the Home Office banned 21 organizations. Many have roots in communities in the UK, e.g. the Kurdistan Workers Party (PKK), International Sikh Youth Federation, Tamil Tigers, et cetera. Indeed, Kurdish communities have regarded the PKK as a means for national self-defence and self-determination against Turkish state oppression.

Since 2000, ordinary political activities have been prosecuted in court as 'terrorism'. Defendants (and their supporters) have been pressurized to act as police informants. In such ways, the bans are used to deter solidarity with resistance against oppressive foreign regimes, often supported by the UK government.

Extra powers of detention and harassment can be exercised beyond any judicial scrutiny. Such powers are triggered by mere suspicion that someone may be involved in so-called 'terrorism'—including conduct that does not constitute a criminal offence, or anticipation of some future activities. People become subject to attacks on civil liberties, such as detention without adequate legal representation. For example, anyone can be held without charge for up to seven days.

After the 11 September attacks, moreover, the Anti-terrorism, Crime and Security Act (ATCSA) 2001 extended police powers of detention and surveillance. It even authorized the internment of non-UK citizens. Thus, inequality before the law was entrenched. That law even imposed a general duty to give the authorities any information about suspected 'terrorist' activities.

Since December 2001, several Muslims have been detained for an indefinite period, with no requirement for disclosure of the supposed evidence against them. In effect, they have been 'disappeared' by the state. Police have warned relatives and friends of the internees against any contact with their families, thus spreading fear about who will be next for internment.

Much use of these powers relates to immigration issues and political activities. Of all the people arrested under the legislation, few have been charged—and those mainly under immigration law. Most could have been arrested under such law or under the ordinary criminal law, instead of 'anti-terrorist' powers (IRR, 2003). Some were charged with membership of a banned organization but were not accused of any specific activity that would be otherwise illegal in the UK (see next section).

After a UK citizen was implicated in a suicide bombing in Israel, the entire family was arrested under the ATCSA 2001. They were accused of failing to pass on information about the intentions of the alleged bomber. Such arrests set an ominous precedent for the extension of police informants and thus for distrust within communities.

## BANS AND PERSECUTION

Bans on organizations, and subsequent prosecutions against a few individuals, have been experienced as an attack on entire communities, e.g. Kurds, Sikhs, Tamils and North Africans. Political activities come under constant surveillance and are subjected to harassment as 'terrorism'. Moreover, there have been attempts to intimidate migrant communities and to turn refugees into police informants. Here are two high-profile examples that illustrate the broader aims and effects.

Kurdish case: in 2002 campaigners for Kurdish rights were prosecuted for 'terrorist' links. Evidence in court included photos of defendants holding placards that listed several banned organizations. In reality they had been among over 6,000 demonstrators ridiculing the bans, e.g. by wearing T-shirts that said 'I am the PKK' (Kurdistan Workers Party). At least one defendant was approached by Special Branch officers asking him to provide information on other political activists, while implying that such cooperation could help him to gain financial benefit and refugee status. Fortunately the defendants obtained a jury trial, and defence witnesses led the jury to question the prosecution case, so that the case was eventually abandoned. In that case, Turkish government persecution of Kurds was extended to the UK.

Vatan case: distributors of the Turkish-language magazine, Vatan, have been harassed since late 2000, and copies have been confiscated. In January 2003 they were arrested on grounds that the magazine was 'terrorist property', i.e. promoting and financing a banned organization. Moreover, Special Branch officers have visited more than a hundred shopkeepers to identify those who have helped to sell the magazine or contributed funds to families of political prisoners in Turkey. They were asked whether they would testify against the defendants. If reluctant, they were told, 'Your job/shop/car is not as secure as you would like to think it is.'

## COMMUNITIES STIGMATIZED AS 'TERRORIST' NETWORKS

'Anti-terrorism' powers have been used in arbitrary ways. Communal, friendship and political networks of migrant communities are readily stigmatized as 'suspected' terrorist activities. Possession of videos with bin Laden has been used to brand refugee circles as an 'al-Qaeda cell'. When Muslims are prosecuted for ordinary illegal activities, e.g. credit-card fraud or forged travel documents, these are portrayed as integral parts of 'terrorist' networks, yet without any evidence of plans for violent activity.

Consequently, entire communities have felt terrorized. For example, police actions have intensified Muslims' feelings that they live in a state of siege, while encouraging popular prejudices against them; mere arrest has undermined people's reputations, livelihoods and freedom to travel; a few dozen arrests, with just a few prosecutions, have effectively intimidated entire communities. Through an apparently random, open-ended series of arrests, 'The use of 'anti-terrorist' powers has now paralysed and terrified significant parts of the Muslim community in this country', according to a solicitor who deals with the human consequences (Peirce, 2003); anticipating arbitrary persecution, many Muslims keep telephone numbers of a solicitor, yet this is interpreted as suspicious by the topsy-turvy logic of the police; refugees fear that the authorities here will persecute them in ways similar to their own governments or deport them back home, so they become more likely to attack the police. This may explain why a policeman was knifed to death in January 2003 in Manchester, yet the mass media linked this attack to a 'ricin plot'.

Economic resources of communities are also threatened. The ATCSA 2001 empowers the authorities to seize property or cash, and to freeze bank accounts, in cases of suspected 'terrorist' purposes. These powers have been used to investigate charities of migrant communities, especially Muslims. Some bank accounts have been frozen.

Regardless of whether any wrongdoing is eventually found, an asset freeze damages reputations and undermines trust within communities. 'Muslim international humanitarian relief agencies and charities have been adversely affected through the discriminatory and disproportionate application of freezing orders. Although most Muslim charities that have been investigated by the Charity Commission due to their possible links with terrorism have been exonerated, they have suffered heavily. The psychological impact of applying freezing orders has meant a haemorrhaging of donations for Muslim charities as a result of the stigma of being affiliated with terrorism' (FAIR, 2003: 10).

Moreover, such communities fear that their cultural custom of cash transactions may be treated as suspicion of terrorist links. 'Muslim and other minority communities in Britain tend to conduct their religious, business, charitable and other transactions largely in cash' (FAIR, 2003). This is especially the case for Muslims, many of whom avoid banks, e.g. because they oppose usury, or because they suffered from the crash of the Bank of Credit & Commerce International (BCCI). Yet investigations may misinterpret and effectively penalize cash transactions, outside any judicial procedure.

## MUSLIM RESPONSES IN THE UK

Combined with anti-Muslim reportage in the mass media, state persecution in the UK has pushed many Muslims into a siege mentality. They distrust institutions such as local government and the Labour Party. In the most recent local elections in May 2003, many shifted to the Liberal Democrats or did not vote at all. Many express ambivalence about being British. Says a 23-year-old, 'I am ashamed to call myself British... Is this how our country fights terrorism, with its own brand of high-tech military terror?' The 'anti-terror' laws have been criticized by organizations such as the Muslim Parliament and the Forum Against Islamophobia & Racism (FAIR, 2003). Like civil liberties organizations, they do so by appealing to traditional legal norms of Britain.

Muslim youth have responded in various ways. Many fearfully avoid any involvement in politics or public life. A significant minority (especially young men) look to religion as a political solution. In some cases, their activities become insular, as a means to avoid persecution; they secretly discuss ways to fight back as Muslims. Some mosques had been a focal point for jihadis, but this role has become more difficult. According to one writer (Nahdi, 2003), 'Pressure from the authorities, combined with the sentiments of most congregations, have pushed many of these extremists out of the mosques'.

By contrast to that small minority, many Muslims (especially young women) break out of insularity. They self-confidently define themselves as British—against the government. For example, 'Just Peace' links Muslim youth with the Stop the War Coalition, thus encouraging links with the wider British society that opposed the attacks on Afghanistan and Iraq.

## EUROPEANIZING THE 'WAR ON TERROR'

The 'war on terror' has been Europeanized, often in the name of 'security', not only by right-wing parties. Scares about refugees' links with terrorism have served as a pretext for harassing or even excluding them, in ways that intimidate entire communities. In 1993, Germany had already banned the PKK and any other Kurdish organizations suspected of financing the party. Later, the SDP-Green government there imposed more stringent rules on refugees, on grounds that 'the restriction of the basic rights of asylum seekers is justified in order to protect national security and public order'.

After the 11 September attacks in the USA, the Socialist-Green government of France enacted a *Loi Sécuritaire Anti-terroriste*, which is used to persecute foreigners, mainly Muslims. In early 2003, the new right-wing government there proposed a *Loi Sécuritaire Quartier*, aimed at regulating everyday behaviour of Muslim youth in the low-income, mainly immigrant *banlieues*. Such measures accommodate racist scares about Islam as being uncivilized, an enemy of peace, et cetera, rather than counter them.

Moreover, state repression is being harmonized. Pressed by the UK and Spain, in December 2001 the EU Council redefined terrorism more broadly, in ways similar to the UK. 'Terrorism' now encompasses any criminal activity which is undertaken for 'unduly compelling a government or international organization to perform or abstain from performing any act'; likewise any criminal activity 'directed against one or more countries, their institutions or their people with the objective to intimidate them and to destroy or seriously change the political, economic and social structures of a country'. Moreover, any 'passive or active support' for such activities was prohibited. On this basis, the Council mandated member states to ban a similar list of 23 organizations and to freeze their assets (EU Council, 2001a). Thus, various political activities readily become 'terrorism'.

Moreover, a state culture of suspicion directs its scrutiny at foreigners and especially Muslims (Fekete, 2002: 12). This suspicion may be intensified as the 'security' services set up a Europe-wide 'anti-terrorist roadmap'. A database will include various political activists and foreigners, thus linking all these categories in practice (EU Council, 2001b).

## CULTURE OF SUSPICION TOWARDS MUSLIMS

In all the ways described here, Muslims are portrayed as a source of 'insecurity' or danger to the general public—simply on grounds of vague suspicion. 'Anti-terrorist/security' measures are presented as a solution to that false problem. In terms of justice, 'security' should mean protection from oppressive regimes, yet for many Muslims it means the opposite—a greater danger from such regimes or from the British state acting as their proxy. Overall, the 'anti-terrorism' legislation is an attack on democracy and especially on migrant communities. Its wording and use has blurred crucial distinctions—between political activity, communal networks, immigration issues and organized violence.

Protecting the European public from violence does not drive or explain the new measures. Rather, they have political purposes, for example, to intimidate minority communities, especially refugees, against taking part in political activities—and to isolate such communities; to attack communal and friendship networks, especially in Muslim communities; to deter support here for internal resistance against oppressive regimes abroad from which refugees have fled; to protect foreign regimes which are supported by the UK government; to give governments unlimited access to information on political activities; to gain extra powers for dealing with immigration, while portraying refugees as dangerous; to justify continued employment for the secret police, in a period when the conflict in Ireland no longer provides a credible threat to the public.

Implicitly, an epidemiological model of terrorism is used to construct Muslim communities as dangerous. Their social networks, cultural practices or minor crimes are treated as 'suspicion' of terrorist links—which therefore must be identified and stopped in advance. Through scare stories and high-profile arrests, Muslims become 'the Other', onto which a society can project its own fears and denials. In particular, citizens can evade the consequences of Britain's support for foreign governments whose state repression generates political violence and refugees. We are all targets of this 'anti-terrorist' propaganda, manipulation, intimidation or repression—the latter directed mainly at migrant communities, especially Muslims (CAMPACC, 2003).

These dynamics set a new European context for Muslim identities and their relationships with the rest of society. I wish to suggest that a research-activist network could take into account these ominous developments, and be part of the way forward.

## REFERENCES

Bedell, G., 'Veiled humour', *The Observer Review*, 20 April 2003.

CAMPACC, 'The 'War on Terror' at Home: we are all targets of the state', February, www.cacc.org.uk, 2003.

EU Council Common Position on Combating Terrorism, available at www.statewatch.org/news/2002/jan/02euter.htm, 2001a.

EU Council Working Party on Terrorism, 'Presentation of a Presidency initiative for the introduction of a standard form for exchanging information on terrorist incidents', December, 2001b.

Fekete, L., *Racism: the Hidden Cost of September 11*, Institute of Race Relations, London, www.irr.org.uk, 2002.

IRR, 'Terror policing brings many arrests but few charges', Institute of Race Relations, London, www.irr.org.uk/2003/march/ak000002/html, 2003.

FAIR, *ATCSA 2001 Review: a submission from FAIR*, London: Forum Against Islamophobia & Racism [May], 2003.

Nahdi, F., 'Young, British and ready to fight', *The Guardian*, 1 April 2003.

Peirce, G., 'Terrorising communities', *Campaign Against Racism and Fascism (CARF)* magazine, Spring, 2003.

## NOTE

1. This chapter was written in 2003, since when major developments have taken place.

# 12

# The Politics of Identity

*Imran Khan*

I was recently reminded by a friend of an old joke told by a famous comedian some years ago. I cannot recall the name of the comedian but I can tell you that the joke has been somewhat updated in terms of personnel. It goes something like this: Jacques Chirac, Fidel Castro and Tony Blair happen to be visiting an art gallery when they come across a painting showing Adam and Eve in classic repose. The three begin to discuss the identity of the painter. Chirac says that the painter is of French origin, stating that the painting shows a romantic scene full of love; Castro says that the painter must be of Eastern European origin as the two are sharing what little they have equally between them. Blair, however, is convinced that the painter is British. Pressed as to why he thinks so, he states that the two are half-clothed and half-starving, yet they still think they are in paradise.

The joke, if it can be called that, was told to illustrate a point: its punchline is only effective if the audience is in on the joke—namely, the nature of the British as viewed by the British. I retell the joke for a particular reason, which is to illustrate the point that there are certain views of the British or Britishness that are held by different parts of our community. One such view came from an Asian man in Burnley about the events that had occurred in his area last summer. He said this, 'Racial attacks—that's what Britain's all about, isn't it?'

To many in the black communities in this country, this comment, perhaps, epitomizes the perception they have of what is at the heart of our society. To these individuals, notions of diversity and multiculturalism are meaningless epithets designed to cloak the reality they face on a daily basis. In a sense, little has changed for the black communities over the past few decades, except for the terminology used to express their existence. We were coloureds, then Asian and Afro-Caribbean, ethnic minorities, minority ethnic communities, visible minorities, people of colour and now part of a diverse community.

For my part I always thought the most appropriate term was the 'black communities'. To treat the issue on the basis of ethnicity alone is to view it in apolitical terms. Yet the question of race is nothing more and nothing less than political in nature. It always struck me as rather odd, for example, to hear of newer and more prosaic terms for the black communities in the US, as if that change in nomenclature alone would somehow redress the reality that black communities faced in that country. For the first time last year the black prison population in the USA passed the 50 per cent mark. The fact that they were now 'people of colour' made not an iota of difference. The point I make somewhat clumsily is that the past few decades have seen attempts at integration on an ethnic/multicultural level and not at a political level. We have allowed ourselves to be 'ethnicized', believing that to be the route to acceptance: understand who I am and you will accept who I am.

This has failed, and failed abysmally in my view. It may be that we all now celebrate Diwali, Eid and Christmas in equal measure but it does not stop the racism that is so rife in society. True equality and enfranchisement comes about through political change and not by virtue of some constructed notion of a rainbow coalition among various ethnic groups. There is no point in celebrating our diversity when it is literally only skin deep.

In my view today's concept of diversity, the successor to multiculturalism, has done the black communities a disservice. It has masked the reality that exists, and suggested progress when there has been little, if any. The history of the West is clear. Black people have been subjected to centuries of slavery, decades of second-class citizenship, widespread legalized discrimination, economic persecution, educational deprivation and cultural stigmatization. We have been bought, sold, killed, beaten, raped, excluded, exploited, shamed and scorned for a very long time. The word racism is hardly an adequate description of our experience.

We now live in very difficult and extraordinary times. As one commentator put it, 'We have come a full and bloody circle.' It started with the toppling of the Twin Towers in New York and ended with the shuffling of rubble in Kabul and the bombing of Baghdad. We now live in an age where an act of terror killing thousands unleashed a war in the poorest country in the world. We live in an age where war was declared illegally against a country that has no known nuclear capability, while diplomacy takes place with a country that has.

We live in an age where the Quran is the best-selling publication in the world and Prime Minister Tony Blair an avid reader of it, yet racist attacks are escalating—you can be attacked on the streets simply because of your faith or your colour.

We live in an age where some long-term enemies have suddenly become sycophantic sweethearts. Ruthless dictators criticized in the past by the USA have become close and faithful allies—just look at Bush and Putin.

We live in an age where you can be sent to prison without trial; where on simple suspicion you can rot in prison for months; where over a thousand citizens can disappear into prisons and no one bats an eye lid; an age where confidential information about you can be disclosed to the police and the intelligence services; where your Internet and e-mail can be monitored and intercepted; where peaceful protest can become a crime.

We live in an age where US and British reaction to 11 September stands against the idea of defending Western civilization, all of this against a backdrop of the 'idea of a common people—the nation—with a shared history and proud culture to defend'. An emotional attachment to the nation has now provided legitimacy to engaging in conflict with those outside the nation. Yet not all in this country share this view: there has been an emergence of identity politics that has come to supply an anchor in the turbulent waters of globalization. Certain minority communities, having rejected assimilation into the national norm, are developing their own identities with a loyalty that is not necessarily tethered to the nation state or marked by geographical boundaries. Recent world events, perhaps, are testament to this emergence of a new British Muslim identity, which some in our community find hard to understand.

US and British reaction to 11 September stands against a background refrain of the defence of a common culture and of 'Western civilization' or 'the democracies' that apparently have a shared history and proud values to defend. This is an entirely constructed notion. Does our common 'Western heritage' also include Nazi history, black segregation in the US, Vietnam, or British colonialism? Emotional attachment to our new, fake community, designed to create a new sense of who is now 'inside' and who is 'outside', is being fastened with lashings of the same sort of media mood music we experienced after the death of Princess Diana.

Yet far from all in the West, let alone Britain, subscribe to this view or indeed support any part of it. The new myths that we all belong to a shared community in the West exclude the experience of millions and millions. For some groups, that exclusion has helped the emergence, as I have said, of identity politics, which has come to supply an anchor in the confusing, insubstantial froth that is the ideological out-wash from globalization. They have rejected assimilation into the freshly minted Western norm, and are developing their own identities with a loyalty not tethered to any inaccessible and unaccountable community called 'the West'.

The politics of identity also lend a content to the widespread anti-Western feelings and protests of the people in countries such as Saudi Arabia, Jordan and Egypt, where the governments' collusion with the USA has led to the growing Islamic militancy of the 'Arab street.' Saudi Arabia is now in serious difficulties and its monarchy, which guards the holy sites, is considered corrupt. Jordan's support for action against Afghanistan, with two-thirds of its population of Palestinian origin, has left its king in serious trouble. The story is much the same in Egypt. It owes more than $30 billion in foreign debt, despite cancellation of billions of dollars of debt during the Gulf war that paid for its anti-Saddam stance.

The more pro-US these governments have become over the past ten years, the more there is civil unrest and a rise in Islamic militancy. Now the globalized 'war against terrorism' has sharpened all these chronic contradictions into an acute stage.

It is in the nature of globalization that it factionalizes traditional leaderships in poorer countries and breaks down multi-ethnic and religious states, unleashing ethnic wars, balkanizing weak nations and displacing peoples. Access to the resources of the USA, the EU or Japan becomes the only basis for survival, and a mad scramble of elites in the poorer world ensues. These political elites seek any basis they can to mobilize a popular base or section of the armed forces in the countries they control, and thereby win the imprimatur of the World Bank or the IMF. But the population of large parts of the world cannot get their noses into this particular trough, even if they wanted to. And their economic and political exclusion can create a vacuum that is presently filling with the politics of identity.

The collapse of the Soviet state in the 1980s pole-axed the potential independence of Arab nationalism, leaving in its wake few choices, again feeding Islamic militancy among the poor. And US-sponsored dictators in the Middle East (and elsewhere) were encouraged to suppress all opposition, leaving any political radicalism to be channelled through the mosque.

We know that the tiniest village in Asia and the grand buildings of the big cities of the West are tied together in a thousand different ways. Globalization has made those links unbreakable. The West produces the poverty and cheap labour of the East and the South. The labour and resources of the East and the South help prop up the elites of the West. But globalization has made that system of relationships much clearer than at any time in human history, and has thereby produced a new and deadly contradiction. The extremes of poverty and wealth now face each other in the modern world. The results of injustice, starvation and war feed through the television screens of the West. The opposite is also true—the hypocrisy, violence and greed of the West are available to everyone else on the planet with eyes to see.

This contradiction has become acute and painfully obvious. The leadership of many poor countries seems, to their populations, to exist only according to the whims of the West. For the refugee, the only place on earth where there is the possibility of a half-decent life is the West. For the child of the East or South, their birthright seems stolen at the behest of the West. The militant and dispossessed with no sense of geographical or national boundary see opposition to the West in whatever form as justified and even—in the absence of any alternative explanation—a sacred duty.

Finally, as we are often told, a free market economy produces winners and losers. That is, of course, true, not only within countries but also between them. What Silvio Berlusconi called a 'clash of civilizations' is right, but without the plural. It is a clash within our one, globalized, market-driven civilization. We are not, fundamentally, in a struggle between peace and terror, or of the fundamentalist Middle East against the liberal West, but in the last analysis, of the rich against the poor. Each side of this struggle looks through its end of the same telescope at the distorted image of the other. Compounding this conflict are not just geographical considerations, and the cultural and political poverty of some of the new leaderships of the oppressed, but also racial segregation.

And how have we dealt with this? Well, a decade ago our security and well-being was said to be under threat from Irish organizations. Anti-terrorist laws had a dramatic and chilling effect on the whole of that community, not just in its freedom of expression but its freedom of movement: if you were Irish you could be singled out by the authorities for no reason other than that you were travelling to or from Ireland. If you were Irish you would have to anticipate family members disappearing into custody along the way, and sometimes wrongly convicted of terrorist offences. That experience of constant fear in the Irish community is being replicated in refugee communities today despite the British Home Secretary belatedly trying to stop the very process his government started by the introduction of the most far-reaching and draconian piece of legislation the UK has ever seen—the Terrorism Act of 2000. What this act did, in fact, was to bring into sharp relief that which had been taking place in a much more covert way over the last few years. Members of refugee communities from Egypt, Algeria, Pakistan, Saudi Arabia and other countries who were concerned about atrocities in their own regions were being detained by the authorities. What was clear was that while they all shared a common purpose in opposing tyranny in their own countries, they also shared what the British state regarded as a common trait—they were devout Muslims and therefore, in the eyes of the British, 'Islamic Fundamentalists'—an extremely racist and pejorative term used interchangeably in the media to describe terrorists. Thus, in one dramatic process whole refugee communities came to be criminalized. Under the Act, it is not just the use of violence that is criminalized, but the use or threat of any action involving violence to people or property or serious risk to health and safety that is designed to influence any government or intimidate members of the public anywhere in the world for political, religious or ideological reasons. That, apparently, is the UK's definition of terrorism, despite the fact there is no accepted definition of the term. The issue has long been the focus of international attention resulting in a proliferation of agreements relating to the issue. However, international consensus has never been achieved on a precise definition of what constitutes terrorism and who can be responsible for it. As some would say, one person's terrorist is another person's freedom fighter. We need only look at US foreign policy to see what we are dealing with. Was it an act of terrorism that led Madeline Albright (US Secretary of State) to say in 1996 that half a million Iraqi children dying as a result of economic sanctions against Iraq was 'a very hard choice'? Was it an act of terrorism that resulted in millions killed in the wars in Korea, Vietnam and Cambodia; or 17,500 killed when Israel (backed by the US) invaded Lebanon in 1982; or 200,000 Iraqis killed in the Gulf War; or thousands of Palestinians dying whilst fighting Israel's occupation of the West Bank? The list goes on, with millions dying in countries such as Yugoslavia, Somalia, Haiti, Chile, Nicaragua, El Salvador, the Dominican Republic and Panama.

But returning to the UK, the anti-terrorism legislation does not talk simply of destabilizing the 'health or safety' of this country but of any country. The act is a gift to the tyrannical regimes that refugees are fleeing from in the first place. If you support democracy and oppose tyranny you are persecuted in your own country and therefore flee. You arrive in the UK as a refugee, protest at what your government is doing and what happens to you? Detention and criminalization. The effect of the legislation is indeed terrifying, as it is intended to be. It is intended to frighten people, individually and collectively, so that among the decisions people will now have to make, for the first time in this country, is whether they intend to go on exercising their right to freedom of speech. Minority and refugee communities have been put into a straitjacket of fear, and those who most experience this fear are those who have already demonstrated immense courage in opposing tyranny in their own countries. Now, legitimate attempts to achieve democracy in their own countries by their actions are being intentionally stifled. The effect of the legislation is to make a mockery of the principles of democracy in this country, and certainly makes the prospect of democracy in others much more difficult.

The key philosophical and legal question at the moment is this: on what grounds and in what circumstances should the state be able to criminalize the activities of its citizens? Lord Woolf, one of the most senior judges in this country, said some months ago that we should not forget the mistakes that were made during the second world war when so-called 'aliens' were rounded up and detained without trial—something which is permissible with so-called 'suspected international terrorists' in the UK. So if you are a foreign national, you can be locked up without trial—indefinitely—when there is no evidence on which you could be prosecuted. This, of course, does not apply if you hold a British passport. The effect of this is best described by a legal journalist who states that it is a bit like the Home Secretary deciding that most muggers are black, so all suspicious-looking black people in an area are rounded up—but no whites, not even those who were thought to be planning an armed robbery. If we are really at risk in the UK from suspected terrorism then we ought to do what naturally should follow from such suspicion—introduce universal internment. If we tried that there would be uproar. The thing is that while the legislation affects so-called foreigners, refugees and asylum seekers, the majority of Britons feel safe in their beds. In doing so they fail the test set by Martin Luther King who said that the ultimate measure of a people is not where we stand in a moment of comfort and convenience, but where we stand in a time of challenge and controversy. What should our response be?

It should be nothing less than justice for the poor of the world: for the Palestinians, the Afghan people, for asylums seeker and refugees. If the huge resources that Western leaders command can be turned to war, then they can also be turned to justice. Terror is wrong—whether against America or by the West. What is the alternative? Justice. The invasion of Iraq must be stopped. State terror against the Palestinians and the Iraqi people must be ended. Is this too much to expect, too much to ask for? Why think that? The poor of the earth, including those in this country, the overwhelming majority of the population of the planet think this way. Why must the majority of the earth be silent while the rulers and the rich are heard? Demonstrations, conferences, pickets, leaflets and petitions helped to stop the war in Vietnam, helped to release Nelson Mandela. The power of the people we have seen in days and months gone by shows that the same result can be achieved with what is happening today.

# Conclusion

## Policy Implications:
## Youth, Gender, and Trans-Islam

*Kasturi Sen*

> Citizenship is not just recognition of formal legal status;
> it creates and sustains identities. Social citizenship
> crucially involves community, participation, identity and
> resources. It is clear that these resources critically involve
> participation in the economy as well as in politics and
> culture (see Turner's chapter).

The European Union was founded on the principles of liberty,
democracy, respect for human rights and fundamental freedoms, and
on the rule of law; principles which are common to all the member
states.[1] However, a recent survey suggests that young people of migrant
origin in many countries of Europe 'believe that a great deal more must
be done to guarantee the fundamental rights of each individual, and
even more importantly, to guarantee the rights of minorities and tackle
all forms of discrimination and racism by all available means.'[2]

This preamble of the European Treaty made in June 2004 is a fitting
introduction to the topic of young people of Muslim origin in Europe,
many of whom are third generation immigrants and were born in
Europe. However, as this book illustrates, many continue to feel
excluded and victimized by the forces of the state—where opportunities
are stillborn, education undermined and the future left uncertain, and
where communities feel threatened by terror legislation that appears to
target those of Muslim origin specifically and disproportionately in
many countries covered by the Accompanying Measure (Samad and
Sen, 2003).

This chapter will consider the origins of the experience of exclusion,
and implications of this for the several million young people of Muslim

origin living in Europe. It will refer to the influence of historical forces and legislative processes, and will assess their impact on the formation of identity and association among migrants of Muslim origin in selected countries of Europe, covered by this book—France, Germany, the Netherlands, the United Kingdom, Belgium and Sweden.

It will explore in particular the policy implications of the current discourse, and the experiences of migrants of Muslim origin in the context of European expansion and the desire for inclusive citizenship.

## HISTORICAL FACTORS

The experience of exploitation, isolation and insecurity is not a new one amongst migrant communities worldwide. There is much evidence in the history of migration to suggest major struggles for recognition and the claim for rights of citizenship amongst migrants in their countries of destination. However, the experience of Muslim migrants over the past few decades appears to be more distinct in nature, redefined and homogenized throughout Europe, despite historical and contextual differences and settlement patterns in each of the countries covered here. Some would suggest that this has occurred because of a long-standing intellectual antipathy, stemming from Orientalist interpretations of Islamic culture and society (as homogenous, unchanging and static), and can be put down to not dissimilar yet dichotomous distinctions elucidated between tradition and modernity in political relations. The aberrations in descriptions of so-called 'Muslim culture and society' are described and critiqued by Kamali, Turner and Samad in chapters of this book.

However, premised upon the low economic status of many migrant communities of Muslim origin throughout Europe, such categories have eventually been meted out in the form of discriminatory treatment and practice in social and legislative terms. This is manifest in the absence of coherent policies for integration in all spheres of society in such areas such as employment, education and housing, all of which are intrinsic to notions of belonging, citizenship and active participation. Most recent immigrants might claim that the experience of exclusion and discrimination is not an uncommon one, but migrants of Muslim origin appear to fall into a special category of exclusion, which is particular to that community alone, reinforcing social isolation and insecurity.

Whilst such discrimination has occurred to varying degrees in the countries under discussion and over a period of time, the situation has become much more visible since the events of 11 September, at institutional level and through individual experiences. The is being articulated through different forms of protest at the level of the community in a growing demand for greater recognition and need for the freedom of association, in particular the freedom to practise religious beliefs as enshrined in the European Constitution and the constitution of the individual countries (Glavanis et al., 1999; Anwar et al., 2001; see Kamali's chapter).

Since the events of 11 September, however, there appears to be a perception among policy-makers throughout Europe and in particular the United States, that terror networks based upon transnational ties may be most closely linked to communities of Muslim origin, and that any cultural associations need not only be controlled, but also to be monitored closely. Security networks and policies have therefore been backed up by legislation in a number of the countries, allowing for the scrutiny of, and monitoring of, associations amongst Muslims in particular (see Levidow's chapter).

Several chapters of this book emphasize the fact that Muslims in Europe (despite the generic terminology utilized for purposes of description) are shaped by different histories, languages and cultures as well as by socio-economic status, and cannot be lumped together as 'one' defined by religion alone. Many do not speak the same language or share the same tradition in diet, dress or prayer. Some are secular whilst others wish to practise their faith. Within this general framework, migrants from rural areas, for example, will have very different expectations and practices compared to their urban counterparts, whether in their own country or in other countries where Muslims form a majority. There is also a minority within a minority that rejects being defined as 'Muslim' as they neither practise nor adhere to any religious tenets. This group would have more in common with their socio-economic and class counterparts among their hosts rather than one that is defined by commonplace assumptions of a **religious** minority. This group, for example, do not wish to be represented either by *imams* or by faith-led organizations, but by secular political parties.

For policy-makers in most European countries, the demand for rights and recognition from communities that, since arrival, have been largely excluded from the public arena, has created a dilemma as to how best to accommodate these demands, particularly in the current climate of fear, of a 'monolithic and troublesome faith'—a perception linked to recent events in the world. From the perspective of these migrant communities, the second generation of migrant youth in countries with four decades of migration (mainly France, Germany and the United Kingdom) battled in the seventies and eighties for political representation of their ideas, better access to employment, education, healthcare, minimum wages and trade union membership. However, during the past decade, a different voice of rebellion has emerged amongst the third generation of migrant youth (particularly among migrants of Muslim origin), one that is expressed in terms of religious identity. Possibly for the first time in migrant politics in recent decades, there may be a generational unity in the demand for such freedoms premised upon a religious rather than a secular political identity.

Arguably, this is a global phenomenon that encompasses all faiths and is not atypical of Muslim populations, where political demands are increasingly expressed in terms of religiosity with aspirations for a national identity replaced by demands for greater cultural and religious representation. To some extent these demands reflect failures of the systems and countries in question to acknowledge the need for political representation among a growing minority who feel increasingly isolated and dispossessed.

A long-standing failure amongst political parties as well as in legislative processes has been to acknowledge the need for equality in diversity, and has resulted in misleading policies and approaches in understanding needs in employment, education, health and social sectors. This in turn has jeopardized opportunities for even partial integration, pushing some sections of the migrant community further into ghettoized isolation. The effects of this upon health, for example, are largely unknown, and this is symptomatic of the neglect of the needs of migrant communities in general (Nazaroo, 2001).

As a result, the experience of discrimination, despite its varied legal and historical nature, is perceived by many migrants of Muslim origin as unique, and is seen as part of combined institutional and more explicit forms of racism based on their religious identity. In particular, the continuity of a history of negative image portrayal, it is argued, is increasingly reflected in legislation that is in theory for the protection of national security. These policies have a more global outlook, and reinforce the exclusion and hostility experienced by European Muslims, regardless of location or generation, through the implementation of punitive anti-terrorist legislation (Feteke, 2003).

A recent report on 'Muslim Voices within Europe', for example, suggests that the particular experience of migrants of Muslim origin is related largely to their 'Muslim-ness' rather than their ethnicity, and has arisen out of an increased 'visibility' related to demands from communities for greater political and social recognition. These include demands for rights to facilitate the practice of traditions: for example, to form cultural associations, establish meeting places and prayer halls, observe dietary requirements in public institutions such as schools and hospitals, follow a dress code, and provide facilities for learning language and religious texts. While many of these demands have been met or facilitated by the communities themselves, others require public resources, in particular in countries such as the United Kingdom, France, Belgium and the Netherlands.

This increase in visibility, or even the demand for it, appears to have resulted in growing resentment from host communities. This resentment is steeped in suspicion and mistrust from the hosts in most European countries, especially in France where secularism has played a key role in the definition of French citizenship. Such reactions are compounded by the attribution of 'otherness' to Muslim communities, culturally and historically. This may in turn become inverted among the communities, and reinforce the sense of exclusion played out in the activities of living apart.

Most writers agree that the issue that causes most hostility is dress code—the right of women to wear the '*hijab*'—since it is viewed as being contrary to the principles of secularism. Some have suggested that the idea of an 'Islamic threat' has replaced the fear of communism to Western societies, with Muslims viewed as both the enemy within and without (Keppel, 1997; Glavanis et al., 1999).

The feeling of exclusion is a common one despite the heterogeneity of communities of Muslim origin, which includes migrants from countries as far apart as Nigeria and Pakistan. Both actual and subjective feelings of exclusion reinforce a sense of otherness. As a result, questions of identity politics have increasingly played a role in defining the meaning of, and the rights to, citizenship among migrants of Muslim origin, since people are defined by, and define themselves, in terms of their relationship to Islam rather than their country of origin.

## COUNTRY EXPERIENCES

In the six countries discussed in this book, there is considerable variation in legislation for the protection of minorities. For example, in France, the main factor underpinning legislation is citizenship rather than minority status; i.e. protection is in theory the same for all on the grounds of French citizenship. Minority status is not acknowledged, thus making difficult the desire for political and cultural expression or activities that highlight differences in treatment. The debates that have raged over the wearing of the *hijab* in France are such a case in point. The public antipathy expressed towards the observation of this dress code is, according to Glavanis et al., based on a misunderstanding of the symbolic nature of the head scarf as opposed to the *hijab* simply representing a form of 'patriarchal oppression' as is commonly perceived. Glavanis et al. argue that this perception has led to disapproval and discrimination, particularly in education and employment. This is in spite of the fact that Christian and Jewish practitioners of their respective faiths are not required to remove the symbols of their faith in the workplace (Glavanis et al., 1999).

Hence the struggles of different groups of immigrants have been to try and establish the right to form associations and to practise freedoms that diverge from this singular criterion of citizenship. The migrant view is that to be French and Muslim is not contradictory, nor undermining of the desire to be French (see Cesari's chapter) and especially so since the experience of being a 'French' citizen has been perceived as unequal citizenship, with young people experiencing front-line discrimination in social, economic and educational opportunities, with little opportunity for redress (see Pêdziwiatr's chapter).

In Belgium, migrants, mainly from Turkey and Morocco and more recently from Bangladesh, have, over the past few decades, experienced hostility and discrimination while theoretically receiving 'equal' treatment under the law. The areas of social and cultural life that arouse most suspicion and hostility include the freedom to worship and to obtain access to basic social and economic services (mainly education and health) as other citizens. But any implicit opposition from the host society has been matched by an increased demand by second-generation youth of both Turkish and Moroccan descent for more equal treatment and better opportunities, particularly in employment and education, which might enable them to leave their ghettoized existence in the suburbs. Migrants of Muslim origin form some 9 per cent of the total population in Belgium.

In Germany, the issue of the 'rights of citizenship' among immigrants does not arise, since the majority have not received official legal status as citizens but are classified as temporary 'guest' workers. This status remains, despite many Turkish families having been in residence for three generations, and causes considerable insecurity, particularly among second and now third generation migrants, many of whom were born in Germany. Fewer than half of the migrants of Muslim origin in Germany have the right to citizenship, and as in Sweden, many belong to different Islamic traditions, though the largest number are Turkish in origin.

Muslim migrants to Sweden arrived during the 1970s and 80s, both as workers but many also as political refugees. Most have become Swedish citizens but remain very diverse with their origins in countries as far apart as Bosnia, Lebanon and Ethiopia. They speak different languages, belong to different ethnic groups and theological branches of Islam and include a substantial group of non-practising Muslims (Anwar et al., 2001). However, Sweden, in contrast to the United Kingdom and Germany, is a highly secularized country where religion is not considered a relevant factor in policy-making. Thus, when policy is formulated, the issue of targeting policies towards minorities who are Muslim is not a relevant factor, so problems that may be faced by Muslims in Sweden are not considered relevant. Swedish immigration policies are concerned mainly with the relationship between the state and the individual rather than between the state and a religious minority. Cultural, ethnic and religious groups have no rights in Swedish legislation (Anwar et al., 2001).

There are about one million Muslims in the Netherlands (out of a population of sixteen million Dutch) who have come from a wide range of countries over the past three decades. These include migrants from Morocco, Algeria, Tunisia and Indonesia, and largely undertake low-paid, unskilled work. This group has until recently been allowed to survive with the relatively liberal multicultural policies of the Netherlands, by receiving grants and subsidies to establish their own specific cultural associations in the country; quite different, for example, from the situation of Muslim migrants either in France or in Germany. But pressures from right wing politics and the institutionalization of deprivation among large sections of the migrant community have, in the past two years, created tension and debate about the multiculturalist policies of Dutch liberal democracy. Growing international tensions, together with the murder by a Muslim radical of the Dutch filmmaker van Gogh in November 2004 for his negative views about Muslim minorities, have resulted in calls for either total assimilation or the encouraging of repatriation of Muslim migrants. Subsequently, there is at present considerable public pressure in the Netherlands to reduce opportunities available to minority groups to organize, in their own right, social and cultural activities with aid from the Dutch government. Anti-Muslim propaganda and racist attacks against religious and cultural organizations are on the increase, creating a very volatile situation for the majority of migrants of Muslim origin.

In the UK, while immigration laws have determined legal status (the right to become a citizen), policies of diversity and equality protect minorities from racial discrimination in housing, employment and welfare, together with the right to practise religious customs. To date these have addressed the needs of ethnicity rather than of religious difference, even though certain religious groups receive specific protection (Sikhs and Jews) of association and practice. Since there is no specific legislation identifying the needs of Muslim minorities either in France or in the UK, people of Muslim origin feel vulnerable, and confront a lack of redress when they experience discrimination or harassment on the grounds of their religion, as has increasingly been the case, due to the growing obsession with security and associated negative stereotyping in the media and in policy circles.

In addition, Choudhury (in this book) suggests that anti-discrimination legislation in the UK can only be viewed as effective when the experience of religious minorities (i.e. Muslims) is monitored, whether at work or in welfare. If there are no such mechanisms or criteria in place to assess the nature of discrimination, then the weakness of the legislation is exposed. It is the testing of the legislation on equality that will act as a measure of the extent to which minorities (Muslims in particular) may feel protected. An ambiguity in current legal status prevents the testing of legislation throughout the countries in question, and is compounded by discrimination and harassment directly linked to the 'war' on terror.

Political representation in countries such as the UK has varied in terms of its strength at the national and local level. Whilst it remains relatively weak at the national level, which includes representation of Muslims among mainstream political parties, experience at the local level has included some changes to the running of schools and local social activities to incorporate the needs of practising Muslims (Glavanis et al., 1999).

On the social and economic front, a high percentage of Muslims in the countries covered in this discussion continue to live in economically and socially disadvantaged areas. The migration of most Muslims to countries such as Britain and France was a result of economic demand during the 1960s and 1970s for cheap labour in the manufacturing industries. Their living conditions were then, and continue to be now, lower than those of non-Muslim citizens. Children attend schools struggling with social, financial and other problems. At least partly due to this situation, children from Muslim backgrounds perform relatively poorly with higher dropout rates. In most of the countries, parents view the education system as failing Muslim pupils. This does not augur well for their future. Yet understanding the effects of social and cultural deprivation and the need for appropriate remedies is more often than not replaced by fatalistic approaches informed by negative, behaviouristic stereotypes of why people perform badly, linked largely to origin. The onus is therefore placed on the immigrant child and his or her family as part of the neo-liberal ideology of individual responsibility, rather than being viewed as a broader issue with responsibility shared by families and the state.

Neo-liberal ideology and policies have reinforced the isolation and exclusion experienced by many sections of the poor and among migrant communities, throughout Europe. Fewer resources are available for publicly funded activities to increase mutual responsibilities, participation in civic life and the promotion of citizenship over and above the making of visible investments in employment, education and the health sectors. There is much evidence to show that the retrenchment of public provision creates a type of exclusion that reinforces the need to revive contact with one's past. While some would argue that such contact is common to all migrant communities, and functions as a key element in coping with the present, it has also become a target of criticism among those who view reliance upon the past as preventing an acknowledgement of the present.

## CONTACT WITH THE PAST

It is clear from the evidence produced in this book and elsewhere that it is as a result of their own experience of alienation and isolation that many migrants turn to their country of origin to establish historical links and a sense of place. This has been common to the processes of immigration throughout the world and at different points in time (Robbens and Orozco, 2000). The need to establish contact with the past is more common to first generation immigrants, and is often a direct result of isolation from the present. It is not a desire to be further excluded from the present, as Engeberson has illustrated in this book for the Netherlands, and Samad for the UK, but rather a desire to re-establish oneself in the present. The findings of research undertaken in the Netherlands suggests that among young people of Muslim origin trans-national ties act as a strengthening factor in the process of adaptation to host society, rather than the opposite, as espoused by theories of integration. These argue that strong ties with the country of origin act as a prohibitive factor to getting on with the present (see Engberson's chapter).

The policy relevance of this debate is directly linked to the undue scrutiny being faced by communities of Muslim origin throughout the European region. In most countries, policy has assumed that all migrants will eventually assimilate into the host societies, although during certain points in time the dominant opinion has allowed for integration rather than assimilation. Glavanis argues that such terms have lacked clear definition, but the main factor underlying them is that it remained the responsibility of individuals to encompass the host society and culture. There continues to be little recognition of the fact that both integration and assimilation are a two-way process, and economic, social, political and legal enabling is the key to whether a group remains marginalized or not. However, there is common agreement among the authors of this book that contact with the past does not in any way suggest the emergence of a transnational Islamic movement that is seeking to destroy the so-called democratic values of European society.

The re-emergence of an Orientalist perspective as the dominant discourse ensures that policy measures, particularly in the realms of security, will not only target Muslim populations but also remain bound by political and cultural misapprehension. This is despite all attempts by communities of Muslim origin to integrate and go about their business successfully and with resilience. As highlighted in several chapters of this book, intrinsic to the latent hostility towards Muslims (whether they are practising Muslims or not) is the perpetuation of negative stereotypes in the media and elsewhere of Muslim communities as 'the other', implying a fundamental and unalterable difference of legendary proportions. This, however, denies the reality of a highly heterogeneous population, whether within the European Union or elsewhere, with varied practices and beliefs as well as socio-economic origins that influence behaviour and levels of adaptation. Stereotypes also tend to ignore the structural and material conditions of daily existence, which have a real impact upon opportunity and realization. This book has already acknowledged that there are considerable variations in legal systems and social cultural frameworks in the countries with resident Muslim populations. The creation of a monolith, however, fits in well with the dominant discourse that is embedded in fear of the 'other' and the resultant essentialization of Islam, thereby feeding into negative stereotypes. With little room for negotiation, self-proclaimed leaders of Muslim communities have themselves accepted this categorization, in order to strengthen hierarchies within migrant communities, and this reinforces the stereotype of 'otherness'. In addition, there are Europe-wide policy measures being implemented, particularly on the security front, that create much greater homogeneity in the experience of fear and insecurity.

In her seminal work on the stressors involved in paths of migration, Orozco argues that the difficulties involved in the migration process and their effect on different generations of migrants have largely been underestimated in most of the writing on the topic. She suggests that immigration is one of the most stressful experiences that individuals can undergo, because it removes from migrants predictable contexts such as extended families, friends, community ties, jobs, living conditions, customs and often language. Immigrants are thus stripped of many of the sustaining social relations and roles that have in the past provided meaning and belonging. Once they have reached their destination area, without a sense of competence, control and belonging, many not only feel a keen sense of loss, but also totally marginalized (Suaraz-Orozco, 2000). Their ability to cope in this situation will depend to a large degree on the support and enablement provided by the host societies. This dimension is often ignored in the discourse on migration, which places the onus on immigrants to adapt. As a result of this misapprehension, policy discussions have been reversed to individualize and pathologize communities on their difficulties in adapting to host societies (see chapters by Samad and Alexander).

'The emergence of essentialist identification, many writers have pointed out, is a result of social exclusion, racism and xenophobia' (Hall,

1996; Gilroy, 1987; Samad, 1997). Sociologists insist on the importance of the social dimension of citizenship. Effective social citizenship is a function of social capital, and low levels of citizenship, due to marginalization and exclusion, reflect low participation rates in community activity (see Turner's chapter).

This is part and parcel of the dominant paradigm in relation to Muslims in general, and youth of Muslim origin in Europe have been framed as a problem and associated too closely with the 'terror threat'. Two main discourses as described by Samad in the introduction are hostile, and view current communities as a potential threat to security, easily linking up to transnational fundamentalist networks whilst providing little evidence to support such a view. The policy reaction premised on the perpetuation of fear has been to generate punitive legislation that creates further fear and alienation. Some authors have suggested that in all countries this population provides a convenient scapegoat for the social friction generated by policies of neo-liberalism.

There are then the two parallel debates concerning Muslim minorities in Europe, one, the re-emergent Orientalist discourse, and the other, the discussions on European identity, both of which have 'problematized' Muslims. The security paradigm has been premised on the assumption of an imported Islamic radicalism establishing itself in the European context through the creation of transnational identities among Muslims whereby, according to Samad in his chapter, 'Jihadis were being parachuted into the fertile terrain of inner city ghettos'.

The second policy theme that intersects with the security issue is the question of the emerging European identity. The predominance of the security paradigm in relation to Muslims that would reinforce the construction of the 'other' within, leads to substantial numbers of people being excluded from this new European identity.

## POLICY IMPLICATIONS

The desire amongst a substantial section of under-privileged Muslim minority communities to be visible and to assert identities that are enshrined in religiosity has created a political uproar throughout Europe. The historic exclusivity attributed to Islam has been self-fulfilling, and negative images derived from this association have been revived and have permeated interpretations of culture and polity of

Muslim minority communities, whether this is in the realms of academia (including European Social Science Research, with some exceptions), in the media or in speeches made by numerous politicians. Moreover, many self-proclaimed leaders in Muslim communities have 'stoked' the fires by reasserting the need for Muslims to return to the essential values of the Quran, and rejecting as far as possible the dictates of liberal democracies. The extent to which this opinion is representative is unknown but has created much turmoil, panic, fear and a resurgence of negativity.

Neo-liberal policies and the systematic reduction of welfare provision throughout Europe, particularly so in countries such as the United Kingdom, have allowed further encroachment of family and church into the domestic sphere. Whilst this is in no way exclusive to Muslim communities, it is this group that remains the most scrutinized. Glavanis et al. (1999) argue that it is not Islamic militancy that is at the root of the current turmoil, but rather the absence of equal access to social, economic and cultural resources that has contributed to the marginalization and social exclusion of these communities, which have aspired to little else other than the basic rights of citizenship: tolerance, justice, employment, education, et cetera. Growing intolerance and misconception have exacerbated the situation in many countries (Glavanis et al., 1999).

A review of the chapters and recent literature on the topic suggests that a number of policy measures would be pertinent at national and European levels in the context of turmoil, mutual suspicion and a growing feeling of exclusion and isolation. These would involve improving knowledge and understanding of the diversity of Islamic history, society and cultures in order to break the myth of 'monolithism' among other stereotypes of Islamic culture and polity. There could also be exploration of ways to increase participation among Muslim youth in mainstream activities, through programmes of positive discrimination and with the allocation of additional resources, particularly in the areas of education and employment. This would enhance multiculturalism and social cohesiveness with less emphasis on the stereotyping of whole communities in a negative manner. It is also likely to increase interaction between communities through support for social and cultural activities in inner city areas that remain particularly deprived.

There is also a need for policy measures that would discourage sensationalist reporting in the media about minority communities, and encourage serious research (with public funding) to enable better understanding and debate about the changing nature of faith politics across all religions. Whilst countries such as France restrict visible manifestations of religiosity in places of work and at schools, this should not target Muslims over others, while maintaining one's faith and personal beliefs should not be castigated as an activity needing to be monitored by the security forces. If restrictions are placed upon religious bodies in the running of schools and other educational establishments, Muslims groups cannot be singled out for exclusion since this is clearly discriminatory. Legislation needs to be applied equally. Above all, there needs to be much more effort to increase understanding of Muslim culture and society in the context of countries of origin and the varied histories of migration, in order to negate the growing essentialization of Islam and the regular harassment of Muslim communities throughout Europe by the security forces in the name of the' war on terror', whose roots, as Turner has indicated, are far beyond recent events and are in the formulation and social construction of 'the other'.

Police understanding of Muslim communities in particular and race relations in general needs to be improved to prevent the targeting and all too regular harassment of Muslim communities, especially the youth. To improve accountability and credibility, this needs to go hand in hand with the establishment of mechanisms for monitoring complaints about police action.

## REFERENCES

Anwar, M., Blaschke, J., and Sander, A., *Policies Towards Muslim Minorities; Sweden, Great Britain and Germany*. Report for European Commission DG Employment and Social Affairs, 2001.

Cesari, J., *Muslim Minorities in the West: The Silent Revolution* in Esposito, John and Burgat, François (eds.), *Modernizing Islam: Religion in the Public Sphere in the Middle East and in Europe*, Rutgers University Press, 2003: 251-269.

European Commission White Paper, 'A new impetus for European youth', DG Justice and Employment, European Commission, Brussels, 2001.

Feteke, L., 'The Politics of Fear: civil society and the security state' in *Race and Class*, Institute of Race Relations, Special Issue, London UK, 2003.

Gilroy, Paul, *There Ain't No Black in the Union Jack*, Hutchinson, London, 1987.

Glavanis, P. M et al., 'Muslim Voices' in the European Union: The Stranger Within: Community, Identity and Employment, Final Report, European Commission, Brussels, Targeted Socio-Economic Research (TSER) SOE1-CT96-3024, 1999.

Hall, Stuart, 'Politics of Identity' in Ranger, T., Samad, Y. and Stuart, O. (eds.), *Culture, Identity and Politics: Ethnic Minorities in Britain*, Avebury, Aldershot, 1996.

Keppel, G., *A L'Quest d'Allah* (Allah in the West), Stanford University Press, Stanford, 1997.

Nazroo, J.Y., *Ethnicity, Class and Health,* Policy Studies Institute, London, 2001.

Samad, Y., 'Ethnicity, Racism and Islam: Identity and Gender and Generational Debates' in *Multiculturalism, Muslims and the Media: Pakistanis in Bradford,* unpublished manuscript produced as part of the research conducted for the ESRC (Award number L126251039), 1997.

Samad, Y. and Sen, K., Final Report, *Youth, Gender, Transnational Identities and Islamophobia,* European Commission, Brussels, 2003.

Sander, A. and Larson G., *'Muslims in Sweden',* 2003, available on http://www.emzberlin. de/projekte/pdf/Muslims_in_Schweden.pdfttp://www.emzberlin.de/projekte/pdf/ Muslims_in_Schweden.pdf

Sander, A., Larsson, G., Kos-Dienes, D. *'State Policies Towards Muslim Minorities in the European Union',* final report, 2001.

Suarez-Orozco, C., 'Identities under siege: immigration stress and social mirroring among children of immigrants', in Robben, A.C.G.M. and Suarez-Orozco, M. (eds.), *Cultures Under Siege – collective violence and trauma,* Cambridge University Press, Cambridge, 2000.

## NOTES

1. Treaty on EU, Preamble.
2. European Commission White Paper 'A new impetus for European youth', 2001: 19.

# Glossary

| | |
|---|---|
| *Azan* | The call to prayer. |
| *Bazari* | Belonging to a market, mercantile; a market-person. |
| *Bhangra* | Dynamic folk dance from the Punjab region in North India and Pakistan. In its more recent history, *bhangra* has been fused with contemporary Western musical styles. |
| *Biraderi* | Patrilineal kinship group in the Punjab. |
| *Burqa* | Women's clothing that covers the whole body from head to toe. |
| Chav | A young person, usually working class, often without a high level of education, who follows a particular fashion consisting of flash jewellery and designer labels. |
| *Dawah* | The call to Islam. |
| Diwali | The Hindu Festival of Lights that marks the victory of good over evil. |
| *Dupatta* | A long scarf worn with a *shalwar kameez* that has long been a symbol of modesty in South Asian dress. |
| Doxa | Belief or glory. |
| Eid | Literally, 'festival' or 'celebration': Eid ul-Adha, 'the Festival of Sacrifice', marks the end of Haj and Eid ul-Fitr, 'the Festival of Fast-Breaking' marks the end of Ramadan. |
| Hadith | Validated recorded saying or tradition of the Prophet Muhammad (PBUH). |
| Halal | Lawful, permitted. |
| Hijab | Literally, 'cover'. It describes the self-covering of the body for the purposes of modesty and dignity, including the hair. |
| Hijrat | Literally, 'migration'. Muhammad (PBUH) and his followers' emigration from Mecca to Medina. |
| Ijtihad | The process of making a legal decision by independent interpretation of the sources of the law, the Quran and the *Sunna*. |
| *Imam* | Literally, 'leader', e.g. a man who leads a community or leads the prayer. |
| *Izzat* | Prestige, honour. |
| Jihad | Literally, 'struggle'. Any earnest striving in the way of Allah for righteousness and against wrong-doing. Greater jihad: internal struggle for the soul against evil and temptation. |

|              | Lesser jihad: fight to protect Islam from attack or oppression. |
| --- | --- |
| Jihadi | Someone committed to jihad. |
| *Lena-dena* | Reciprocal exchange of gifts and services. |
| Madrassa | An Islamic religious school. |
| Mujahedeen | Fighters for Islam. Singular, mujahid. |
| *Purdah* | Means 'curtain' in Persian. Metaphorically, refers to the practice of secluding women. |
| Quran | Revealed scriptures of Islam. |
| Salafi | In modern discourse, the term 'Salafi' describes various 'purist' and especially militant forms of Sunni Islam. |
| *Shalwar kameez* | *Shalwar* is a sort of loose, pyjama-like pair of trousers. The *kameez* is a long shirt or tunic. |
| *Shariah* | Islamic law based on the Quran and *Sunna*. |
| Shia | The second largest sect in Islam. |
| *Sufi* | A Muslim mystic |
| Sunni | The largest sect in Islam, with no single central authority. |
| *Ulama* | Religious Islamic scholars. Singular, *alim*. |
| *Ummah* | The global Muslim community. |
| *Wahabi* | Follower of Wahabism, a movement of Islam named after Muhammad ibn Abd al Wahhab Muhammad ibn Abd al Wahhab. The term is considered offensive by some members who prefer to call themselves al-Muwahhidun (the monotheists) or Salafi. |

# Bibliography

Abercrombie, N. Hill, S. and Turner, B.S., *Sovereign individuals of capitalism*, Allen & Unwin, London, 1986.

Ahmad, Feroz, *The Turkish Experiment in Democracy 1950-1975*, London, 1977.

Ahmad, Feroz, *The Making of Modern Turkey*, Routledge, London, 1993.

Ahmed, Akbar S., *Postmodernism and Islam. Predicament and Promise*, Routledge, London, 1992.

Ahmed, Akbar S., Discovering Islam. Making Sense of Muslim History and Society, Routledge, 1998.

Al-Ali, Nadje, Black, Richard and Koser, Khalid, Refugees and transnationalism: the experience of Bosnians and Eritreans in Europe, Journal of Ethnic and Migration Studies, Vol. 27, No. 4, 2001: 615-634.

Alexander, C., *The Asian Gang: ethnicity, identity, masculinity*, Berg, Oxford, 2000.

Alexander, C., '[Dis]Entangling the Asian Gang' in Hesse B. (ed.), *Un/Settled Multiculturalisms*, Zed Press, London, 2000.

Alexander, C., 'Beyond Black: rethinking the colour/culture divide', *Ethnic and Racial Studies*, Vol. 25, No. 4, 2003: 552-571.

Alexander, C., 'The Next Generation', in Ali, N., Kalra, V. & Sayyid, S. (eds.) *Asian Nation*, Christopher Hurst, London, forthcoming.

Alexander, Jeffrey (ed.), *Real Civil Societies: Dilemmas of Institutionalization*, Sage Publications, London, 1997.

Ali, Y., 'Muslim Women and the Politics of Ethnicity and Culture in Northern England', in Sahgal, G. & Yuval-Davis, N. (eds.), *Refusing Holy Orders: Women and Fundamentalism in Britain*, Virago, London, 1992.

Allen, Christopher and Nielsen, Jorgen S., Summary Report on Islamophobia in the EU after 11 September 2001, European Monitoring Centre on Racism and Xenophobia, Vienna, 2002.

Amin, A., *'Ethnicity and the Multicultural City'*, Report for the Department of Transport, Local Government and the Regions, 2002. *Amiraux, V.,* EU Accession Monitoring Program (EUMAP), Report on France: *'Monitoring Minority Protection in EU Member States'*, 2002.

Amiraux, V., *Studying Islam in Europe: Are there ties binding academics and politics*, Conference paper, Erfurt, 2001.

Amit-Talai, Vered and Wulff, Helena (eds.), *Youth Cultures: A Cross-Cultural Perspective*, Routledge, London, 1995.

Angell, Norman, *The Great Illusion*, Heinemann, London, 1910.

An-Nisa Society, *Second Review of the Race Relations Act 1976—A Response*, Wembley.

Anwar, M., *Myth of Return: Pakistanis in Britain*, Heinemann, London, 1979.

Anwar, M., Blaschke, J., and Sander, A., *Policies Towards Muslim Minorities; Sweden, Great Britain and Germany*. Report for European Commission DG Employment and Social Affairs, 2001.

Appadurai, A., 'Disjuncture and Difference in the Global Cultural Economy' in Featherstone, M. (ed.), *Global Culture, Nationalism, Globalization and Modernity*, Sage Publications, London, 1990.

Arnason, Johan *The Future that Failed: Origins and Destinies of the Soviet Model*, Routledge, London, 1993.

Audrad, C., 'Multiculturalisme et tranformation de la citoyennete' (Multiculturalism and the transformation of citizenship), *Archives de philosophie du droit*, 2001: 45.

Back, L., 'Aryans Reading Adorno: cyber-culture and 21st century racism', *Ethnic and Racial Studies*, Vol. 25, No. 4, 2002: 628-651.

Back, L., 'Guess Who's Coming to Dinner? The political morality of investigating whiteness in the grey zone', in Ware, V. & Back, L., *Out of Whiteness*, University of Chicago, Chicago, 2002.

Ballard, R., *Desh Pardesh—The South Asian Presence in Britain*, Hurst & Company, London, 1994.

Barber, B. R., *Jihad vs McWorld. How globalism and tribalism are reshaping the world*, Ballantine Books, New York, 2001.

Barker, Martin, *The New Racism*, Junction Books, London, 1981.

Bash, L., Glick Schiller, N. and Blanc-Szanton C., *Nations Unbound: Transnational Projects, Post-Colonial Predicaments and De-Territorialized Nation States*, Gordon and Breach, Amsterdam. 1999.

Beck, Ulrich, Giddens, Anthony & Lash, Scott, *Reflexive Modernization: Politics, Tradition and Aesthetics in the Modern Social Order*, Polity Press, Cambridge, 1994.

Bedell, G., 'Veiled humour', *The Observer Review*, 20 April, 2003.

Berger, P., *The Social Reality of Religion*, Faber & Faber, London, 1969.

Bhabha, Homi, *The Location of Culture*, Routledge, London, 1994.

Birand, Mehmed Ali, *The Generals' Coup in Turkey: An Inside Story of 12 September 1980*, Brassey's, London, 1987.

Bonney, Richard *Jihad: From Qur'an to bin Laden*, Palgrave Macmillan, Basingstoke, 2004.

Borillo, D., *Les instruments juridique francais et europeens dans la mise en place du principe d'egalite et de non-discrimination*m (French and European legal tools in the implementation of the principle of equality and non-discrimination).

Bousetta, H. and Maréchal, B., *L'Islam et les musulmans en Belgique: Enjeux locaux et cadres de reflexion globaux*, Fundation Roi Baudouin, 2003.

The Bradford Commission Report, *The report of an inquiry into the wider implications of public disorders in Bradford which occurred on 9, 10 and 11 June 1995*, HMSO, London, 1996.

Buijs, F. and Rath, J., *Muslims in Europe: The State of Research*, essay prepared for the Russell Sage Foundation, New York, 2002.

Cabinet Office Strategy Unit, *Ethnic Minorities and the Labour Market: final report*, Cabinet Office, London, 2003.

CAMPACC, 'The 'War on Terror' at Home: we are all targets of the state', February, www.cacc.org.uk, 2003.

Cantle, Ted, *Community Cohesion*, HMSO, London, 2001.

Castles, S. & Miller, M., *The Age of Migration: International Population Movements in the Modern world*, The Macmillan Press, Hampshire, 1994.

CCCS Collective, *The Empire Strikes Back*, Hutchinson, London, 1981.

Cesari, Jocelyne, Musulmans et republicains: Les jeunes, l'Islam et la France, Complexe, Brussels, 1998.

Cesari, Jocelyne, 'Intégrisme Islamique' and 'Sectes' in Dictionnaire des Idées Rebelles, Larousse, 1999: 295-296 and 556-557.

Cesari, Jocelyne (ed.), Musulmans d'Europe, Cemoti, Paris, 2002.

Cesari, Jocelyne., Muslim Minorities in the West: The Silent Revolution in Esposito, John and Burgat, François (eds.), Modernizing Islam: Religion in the Public Sphere in the Middle East and in Europe, Rutgers University Press, 2003: 251-269.

Chomsky, Noam & Herman, E. S., The Washington Connection and Third World Fascism, South End Press, Boston, 1979.

Cohen, Robin, Global Diaspora: an Introduction, UCL Press, London, 1997.

Commission of the European Communities, Communication from the Commission to the Council, The European Parliament, The European Economic and Social Committee and the Committee of the Regions on Immigration, Integration and Employment, Com (2003) 336 final, Brussels, 2003.

Connell, R.W., Masculinities, Polity, London, 1995.

Cook, David, Understanding Jihad, University of California Press, Berkeley, 2005.

Daedalus, Special Issue on Early Modernities, Vol. 127 (3), 1998.

Daedalus, Special Issue on Multiple Modernities, Vol. 129 (1), 2000.

Daniel N. Islam and the West: the Making of an Image, Edinburgh University Press, Edinburgh, 1960.

Dassetto, Felice, La Construction de l'Islam Européen, L'Harmattan, Paris, 1996.

Dayha, B., 'The nature of Pakistani ethnicity in industrial cities in Britain', in Cohen, A. (ed.) Urban Ethnicity, Tavistock, London, 1974.

Delanty, G., Rethinking Europe and Modernity in Light of Global Transformations: The Making of a Post-Western Europe, paper presented at Koc University, Istanbul, 2 May 2003.

Delanty, Gerard, Citizenship in a global age: society, culture, politics, Open University Press, Buckingham, 2000.

Delanty, Gerard, Inventing Europe: Idea, Identity, Reality, Macmillan, Basingstoke, 1995.

Denham, Lord, Building Cohesive Communities, HMSO, London, 2001.

Derrida, J., 'Faith and Knowledge: the two sources of 'religion' at the limits of reason alone' in Derrida, J. and Vattimo, G. (eds.), Religion, Polity Press, Cambridge, 1998: 1-78.

Dorronsoro, G., 'Pakistan's Afghanistan Policy' in Mumtaz, S., Racine, Jean-Luc, Ali, Imran, Anwar (eds.), Pakistan The Contours of State and Society, Oxford University Press, 2002.

DTI (Department of Trade and Industry), Towards Equality and Diversity: Implementing the Employment and Race Directives, London, 2002.

Eade, John, 'Ethnicity and the Politics of Cultural Difference: An Agenda for the 1990s' in Ranger, T., Samad, Y. and Stuart, O. (eds.), Culture, Identity and Politics: Ethnic Minorities in Britain, Avebury, Aldershot, 1996.

Eickelman, Dale F., 'The Coming Transformation of the Muslim World' in: Global Politics and Islam, 1999: 1-5.

Eisenstadt, Shmuel N., Modernization: Protest and change, Englewood Cliffs, New York, 1966.

Engbersen, G. and van der Leun, J.P., 'The Social Construction of Illegality and Criminality' in European Journal on Criminal Policy and Research, jrg. 9, nr. 1, 2001: 51-70.

Engbersen, G., Snel, E., de Boom J. en Heyl, E., *Migration, Immigrants and Policy in the Netherlands. Report for the continuous Reporting System on Migration (SOPEMI) of the Organization of Economic Co-operation and Development (OECD)*, Risbo, Rotterdam, 2002: 93.

Engbersen, G., Leerkes, A., Snel E. and van San, M., *Transnationale activiteiten en identiteiten*, Risbo/EUR, Rotterdam, 2003.

Eren, Nuri, *Turkey Today and Tomorrow: An Experiment in Westernization*, Praeger, New York, 1963.

Esposito, John L., *The Iranian Revolution: Its Global Impact*, Florida International University Press, Miami, 1990.

EU Business, www.eubusiness.com/ 11 September 2003.

EU Council Common Position on Combating Terrorism, available at www.statewatch.org/news/2002/jan/02euter.htm, 2001.

EU Council Working Party on Terrorism, 'Presentation of a Presidency initiative for the introduction of a standard form for exchanging information on terrorist incidents', December, 2001.

European Commission White Paper, '*A new impetus for European youth*', DG Justice and Employment, European Commission, Brussels, 2001.

The European Convention, Draft Treaty Establishing a Constitution for Europe, submitted by the President of the Convention to the European Council meeting in Thessaloniki on 20 June 2003, CONV 820/03.797/1/02 REV 1, 2003.

Eurostat Statistics in Focus: Why do People Migrate? 2001.

Eurostat Statistics in Focus, 2002.

Eurostat Yearbook 2003.

Eze, Emanuel Chukwudi, *Race and Enlightenment*, Blackwell, Cambridge, Mass., 1997.

FAIR (Forum Against Islamophobia and Racism), *Towards Equality and Diversity— Implementing the Employment and Race Directives: Response from the Forum Against Islamophobia and Racism*, London, 2002.

FAIR, (Forum Against Islamophobia and Racism) *ATCSA 2001 Review: a submission from FAIR*, London: Forum Against Islamophobia & Racism [May], 2003.

Faist, T., 'Transnationalization in international migration: implications for the study of citizenship and culture' in *Ethnic and Racial Studies, 23*, 2000: 189-222.

Faist, T., *The volume and dynamics of international migration and transnational spaces*, Oxford University Press, Oxford, 2000.

Farrar, M., 'The Northern 'Race riots' of the summer of 2001—were they riots, were they racial?', presentation to *Parallel Lives and Polarisation* workshop, BSA 'Race' Forum, City University, 2002.

Featherstone, M., *Consumer Culture and Postmodernism*, Sage, London, 1991.

Fekete, L., *Racism: the Hidden Cost of September 11*, Institute of Race Relations, London, www.irr.org.uk, 2002.

Feteke, L., 'The Politics of Fear: civil society and the security state' in *Race and Class*, Institute of Race Relations, Special Issue, London UK, 2003.

Franks, M., 'Crossing the borders of whiteness? White Muslim women who wear the *hijab* in Britain today', *Ethnic and Racial Studies*, Vol. 23 (5), 2000.

Fredman, S., 'Equality: A New Generation?' *Industrial Law Journal*, Vol. 30, No. 2, 2000.

Fredman, S., *Discrimination Law*, Oxford University Press, Oxford, 2001.

The Freedom House evaluation, 2003: http://www.freedomhouse.org/research/freeworld/2003/tables.htm

Ghods, M. Reza, *Iran in the Twentieth Century: A Political History*, Lynne Rienner Publishers, Boulder, Co., 1989.

Giddens, Anthony, *The Consequence of Modernity*, Polity Press, Cambridge, 1990.

Giddens, Anthony, 'The Third Way Can Beat the Far Right' in *The Independent*, 3 May 2002, London.

Gilroy, Paul, *There Ain't No Black in the Union Jack*, Hutchinson, London, 1987.

Glavanis, Pandeli M., 'Political Islam within Europe: A Contribution to an Analytical Framework', *Innovation*, Vol. 11, No. 4, 1998.

Glavanis, P. M., *'Muslim Voices' in the European Union: The Stranger Within. Community, Identity and Employment*, Final Report, Targeted Socio-Economic Research (TSER) SOE1-CT96-3024, European Commission, Brussels, 1999.

Gohari, M.J., *The Taliban: Ascent to Power*, Oxford University Press, 2001.

Goodey, J., Victims of Racism and Racial Violence: experiences among boys and young men', *International Review of Victimology*, Vol. 5, No. 3, 1999.

Gordon, David C. *Images of the West: A Third World Perspective*, Rowman & Littlefield Inc., New York, 1989.

Greaves, R., *Sectarian Influences within Islam in Britain*, University of Leeds, 1996.

Grunebaum, G. von, *Medieval Islam*, University of Chicago Press, Chicago, 1953.

Guessous, F., Hooper N. and Moorthy, U., *Religion in Prisons 1999 and 2000*, Home Office, London, 2001.

Habermas, Jurgen, *The Inclusion of Other: Studies in Political Theory*, MIT Press, Cambridge, MA, 1998.

Hall, S. et al., *Policing the Crisis*, Hutchinson, London, 1978.

Hall, S., 'New Ethnicities' in Donald, J. & Rattanis, A. (eds.), *'Race', Culture and Difference*, Sage, London, 1992.

Hall, Stuart, Held, David & McGrew, Tony, *Modernity and Its Future*, Polity Press, Cambridge, 1992.

Hall, Stuart 'Politics of Identity' in Ranger, T., Samad, Y. and Stuart, O. (eds.), *Culture, Identity and Politics: Ethnic Minorities in Britain*, Avebury, Aldershot, 1996.

Halliday, Fred, 'The politics of Islamic fundamentalism, Iran, Tunisia and the Challenge to the Secular state' in Ahmed, Akbar S. and Donnan, Hastings (eds.), *Islam, Globalisation and Postmodernity*, Routledge, London, 1994: 91-113.

Halliday, F., 'Islamophobia Reconsidered', *Ethnic and Racial Studies*, Vol. 22, No. 5, 1999: 892-902.

HCI Report (Haut Conseil à l'Intégration HCI), *L'Islam dans la République*, Documentation Française, Paris, 2001.

Heller, A. *A Theory of History*, Blackwell, Oxford, 1994.

Hoeber-Rudolph, Susanne, 'Dissing the State? Religion and Transnational Civil Society', *International Political Science Association Congress*, Quebec City, 1-5 August 2000.

Hoexter, Miriam, Eisenstadt, Shmuel N. and Levtzion, Nehemia, *The Public Sphere in Muslim Societies*, State University of New York Press, New York, 2002.

Home Office, *Prison Statistics England and Wales 2000*, Cm. 5250, London, 2001.

hooks, b., *Black Looks: Race and Representation*, Turnaround, London, 1992.

Humphrey, M., Islam, Multiculturalism and Transnationalism in *The Lebanese Diaspora*, IB Tauris, Oxford, 1998: 18.

Huntington, S., *The Clash of Civilizations and the Remaking of the World Order*, Simon & Schuster, New York, 1996.

Hussain, D., 'Representation and Relationship with the State' in Esposito, John and Burgat, François (eds.), *Modernizing Islam: Religion in the Public Sphere in the Middle East and in Europe*, Rutgers University Press, 2003:251-269.

ICG, *Bin Laden and the Balkans: the Politics of Anti-Terrorism*. International Crisis Group Balkans Report No.119, 2001.

Ignatieff, M., *Virtual war: Kosovo and Beyond*, Vintage, London, 2001.

IRR, 'Terror policing brings many arrests but few charges', Institute of Race Relations, London, www.irr.org.uk/2003/march/ak000002/html, 2003.

Itzigsohn, J. and Saucedo, S., 'Immigrant Incorporation and Sociocultural Transnationalism', *The International Migration Review*, Vol. 36 (3), 2002: 766-798.

Jackson, Peter & Penrose, Jan (eds.), *Constructions of Race, Place and Nation*, UCL Press, London, 1993.

Joas, Hans, 'The Modernity of War: Modernization Theory and the Problem of Violence', in *International Sociology*, Vol. 14, No. 4, 1999.

Jones, T., *Britain's Ethnic Minority*, PSI, London, 1993.

Kaldor, M., *Global Civil Society: An Answer to War*, Polity Press, Cambridge, 2003.

Kamali, M., *Revolutionary Iran: Civil Society and State in the Modernization Process*, Ashgate, Aldershot, 1998.

Kamali, M., *Multiple Modernities: The case of Turkey and Iran*, Liverpool University Press, Liverpool, 2004.

Kaya, I., *Social Theory and later Modernities: The Turkish Experience*, Liverpool University Press, Liverpool, 2003.

Kaye, James & Stråth, Bo (eds.), *Enlightenment and Genocide, Contradictions of Modernity*, PIE-Peter Lang, Brussels, 2000.

Keith, M., 'Making the Street Visible: placing racial violence in context', *New Community*, Vol. 21, No. 4, 1995: 551-565.

Kepel, Gilles and Richard, Yann (eds.), *Intellectuels et militants de l'Islam contemporain*, Seuil, Paris, 1990.

Kepel, Gilles, *Jihad: The Trail of Political Islam*, I.B. Tauris Publishers, London, 2002.

Keppel, G., *'A L'Quest d'Allah'* (Allah in the West), Stanford University Press, Stanford, 1997.

Khan, K., 'Where's the Muslim in MacPherson's Black and White Britain?' *Q-News*, March 1999.

Khosrokhavar, Farhad, 'L'identité voilée', *Confluences—Méditerranée*, L'Harmattan, Paris, 16, Winter, 1995-1996.

Khosrokhavar, Farhad, *L'islam des jeunes*, Flammarion, Paris, 1997.

Koser, K. and Lutz, H. (eds.), *The new migration in Europe: Social constructions and social realities*. Macmillan Press, Houndmills, 1998: 185-198.

Kundnani, A., 'From Oldham to Bradford: the violence of the violated', *Race and Class*, Vol. 43, No. 2, 2001: 105-110.

Kundnani, A., 'The Death of Multiculturalism', Institute of Race Relations, (Online Resources), 2002.

Kurzman, Charles (ed.), *Liberal Islam: A Sourcebook*, Oxford University Press, 1998.

Lash, S. and Urry, J., *Economies of Signs and Space*, London, Sage, 1994.

Lash, Scott, *Another modernity, a different rationality: space, society, experience, judgment, objects*, Blackwell, Oxford, 1999.

Lathion, S., *Musulmans d'Europe*, L'Harmattan, Paris, 2003.

Lawrence, Philip K., *Modernity and War: The Creed of Absolute Violence*, Macmillan, New York, 1997.

Lawrence, Philip K., *Preparing for Armageddon: a critique of western strategy*, Wheatsheaf, Brighton, 1988.

Lechner, F.J., 'Global fundamentalism' in Benyon, J. and Dunkerley, D. (eds.), *Globalization Reader*, Athlone Press, London, 2000: 155-59.

Lee, Robert D., *Overcoming Tradition and Modernity, The Search for Islamic Authenticity*, Westview Press, Boulder, CO, 1997.

Lewis, Bernard, 'The Roots of Muslim Rage', *The Atlantic*, September 1990.

Lewis, John, *Max Weber and value-free-sociology*, Lawrence and Wishart, London, 1975.

Lewis, Philip, *Islamic Britain*, I.B. Tauris, London, 1994.

Lewis, Philip 'British Muslims and the Search for Religious Guidance', Conference paper, in 'From Generation to Generation: Religious Reconstruction in the South Asian Diaspora', at SOAS, London University, 1996.

Lipset, S. M. & Marks, G., *It didn't happen here—Why Socialism failed in the United States*, WW Norton & Company, New York, 2000.

Lubeck, P., Lipschutz, R. and Weeks, E., 'The Globality of Islam: Sharia as a Nigerian 'Self-Determination' Movement', Conference on Globalisation and Self-Determination, Queen Elizabeth House, University of Oxford, 4 April 2003.

Mac An Ghaill, M., 'The Making of Black English Masculinities' in Brod, H. & Kaufmann, M. (eds.), *Theorising Masculinity*, Sage, London, 1994.

Macey, M., 'Gender, class and religious influences on changing patterns of Pakistani Muslim male violence in Bradford', *Ethnic and Racial Studies*, Vol. 22, No. 5, 1999: 845-866.

Macey, M., 'Interpreting Islam: young Muslim men's involvement in criminal activity in Bradford' in Spalek, B. (ed.), *Islam, Crime and Criminal Justice*, Willan Publishing, Cullompton, 2002.

Mandaville, Peter, 'Information Technology and the Changing Boundaries of European Islam' in Dassetto, Felice (ed.), *Islamic Words, Individuals, Societies and Discourses in Contemporary European Islam*, Maisonneuve Larose, Paris, 2000: 281-297.

Maréchal, B., (coord.), *A Guidebook on Islam and Muslims in the Wide Contemporary Europe*, Bruylant-Academia, Louvain-la-Neuve, 2002.

Maschino, M., 'Liberty, Equality, Identity: Do you eat couscous at home?' *Le Monde diplomatique*, June 2002.

Mason, D., *Race and Ethnicity in Modern Britain*, Oxford University Press, Oxford, 2000.

Matar, N., *Islam in Britain 1558-1685*, Cambridge University Press, Cambridge, 1998.

Matinuddin, Kamal, *The Taliban Phenomenon: Afghanistan 1994-1997*, Oxford University Press, 1999.

McGhee, D., 'Moving to 'our' common ground—a critical examination of community cohesion discourse in 21st century Britain', *Sociological Review*, forthcoming.

McLoughlin, Sean, ' 'An Underclass in Purdah?' Discrepant Representations of Identity and the Experiences of Young-British-Asian-Muslim Women', *Bulletin, John Rylands Library*, (nd).

Minault, G., *The Khilafat Movement. Religious Symbolism and Political Mobilisation in India*, Columbia University Press, 1982.

Modood, T., *Not Easy Being British*, Trentham, Stoke on Trent, 1992.

Modood, T. et al., *Ethnic Minorities in Britain: Diversity and Disadvantage*, Policy Studies Institute, London, 1997.

Mohammad-Arif, Aminah, 'A Masala Identity: Young South Asian Muslims in the US', *Comparative Studies of South Asia, Africa and the Middle East*, XX (1 & 2), 2000: 84.

Mohammad-Arif, Aminah, 'Ilyâs et Maudûdî au pays des yankees', *Archives de Sciences Sociales des Religions*, EHESS, Paris, 117, janvier-mars, 2002.

Mohammad-Arif, Aminah, 'The Impact of September 11 on the Muslims from the Indian Subcontinent in New York', in Grare, Frédéric (ed.), *The Muslims of the Indian Subcontinent after the 11th September Attacks*, India Research Press, Delhi, 2002.

Mohammad-Arif, Aminah, *Salam America: L'islam indien en diaspora*, CNRS Editions Paris, 2000. Translated into English as *Salaam America: South Muslims in New York*, Anthem Press, London, 2002.

Moore, Kathleen, 'The Politics of Transfiguration: Constitutive Aspects of the International Religious Freedom Act of 1998', in Yazbeck Haddad, Yvonne and Smith, Jane I. (eds.), *Muslim Minorities in the West: Visible and Invisible*, Altamira Press, Walnut Creek, 2002.

Morris, Jan &. Raaflaub, Kurt A. (eds.), *Democracy 2500? Questions and Challenges*, 2000.

Myrdal, Gretty, 'The Construction of Muslim Identities in Contemporary Europe' in Dassetto, Felice, (ed.), *Islamic Words, Individuals, Societies and Discourses in Contemporary European Islam*, Maisonneuve Larose, Paris, 2000: 35-47.

Naguib, Saphinaz-Amal, 'The Northern Way: Muslim Communities in Norway' in Yazbeck Haddad, Yvonne and Smith, Jane I. (eds.), *Muslim Minorities in the West: Visible and Invisible*, Altamira Press, Walnut Creek, 2002.

Nahdi, F., 'Young, British and ready to fight', *The Guardian*, 1 April 2003.

Nasr, S.V.R., 'Islam, the State and the Rise of Sectarian Militancy in Pakistan' in Jaffrelot, C. (ed.), *Pakistan. Nationalism Without a Nation?*, Manohar, 2002.

National Statistics, Labour Force Survey, Spring, 2000.

Nazroo, J.Y., *Ethnicity, Class and Health*, Policy Studies Institute, London, 2001.

Nederveen Pieterse, Jan & Parekh, Bhikhu, (eds.), *Decolonization of the imagination: Culture, Knowledge and Power*, Zed, London, 1973.

Nielsen, J., *Fluid Identities: Muslims and Western Europe's Nation States*. Paper written for the project 'identity and citizenship' conducted by the International Center for Ethnicity, Migration and Citizenship, New School University, New York, 2000.

Nielsen, J., *Muslims in Western Europe*, Edinburgh University Press, Edinburgh, 1992.

Office of National Statistics, *Religion: Scoping Report*, London, 2002.

Open Society Institute EU Accession Monitoring Program, *Monitoring the EU Accession Process: Minority Protection Volume II Case Studies in selected Member States*, Open Society Institute, Budapest, 2002.

Othman, N., 'Grounding Human Rights Arguments in Non-Western Culture: Shari'a and the citizenship rights of women in a modern Islamic state' in Bauer, J.R. and Bell, D.A. (eds.), *The East Asian Challenge for Human Rights*, Cambridge University Press, Cambridge, 1999: 169-192.

Pakistan Commission on the Status of Women, *Report of the Pakistan Commission on the Status of Women*, 1989.

Palidda, S., Frangoulis, M. and Papantoniou, A., *Deviant Behaviour and Criminalisation of Immigrants*, European Commission, Brussels, 1999.

Parekh, B., 'Foreword' in Modood, T. et al., *Ethnic Minorities in Britain: Diversity and Disadvantage*, Policy Studies Institute, London, 1997.

Parekh, B., *The Future of Multi-Ethnic Britain* (The Parekh Report), Profile Books, London, 2000.

Parson, T., 'Religion in Postindustrial America: the problem of secularization' in Turner B. S. (ed.), *The Talcott Parsons Reader*, Blackwell, Oxford, 1999: 300-320.

Peirce, G., 'Terrorising communities', *Campaign Against Racism and Fascism (CARF)* magazine, Spring, 2003. www.irr.org.uk

Phalet, Karen, van Lotringen, Claudia and Entzinger, Han *Islam in de multiculturele samenleving: opvattingen van jongeren in Rotterdam*, Ercomer, Utrecht, 2001.

Pippin, Robert, *Modernism as a Philosophical Problem*, Blackwell, Oxford, 1991.

Portes, A., Guarnizo, L. and Landholt, P., 'The study of transnationalism: pitfalls and promise of an emergent research field', *Ethnic and Racial Studies*, Vol. 22 (3), 1999: 217- 237.

Portes, A., Haller, W. and Guarnizo, L., 'Transnational entrepreneurs: an alternative form of immigrant economic adaptation', *American Sociological Review*, Vol. 67, (4), 2002: 278-298.

Prévélakis, George (ed.), *The Networks of Diasporas*, L'Harmattan, Paris, pp. 37-46.

Raj, Dhooleka S., 'Who the hell do you think you are? Promoting religious identity among young Hindus in Britain', *Ethnic and Racial studies*, Special Issue Vol. 23, No. 3, 2000.

Ranger, Terence, 'Introduction' in Ranger, T., Samad, Y. and Stuart, O. (eds.) *Culture, Identity and Politics: Ethnic Minorities in Britain*, Avebury, Aldershot, 1996.

Religious Studies Media and Information Service (REMID). www.remid.de

Report of the Runnymede Trust Commission on British Muslims and Islamophobia, *Islamophobia: a challenge for us all*, The Runnymede Trust, London, 1997.

Reyneri, E., *Migrant Insertion in the Informal Economy, Deviant Behaviour and the Impact on Receiving Societies*. Targeted Socio-economic Research (TSER) SOE-2-CT95-3005. European Commission, Brussels, 1999.

Robertson, R. *The Sociological Interpretation of Religion*, Basil Blackwell, Oxford, 1970).

Robertson, Roland, *Globalisation: Social Theory and Global Culture*, Sage, London, 1992.

Rojek, C., *Celebrity*, Reaktion Press, London, 2001.

Roy, Olivier, *L'islam mondialisé*, Seuil, Paris, 2002.

The Runnymede Trust Commission on British Muslims and Islamophobia, *Islamophobia—a challenge for us all*, London, 1997.

The Runnymede Trust Commission on the Future of Multi-Ethnic Britain, *The Future of Multi-ethnic Britain—The Parekh Report*, Profile Books, London, 2000.

Safai, Ebrahim, *Zendeginameh-ye sepahbod Zahedi* (The Biography of General Zahedi), Entesharat-e Elmi, Tehran, 1373/1994.

Safari, Muhammad Ali, *Qalam va siyasat*, Nashr-e Namak, Tehran, 1373/1994.

Said, E., *Covering Islam. How the Media and Experts Determine How We See the Rest of the World*, Pantheon Books, 1981.

Said, E., *Orientalism*, Routledge Kegan & Paul, London, 1978.

Saifullah-Khan, Verity, 'Pakistanis in Britain: Perceptions of a Population', *New Community*, 5 (3), 1976.

*Saint John of Damascus: Writings* translated by Frederic H. Chase, Jr., Father of the Church Inc., New York 1958

Samad, Y., 'Book Burning and Race Relations: the political mobilisation of Bradford Muslims', *New Community*, Vol. 18, No. 4, 1992: 507-519.

Samad, Y., 'The Politics of Islamic Identity among Bangladeshis and Pakistanis in Britain' in Ranger, T., Samad, Y. & Stuart, O. (eds.), *Culture, Identity and Politics: Ethnic Minorities in Britain*, Avebury, Aldershot, 1996.

Samad, Y., 'Ethnicity, Racism and Islam: Identity and Gender and Generational Debates' in *Multiculturalism, Muslims and the Media: Pakistanis in Bradford*, unpublished manuscript produced as part of the research conducted for the ESRC (Award number L126251039), 1997.

Samad, Yunas, 'Media and Muslim Identity: Intersection of Generation and Gender', *Innovation*, Vol. 11, No. 4, 1998.

Samad, Y. and Sen, K., Final Report, *Youth, Gender, Transnational Identities and Islamophobia*, European Commission, Brussels, 2003.

Sander, Å. 'The Road From Musalla To Mosque: Reflections on the Process of Integration and Institutionalisation of Islam in Sweden' in Shadid, W.A.R. & van Koningsveld, P.S. (eds.), *The Integration of Islam and Hinduism in Western Europe*, Pharos, Leiden, 1991.

Sander Å., Larsson G. and Kos-Dienes, D., 'State Policies Towards Muslim Minorities in the European Union', final report, 2001.

Sander Å. and Larson G. 'Muslims in Sweden', 2003, *available on* http://www.emz-berlin.de/projekte/pdf/Muslims_in_Schweden.pdf

Sassen, Sasskia, 'La métropole: site stratégique et nouvelle frontière' in Cesari, Jocelyne (ed.), *Les anonymes de la mondialisation, Culture et Conflit*, Paris, no. 33/34, Summer 1999.

Sharma, A., Hutnyk J. & Sharma, S. (eds.), *Dis-Orienting Rhythms: the politics of the new Asian dance music*, Zed Press, London, 1996.

Shaw, A. 'The Pakistani Community' in Ballard, *Desh Pardesh—The South Asian Presence in Britain*, Hurst & Company London, 1994.

Shaw, A., *A Pakistani Community in Britain*, Blackwell, Oxford, 1988.

Smith, J.I., *Islam in America*, Columbia University Press, New York, 1999.

Snel. E. en Engbersen G., Op weg naar transnationaal burgerschap. De schuivende panelen van internationale migratie. In: F. Becker, W. van Hennekeler, M. Sie Dhian Ho en B. Tromp (red.), *Transnationaal Nederland. Het drieentwintigste jaarboek voor het democratisch socialisme*, Wiardi Beckman Stichting, Amsterdam, , 2002: 23-48.

Sonyel, S.R., *The Muslims of Bosnia: Genocide of a People*, the Islamic Foundation, Leicester, 1994.

Southern, R.W., *Western Views of Islam in the Middle Ages*, Harvard University Press, Cambridge, Mass., 1962.

*Stephen Lawrence Inquiry*, Report of an Inquiry by Sir William MacPherson of Cluny, Cm. 4262-I, London: HMSO, 1999.

Suarez-Orozco, C., 'Identities Under Siege: Immigration Stress and Social Mirroring Among Children of Immigrants', in Robben, A.C.G.M. and Suarez-Orozco, M. (eds.), *Cultures Under Siege—Collective Violence and Trauma*, Cambridge University Press, Cambridge, 2000.

Sweetman, J., *The Oriental Obsession. Islamic Inspiration in British and American Art and Architecture 1500-1920*, Cambridge University Press, Cambridge, 1988.

Talbot, I., *Pakistan A Modern History*, Hurst, 1998.

Talbot, I., 'Pakistan in 2002: Democracy, Terrorism and Brinkmanship', *Asian Survey* xliii, 1 (January/February, 2003), 2003.

Taylor, Peter J., *Modernities: A Geohistorical Interpretation*, University of Minnesota Press, Minneapolis, 1999.

Therborn, Göran, 'The Right to Vote and the Four World Routes to/through Modernity', in Torstendahl, Rolf (ed.), *State Theory and State History*, Sage, London, 1992.

Thomas, S.M., 'Taking Religion and Cultural Pluralism Seriously', *Millennium: Journal of International Relations*, 29 (3), 2000: 815-843.

Thomas, William I. and Znaniecke, Florian, *The Polish Peasant in Europe and America*, Dover Publications, New York, 1958.

Tibi, B., *The Challenge of Fundamentalism. Political Islam and the New World Disorder*, University of California Press, Berkeley, 1998.

Tiryakian, Edward A., 'War: The Covered Side of Modernity', in *International Sociology*, Vol. 14, No. 4, 1999.

Toprak, Binnaz, *Islam and Political Development in Turkey*, E.J. Brill, Leiden, 1981.

Torstendahl, Rolf (ed.), *State Theory and State History*, Sage, London, 1992.

Touraine, A., *Can We Live Together? Equality and Difference*, Polity Press, Cambridge, 2000.

Tunaya, Tarik Zefer, *Islamcilik Cereyani*, Baha Matbaasi, Istanbul, 1962.

Turner, Bryan S. *Orientalism, Postmodernism and Globalism*, Routledge, London, 1994.

Turner, B.S., 'On the Concept of Axial Space: Orientalism and the Originary', *Journal of Social Archaeology* 1(1), 2001: 62-74.

Vali Reza Nasr, Seyyed, *The Vanguard of the Islamic Revolution: the Jama'at-i Islami of Pakistan*, I.B. Tauris, London/New York, 1994.

Van den Tilaart, H. *Monitor Etnisch Ondernemerschap 2000. Zelstandig ondernemerschap van etnische minderheden in Nederland in de periode 1990-2000*, Instituut voor Sociale Wetenschappen, Nijmegen, 2001.

Van der Veer, Peter (ed.), *Nation and Migration: The Politics of Space in the South Asian Diaspora*, University of Pennsylvania Press, Philadelphia, 1995.

Van Engelen, *National Employment Strategy*, 2003.

Verkuyten, M. *Etnische identiteit. Theoretische en empirische benaderingen*, Het Spinhuis, Amsterdam, 1999.

Vertovec, S. 'Conceiving and researching transnationalism', *Ethnic and Racial Studies*, 2 (2), 1999: 447-462.

Vertovec, S. Transnational challenges to the 'New Multiculturalism'. Working paper on Transnational Communities, Programme WPTC-01-06, 2001.

Vogel, D. and Cyrus, N., 'Immigration as a side effect of other policies: principles and consequences of the German non-immigration policy' in Triandafyllidou, A., (ed.), *Does Implementation Matter? Informal Administration Practices and Shifting Immigrant Strategies in Four Member States*, Targeted Socio-Economic Research (TSER) HPSE-CT-1999-00001, European Commission, Brussels, 2001: 9-38.

Webster, C., 'The Construction of British 'Asian' Criminality', *International Journal of the Sociology of Law*, Vol. 25, 1997: 65-86.

Weibel, Nadine, 'Islamité, égalité et complémentarité: vers une nouvelle approche de l'identité féminine', *Archives de sciences sociales des Religions*, no. 19, July-September, 1996.

Weiker, Walter F., *Political Tutelage and Democracy in Turkey: The Free Party and its Aftermath*, E. J. Brill, Leiden, 1973: 219.

Werbner, P., *The Migration Process: Capital, Gifts and Offerings among British Pakistanis*, Berg, Oxford, 1999.

White, A., (ed.) *Ethnicity*, (2002) available on http://www.statistics.gov.uk

Wieviorka, Michel, *The Arena of Racism*, Sage Publications, London, 1995.

Wittrock, Björn, 'Modernity: One, None or Many? European Origins and Modernity as a Global Condition' in *Daedalus*, Winter, 2000: 31-60.

The World Audit on Democracy: http://www.worldaudit.org/democracy.htm

Yack, Bernard, *The Fetishism of Modernities: Epochal Self Consciousness in Contemporary Social and Political Thought*, University of Notre Dame Press, Notre Dame, Indiana, 1997.

Yegenoglu, M., *Colonial Fantasies: Towards a Feminist Reading of Orientalism*, Cambridge University Press, Cambridge, 1998.

Ziring, L., *Pakistan in the Twentieth Century. A Political History*, Oxford University Press, 1998: 490 ff.

Websites of National Statistical Offices

Institut national de la statistique et des études économiques (INSEE) www.insee.fr
Statistisches Bundesamt Deutschland (SBD) www.destatis.de
Office for National Statistics (ONS) www.statistics.gov.uk
General Register Office, Scotland www.gro-scotland.gov.uk
Statistics Netherlands (CBN) www.cbn.nl
Statistica Centralbyrån (SCS) www.scb.se

Websites of Muslim Organizations

Belgium:
EMB www.embnet.be
AEL www.arabeuropean.org
MJM www.mvjm.be
PCP www.particp.be

France:
UOIF www.uoif-online.com
IMMP www.mosquee-de-paris.org
CMTF www.diyanet.go.tr

Germany:
ISLAMRAT BD www.islamrat.de
ZENTRALRAT MD www.islam.de/?tree=zmd
AMGT www.igmg.de
VIKZ www.vikz.de

Great Britain:
MCB www.mcb.org.uk
UMO www.theredirectory.org.uk/orgs/umouk.html
MAB www.mabonline.net

Netherlands:
UMMON www.emim.be/assoc.php
MG www.milligorus.nl

# Index